FAULTLINES

Debating the Issues in American Politics

Fifth Edition

FAULTLINES

Debating the Issues in American Politics

Fifth Edition

A brief edition of *The Enduring Debate*, Eighth Edition

David T. Canon
University of Wisconsin–Madison

John J. Coleman
University of Minnesota

Kenneth R. Mayer
University of Wisconsin–Madison

W. W. Norton & Company
New York London

W. W. Norton & Company has been independent since its founding in 1923, when William Warder Norton and Mary D. Herter Norton first published lectures delivered at the People's Institute, the adult education division of New York City's Cooper Union. The Nortons soon expanded their program beyond the Institute, publishing books by celebrated academics from America and abroad. By mid-century, the two major pillars of Norton's publishing program—trade books and college texts—were firmly established. In the 1950s, the Norton family transferred control of the company to its employees, and today—with a staff of 400 and a comparable number of trade, college, and professional titles published each year—W. W. Norton & Company stands as the largest and oldest publishing house owned wholly by its employees.

Composition: Westchester Publishing Services
Production supervisor: Elizabeth Marotta
Manufacturing by Sheridan Books, Inc.

Library of Congress Cataloging-in-Publication Data

Names: Canon, David T., editor. | Coleman, John J., 1959– editor. | Mayer, Kenneth R., 1960– editor.
Title: Faultlines : debating the issues in american politics / David T. Canon, John J. Coleman, Kenneth R. Mayer, [editors].
Other titles: Enduring debate.
Description: Fifth edition. | New York : W. W. Norton & Company, 2017. | "A brief edition of The Enduring Debate, Eighth Edition." | Includes bibliographical references.
Identifiers: LCCN 2017025063 | ISBN 9780393603446 (pbk.)
Subjects: LCSH: United States—Politics and government.
Classification: LCC JK31 .F37 2017 | DDC 320.973—dc23
LC record available at https://lccn.loc.gov/2017025063

W. W. Norton & Company Inc., 500 Fifth Avenue, New York, N.Y. 10110
www.wwnorton.com
W. W. Norton & Company Ltd., 15 Carlisle Street, London W1D 3BS

3   4   5   6   7   8   9   0

Contents

FAULTLINES

Debating the Issues in American Politics

Fifth Edition

1

Political Culture: What Does It Mean to Be an American?

What does it mean to be an American? This deceptively simple question is challenging to answer. Because the United States encompasses a vast array of ethnicities, religions, and cultures, it can be difficult to define "American" by reference to those criteria. The country's geography differs dramatically from region to region, and economic ways of life accordingly differ greatly as well. In many ways, diverse groups of Americans have experienced American history differently, so a common historical identity is not obviously the answer either. One popular argument is that the United States is united by a set of political ideals. As far back as the early nineteenth century, scholars have tried to identify the nature of American political culture: Is it a commitment to individualism? A belief in equality? A shared set of values about the appropriate role of government? Openness?

The events of September 11, 2001, created for most Americans a profound sense of national unity. Writing ten years later, Daniel Cox, E.J. Dionne, Robert Jones, and William Galston examine survey data and report that "Americans continue to grapple with issues of security, tolerance, religious freedom, and pluralism—matters that lie at the heart of what it means to be American." Public opinion data show the country embracing diversity and tolerance, but also divided along sharp political lines. The authors suggest that these political differences may create problems beyond the inevitable tensions that emerge in a diverse and dynamic society. In their conclusion, the authors argue that what it means to be an American has been evolving. They portray a pattern of "the classic American bargain" where new groups "become American" over a generation or two, adopting the language and culture and customs of Americans. These groups, in turn, change the nature of what it means to be an American, and later groups become American in this newly revised sense, and they themselves revise what it means to be American. In this view, the answer to "what does it mean to be an American" depends on when the question is being asked.

Steven Warshawsky argues that American identity centers around a commonly held set of ideas that can be considered the American way of life. This way of life includes beliefs in liberty, equality, property rights, religious freedom, limited government, and a common language for conducting political and economic affairs. Although America has always been a nation of immigrants, from the original European settlers to the mass immigration of the late nineteenth and early twentieth centuries, Warshawsky sees assimilation into American political culture as critical to American national identity. He also notes that America, including the scope and reach of government, has changed dramatically over time. Warshawsky asks whether these changes have also changed what it means to be an American. He argues this is a difficult question but concludes that straying too far from the principles of the Founders means "we will cease to be 'Americans' in any meaningful sense of the word."

Robert P. Jones, Daniel Cox, E.J. Dionne, and William A. Galston

What It Means to Be American: Attitudes in an Increasingly Diverse America Ten Years after 9/11

Ten years after the September 11th terrorist attacks, Americans believe they are more safe but have less personal freedom and that the country is less respected in the world than it was prior to September 11, 2001. A small majority (53 percent) of Americans say that today the country is safer from terrorism than it was prior to the September 11th attacks. In contrast, nearly 8 in 10 say that Americans today have less personal freedom and nearly 7 in 10 say that America is less respected in the world today than before the terrorist attacks.

Americans strongly affirm the principles of religious freedom, religious tolerance, and separation of church and state. Nearly 9 in 10 (88 percent) Americans agree that America was founded on the idea of religious freedom for everyone, including religious groups that are unpopular. Ninety-five percent of Americans agree that all religious books should be treated with respect even if we don't share the religious beliefs of those who use them. Nearly two-thirds (66 percent) of Americans agree that we must maintain a strict separation of church and state. Americans' views of Muslims and Islam are mixed, however. As with other previously marginalized religious groups in U.S. history, Americans are grappling with the questions Islam poses to America's founding principles and way of life.

Americans who are part of the Millennial generation (ages 18–29) are twice as likely as seniors (ages 65 and older) to have daily interactions with African Americans (51 percent vs. 25 percent respectively) and Hispanics (44 percent vs. 17 percent respectively), and to speak at least occasionally to Muslims (34 percent vs. 16 percent respectively).

Nearly half (46 percent) of Americans agree that discrimination against whites has become as big a problem as discrimination against blacks and other minorities. A slim majority (51 percent) disagree.

- A slim majority of whites agree that discrimination against whites has become as big a problem as discrimination against minority groups, compared to only about 3 in 10 blacks and Hispanics who agree.
- Approximately 6 in 10 Republicans and those identifying with the Tea Party agree that discrimination against whites is as big a problem as discrimination against minority groups.
- Nearly 7 in 10 Americans who say they most trust Fox News say that discrimination against whites has become as big a problem as discrimination against blacks and other minorities. In stark contrast, less than 1 in 4 Americans who most trust public television for their news agree.

Americans are evenly divided over whether the values of Islam are at odds with American values and way of life (47 percent agree, 48 percent disagree).

- Approximately two-thirds of Republicans, Americans who identify with the Tea Party movement, and Americans who most trust Fox News agree that the values of Islam are at odds with American values. A majority of Democrats, Independents, and those who most trust CNN or public television disagree.

- Major religious groups are divided on this question. Nearly 6 in 10 white evangelical Protestants believe the values of Islam are at odds with American values, but majorities of Catholics, non-Christian religiously unaffiliated Americans, and religiously unaffiliated Americans disagree.

By a margin of 2-to-1, the general public rejects the notion that American Muslims ultimately want to establish Shari'a law as the law of the land in the United States (61 percent disagree, 30 percent agree).

- Over the last 8 months agreement with this question has increased by 7 points, from 23 percent in February 2011 to 30 percent today.
- Nearly 6 in 10 Republicans who most trust Fox News believe that American Muslims are trying to establish Shari'a law in the U.S. The attitudes of Republicans who most trust other news sources look similar to the general population.

A majority (54 percent) of the general public agree that American Muslims are an important part of the religious community in the United States, compared to 43 percent who disagree.

Nearly 8 in 10 (79 percent) Americans say people in Muslim countries have an unfavorable opinion of the United States, including 46 percent who say Muslims have a very unfavorable opinion of the United States. Among Americans who believe that people in Muslim countries have an unfavorable view of the United States, three-quarters believe that such views are not justified.

Americans employ a double standard when evaluating violence committed by self-identified Christians and Muslims. More than 8 in 10 (83 percent) Americans say that self-proclaimed Christians who commit acts of violence in the name of Christianity are not really Christians. In contrast, less than half (48 percent) of Americans say that self-proclaimed Muslims who commit acts of violence in the name of Islam are not really Muslims.

Americans hold a number of positive views about immigrants, but also have some reservations.

- Overwhelming majorities of Americans believe immigrants are hard working (87 percent) and have strong family values (80 percent), and a majority (53 percent) say newcomers from other countries strengthen American society.

- On the other hand, more than 7 in 10 (72 percent) also believe immigrants mostly keep to themselves, and a slim majority (51 percent) say they do not make an effort to learn English.

Americans are significantly more likely to say that immigrants are changing American society than their own community. A majority (53 percent) of Americans say that immigrants are changing American society and way of life a lot, compared to less than 4 in 10 (38 percent) who say immigrants are changing their community and way of life a lot. Conservatives are not more likely than liberals to say immigrants are changing their own communities a lot, but conservatives are significantly more likely than liberals to say that immigrants are changing American society a lot.

Americans' views on immigration policy are complex, but when Americans are asked to choose between a comprehensive approach to immigration reform that couples enforcement with a path to citizenship on the one hand, and an enforcement and deportation only approach on the other, Americans prefer the comprehensive approach to immigration reform over the enforcement only approach by a large margin (62 percent vs. 36 percent).

- Nearly three-quarters of Democrats and more than 6 in 10 political independents say that both securing the border and providing an earned path to citizenship is the best way to solve the illegal immigration problem. Republicans are nearly evenly divided. In contrast, nearly 6 in 10 of Americans who identify with the Tea Party movement say that securing the border and deporting all illegal immigrants is the best way to solve the illegal immigration problem.
- Majorities of every religious group say that the best way to solve the country's illegal immigration problem is to both secure the borders and provide an earned path to citizenship.

Americans express strong support for the basic tenets of the DREAM Act: allowing illegal immigrants brought to the United States as children to gain legal resident status if they join the military or go to college (57 percent favor, 40 percent oppose). And opposition to the DREAM Act is less fierce than opposition to broader reform proposals, suggesting that partial reforms based on an earned path to citizenship are likely to have a better chance of passing than broader legislation.

[These] survey findings suggest that we are in the midst of a struggle over what growing religious, racial and ethnic diversity means for American politics and society, and that partisan and ideological polarization around these questions will make them difficult to resolve. Nonetheless, this is a battle that has been waged before, and one that is likely to reach the same conclusion: New groups will—through hard work, community and an embrace of our founding values—become "American" while at the same time changing the meaning of being American in ways that, historically, have enriched the nation.

* * *

A Nation United *and* Divided on Pluralism and Diversity

Americans are a tolerant people, but we are divided by tolerance itself. We are united in our support for religious freedom, but divided over what it means. A substantial majority would like to create a path to citizenship for illegal immigrants even as—at the very same time—a small majority would also deport all illegal immigrants.

The future points to an even more tolerant and open nation because young Americans are far more comfortable with and sympathetic to ethnic, racial and religious diversity than are older Americans. But this generational divide also translates into a political divide. If conservatives and Republicans disagree sharply with liberals and Democrats on matters of taxing and spending, they also differ substantially on a broad range of issues related to immigration and to the implications of racial, religious and ethnic diversity.

Ten years after September 11, 2001, we seem far less united as a nation. As a pioneer in the struggle for religious liberty and as a nation defined by immigration, we remain an exceptionally open country. Even Americans uneasy with diversity accept it in important ways as a norm. But we are so divided across partisan, ideological and generational lines that resolving the inevitable tensions that arise in a pluralistic society may prove to be less of a challenge than settling our *political* differences over what pluralism implies, and what it requires of us. Our national motto is "Out of many, one." We find ourselves a very considerable distance from this aspiration—and politics, more than ethnicity, religion or race, is the reason why.

* * *

Conclusion: The Future of American Pluralism

It would be foolish to extrapolate the future from a single survey. But these findings do reinforce a hunch: that the country is in the midst of the kind of argument it has had again and again over diversity and immigration—and that this one will be resolved as the others have been. The American pattern has been to battle fiercely over the inclusion of new groups, to ask whether this or that new group can ever "Americanize" and whether it will push the country away from its founding principles and commitments.

And then several things happen that culminate in the classic American bargain. The new groups turn out to be, or quickly become, very committed to the underlying values and principles of our democratic republic—sometimes more passionately than those who were here earlier and may have come to take them for granted. Over a generation or two, the new arrivals work hard, build strong communities, and in the process, master the English language. They become "American." But they also change the meaning of being American in ways that, historically, have enriched the nation. And the country moves forward, still very much itself, and also transformed. Similarly, we have battled from the very beginning of our republic over the inclusion of African Americans as full citizens. Steadily, albeit with many reversals, the country has sought to live up to Martin Luther King Jr.'s insistence that the long arc of history does bend toward justice.

The generational patterns discerned in this survey suggest that while we are in for some transitional turbulence on these matters, the arc of American history will, again, bend toward inclusion.

Steven M. Warshawsky

What Does It Mean to Be an American?

"Undocumented Americans." This is how Senate Majority Leader Harry Reid recently described the estimated 12–20 million illegal aliens living in America. What was once a Mark Steyn joke has now become the ideological orthodoxy of the Democratic Party.

Reid's comment triggered an avalanche of outrage among commentators, bloggers, and the general public. Why? Because it strikes at the heart of the American people's understanding of themselves as a nation and a civilization.

Indeed, opposition to the ongoing push for "comprehensive immigration reform"—i.e., amnesty and a guest worker program—is being driven by a growing concern among millions of Americans that massive waves of legal and illegal immigration—mainly from Mexico, Latin America, and Asia—coupled with the unwillingness of our political and economic elites to mold these newcomers into red-white-and-blue Americans, is threatening to change the very character of our country. For the worse.

I share this concern. I agree with the political, economic, and cultural arguments in favor of sharply curtailing immigration into the United States, as well as refocusing our immigration efforts on admitting those foreigners who bring the greatest value to—and are most easily assimilated into—American society. * * * But this essay is not intended to rehash these arguments. Rather, I wish to explore the question that underlies this entire debate: What does it mean to be an American? This may seem like an easy question to answer, but it's not. The harder one thinks about this question, the more complex it becomes.

Clearly, Harry Reid has not given this question much thought. His implicit definition of "an American" is simply: Anyone living within the geopolitical boundaries of the United States. In other words, mere physical location on Earth determines whether or not someone is "an American." Presumably, Reid's definition is not intended to apply to tourists and other temporary visitors. Some degree of permanency—what the law in other contexts calls "residency," i.e., a subjective intention to establish one's home or domicile—is required. In Reid's view, therefore, a Mexican from Guadalajara, a Chinese from Shanghai [sic], an Indian from Delhi, or a [fill in the blank] become "Americans" as soon as they cross into U.S. territory and decide to live here permanently, legally or not. Nothing more is needed.

This is poppycock, of course. A Mexican or a Chinese or an Indian, for example, cannot transform themselves into Americans simply by moving to this country, any more than I can become a Mexican, a Chinese, or an Indian simply by moving to their countries. Yet contemporary liberals have a vested interest in believing that they can. This is not just a function of immigrant politics, which strongly favors the Democratic Party (hence the Democrats' growing support for voting rights for non-citizens). It also reflects the liberals' (and some libertarians') multicultural faith, which insists that it is morally wrong to make distinctions among different groups of people, let alone to impose a particular way of life—what heretofore has been known as the American way of life—on those who believe, speak, and act differently. Even in our own country.

In short, diversity, not Americanism, is the multicultural touchstone.

What's more, the principle of diversity, taken to its logical extreme, inevitably leads to a *rejection* of Americanism. Indeed, the ideology of multiculturalism has its roots in the radical—and anti-American—New Left and Black Power movements of the 1960s and 1970s. Thus the sorry state of U.S. history and civics education in today's schools and universities, which are dominated by adherents of this intellectual poison. Moreover, when it comes to immigration, multiculturalists actually *prefer* those immigrants who are as unlike ordinary Americans as possible. This stems from their deep-rooted opposition to traditional American society, which they hope to undermine through an influx of non-western peoples and cultures.

This, in fact, describes present U.S. immigration policy, which largely is a product of the 1965 Immigration Act (perhaps Ted Kennedy's most notorious legislative achievement). The 1965 Immigration Act eliminated the legal preferences traditionally given to European immigrants, and opened the floodgates to immigration from less-developed and non-western countries. For example, in 2006 more immigrants came to the United States from Columbia, Peru, Vietnam, and Haiti (not to mention Mexico, China, and India), than from the United Kingdom, Germany, Italy, and Greece. And once these immigrants arrive here, multiculturalists believe we should accommodate *our* society to the needs and desires of the newcomers, not the other way around. Thus, our government prints election ballots, school books, and welfare applications in foreign languages, while corporate America asks customers to "press one for English."

Patriotic Americans—those who love our country for its people, its history, its culture, and its ideals—reject the multiculturalists' denuded, and ultimately subversive, vision of what it means to be "an American." While the American identity is arguably the most "universal" of all major nationalities—as evidenced by the millions of immigrants the world over who have successfully assimilated into our country over the years—it is not an empty, meaningless concept. It has substance. Being "an American" is *not* the same thing as simply living in the United States. Nor, I would add, is it the same thing as holding U.S. citizenship. After all, a baby born on U.S. soil to an illegal alien is a citizen. This hardly guarantees that this baby will grow up to be *an American*.

So what, then, does it mean to be an American? I suspect that most of us believe, like Supreme Court Justice Potter Stewart in describing pornography, that we "know it when we see it." For example, John Wayne, Amelia Earhart, and Bill Cosby definitely are Americans. The day laborers standing on the street corner probably are not. But how do we put this inner understanding into words?

It's not easy. Unlike most other nations on Earth, the American nation is not strictly defined in terms of race or ethnicity or ancestry or religion. George Washington may be the Father of Our Country (in my opinion, the greatest American who ever lived), but there have been in the past, and are today, many millions of patriotic, hardworking, upstanding Americans who are not Caucasian, or Christian, or of Western European ancestry. Yet they are undeniably as American as you or I (by the way, I am Jewish of predominantly Eastern European ancestry). Any definition of "American" that excludes such folks—let alone one that excludes me!—cannot be right.

Consequently, it is just not good enough to say, as some immigration restrictionists do, that this is a "white-majority, Western country." Yes, it is. But so are, for example, Ireland and Sweden and Portugal. Clearly, this level of abstraction does not take us very far towards understanding what it means to be "an American." Nor is it all that helpful to say that this is an English-speaking, predominately Christian country. While I think these features get us closer to the answer, there are millions of English-speaking (and non-English-speaking) Christians in the world who are not Americans, and millions of non-Christians who are. Certainly, these fundamental historical characteristics are important elements in determining who we are as a nation. Like other restrictionists, I am opposed to public policies that seek, by design or by default, to significantly alter the nation's "demographic profile." Still, it must be recognized that demography alone does not, and cannot, explain what it means to be an American.

So where does that leave us? I think the answer to our question, ultimately, must be found in the realms of ideology and culture. What distinguishes the United States from other nations, and what unites the disparate peoples who make up our country, are our unique political, economic, and social values, beliefs, and institutions. Not race, or religion, or ancestry.

Whether described as a "proposition nation" or a "creedal nation" or simply just "an idea," the United States of America is defined by *our way of life*. This way of life is rooted in the ideals proclaimed in the Declaration of Independence; in the system of personal liberty and limited government established by the Constitution; in our traditions of self-reliance, personal responsibility, and entrepreneurism; in our emphasis on private property, freedom of contract, and merit-based achievement; in our respect for the rule of law; and in our commitment to affording equal justice to all. Perhaps above all, it is marked by our abiding belief that, as Americans, we have been called to a higher duty in human history. We are the "city upon a hill." We are "the last, best hope of earth."

Many immigration restrictionists and so-called traditionalists chafe at the notion that the American people are not defined by "blood and soil." Yet the truth of the matter is, we aren't. One of the greatest patriots who ever graced this nation's history, Teddy Roosevelt, said it best: "Americanism is a matter of the spirit and of the soul." Roosevelt deplored what he called "hyphenated Americanism," which refers to citizens whose primary loyalties lie with their particular ethnic groups or ancestral lands. Such a man, Roosevelt counseled, is to be "unsparingly condemn[ed]."

But Roosevelt also recognized that "if he is heartily and singly loyal to this Republic, then no matter where he was born, he is just as good an American as anyone else." Roosevelt's words are not offered here to suggest that all foreigners are equally capable of assimilating into our country. Clearly, they aren't. Nevertheless, the appellation "American" is open to anyone who adopts our way of life and loves this country above all others.

Which brings me to the final, and most difficult, aspect of this question: How do we define the "American way of life"? This is the issue over which our nation's "culture wars" are being fought. Today the country is divided between those who maintain their allegiance to certain historically American values, beliefs, and institutions (but not all—see racial segregation), and those who want to replace them with a very different set of ideas about the role of government, the nature of political and economic liberty, and the meaning of right and wrong. Are both sides in this struggle equally "American"?

Moreover, the "American way of life" has changed over time. We no longer have the Republic that existed in TR's days. The New Deal and Great Society revolutions—enthusiastically supported, I note, by millions of white, Christian, English-speaking citizens—significantly altered the political, economic, and social foundations of this country. Did they also change what it means to be "an American"? Is being an American equally compatible, for example, with support for big government versus small government? The welfare state versus rugged individualism? Socialism versus capitalism? And so on. Plainly, this is a much harder historical and intellectual problem than at first meets the eye.

Personally, I do not think the meaning of America is nearly so malleable as today's multiculturalists assume. But neither is it quite as narrow as many restrictionists contend. Nevertheless, I am convinced that being *an American* requires something more than merely living in this country, speaking English, obeying the law, and holding a job (although this would be a very good start!). What this "something more" is, however, is not self-evident, and, indeed, is the subject of increasingly bitter debate in this country.

Yet one thing is certain: If we stray too far from the lines laid down by the Founding Fathers and the generations of great American men and women who built on their legacy, we will cease to be "Americans" in any meaningful sense of the word. As Abraham Lincoln warned during the secession era, "America will never be destroyed from the outside. If we falter and lose our freedoms, it will be because we destroyed ourselves." Today the danger is not armed rebellion, but the slow erasing of the American national character through a process of political and cultural redefinition. If this ever happens, it will be a terrible day for this country, and for the world.

DISCUSSION QUESTIONS

1. Is it important for the United States to have a sense of shared values or not? What are the risks and benefits for individuals and the country of having a sense of shared values?

2. Political scientists and historians often refer to "American exceptionalism," or the idea that the United States was founded and grew from historically unique circumstances that gave it a distinctive political culture, set of values, and sense of how government, the economy, society, and individuals intersect. For example, compared to other democratic countries, Americans place more emphasis on individual rights, and the United States features much greater decentralization of political power across the branches and levels of government. Do these outcomes *require* the kind of shared beliefs discussed by Warshawsky or could they also be sustained in the absence of shared beliefs?

3. Occasionally in political campaigns a candidate's beliefs or actions will be described as "un-American." What do you think people mean when they use this term? Would you describe any of the views presented in the Jones et al. survey data as un-American? If so, what makes a view un-American to you? If not, are there any beliefs that you would define as un-American?

4. A visitor from another country asks you, "What does it mean to be an American?" What do you say?

2

The Founding and the Constitution: Should the Constitution Be Fundamentally Changed?

Veneration for the Constitution is a classic American value; indeed, it is often said that the essence of being an American is a set of shared values and commitments expressed within the four corners of that document, most notably equality and liberty. The Constitution is the embodiment of those values, celebrated as the first, and most enduring, written constitution in human history. We celebrate the first words of the Preamble, "We the People," salute the framers as men of historic wisdom and judgment, and honor the structures and processes of government.

We also note the practical wisdom of the framers, in their ability to reconcile competing tensions by creating a government powerful enough to function, but not at the risk of giving majorities the right to trample minority rights. Political theory at the time held that efforts to create democracies inevitably devolved into one of two end results: either mob rule, as majorities took control and used their power to oppress political minorities; or autocracy, as elites assumed control and did not give it up. The many carefully considered elements of constitutional structure—bicameralism, the balance between federal and state power, the equilibrium of checks and balances—have lasted for more than two centuries. And apart from one exceptional period of civil war, the structures have channeled political conflict peacefully.

Is that veneration truly warranted? Sanford Levinson, a professor at the University of Texas Law School, thinks not. He considers the Constitution to be a seriously flawed document in need of fundamental change. As originally written, the Constitution came nowhere near the aspirations of the Preamble, explicitly allowing slavery, and even after amendments retains several antidemocratic elements, including the electoral college (which elected another popular vote loser to the presidency in 2016); the vastly unequal representation in the Senate, in which Wyoming (population 587,000) has the same voting power as California (population over 39 million, over sixty-five times as large); and lifetime tenure for judges. These features fail to live up to the Preamble, which Levinson considers to be the foundation of the rest of the Constitution—the whole point of the constitutional enterprise. Levinson points out that several key figures of the American Founding—Thomas Jefferson especially—believed that the Constitution would require frequent updating. This was the purpose of Article V, which sets out the process for amending the document. And, Levinson notes, many of the features of the Constitution that we venerate were not thought through but were instead the product of pure compromise, in which the framers took vastly inconsistent positions when necessary in order to secure sufficient support for ratification. So, far from being a philosophically perfect document or system, the Constitution created a cumbersome and inequitable system, one that no other democratic system has chosen to copy since.

The problem with amending the Constitution is that the features Levinson considers most offensive are very difficult or, in the case of unequal representation in the Senate, virtually impossible to change. Article V specifies that no state can be deprived of its equal representation in the Senate without its consent (something that no state could ever be expected to do). The only recourse is a constitutional convention, in which delegates would consider fundamental reform. Levinson regards this as essential in order to allow the national government to respond to the challenge of modern economic and political times.

Greg Abbott and Walter Olson weigh in on opposing sides of the wisdom of calling a constitutional convention. Abbott, the governor of Texas, hails a convention as a way to "restore the rule of law," and counters fears about a "runaway convention." He points out that the scope of a convention could be constrained by each state legislature that endorses the idea, and even if the convention ends up "throwing the entire Constitution in the trashcan," anything the convention proposes would still have to be ratified by three-fourths of the states. Abbott concludes that we cannot allow the "federal government to continue ignoring the very document that created it."

Walter Olson, a senior fellow at the libertarian Cato Institute, argues that to hold a constitutional convention would be too big a risk. Olson points out that the actual language in the Constitution about how a convention would work is very sparse. The Constitution does not say if voting power at the convention would be equally distributed (like in the Senate) or based on population (like in the House). It also does not specify the actual mechanism for triggering a convention: Does each state need to agree on the same language of the topics to be discussed at the convention? He concludes that we always should "beware of a cure that might kill the patient."

Sanford Levinson

The Ratification Referendum: Sending the Constitution to a New Convention for Repair

The U.S. Constitution is radically defective in a number of important ways. Unfortunately, changing the Constitution is extremely difficult, for both political and constitutional reasons. But the difficulty of the task does not make it any less important that we first become aware of the magnitude of the deficiencies in the current Constitution and then turn our minds, as a community of concerned citizens, to figuring out potential solutions. This [reading] is organized around the conceit that Americans [should] have the opportunity to vote on the following proposal: "Shall Congress call a constitutional convention empowered to consider the adequacy of the Constitution, and, if thought necessary, to draft a new constitution that, upon completion, will be submitted to the electorate for its approval or disapproval by majority vote? Unless and until a new constitution gains popular approval, the current Constitution will continue in place."

Although such a referendum would be unprecedented with regard to the U.S. Constitution, there is certainly nothing "un-American" about such a procedure. As Professor John J. Dinan has noted in his recent comprehensive study of what he terms "the American state constitutional tradition," fourteen American states in their own constitutions explicitly give the people an opportunity "to periodically vote on whether a convention should be called." Article XIX of the New York Constitution, for example, provides that the state electorate be given the opportunity every twenty years to vote on the following question: "Shall there be a convention to revise the constitution and amend the same?" Should the majority answer in the affirmative, then the voters in each senate district will elect three delegates "at the next ensuring general election," while the statewide electorate "shall elect fifteen delegates-at-large." It should occasion no surprise that one author has described such a "mandatory referendum" as a means of "enforcing the people's right to reform their government."

It is no small matter to give people a choice with regard to the mechanisms—as well as the abstract principles—by which they are to be governed. The imagined referendum would allow "We the People of the United States of America," in whose name the document is ostensibly "ordain[ed]," to examine the fit between our national aspirations, set out in the Preamble to the Constitution, and the particular means chosen to realize those goals.

I am assuming that those reading this * * * are fellow Americans united by a deep and common concern about the future of our country. * * * I hope to convince you that, as patriotic Americans truly committed to the deepest principles of the Constitution, we should vote yes and thus trigger a new convention. My task is to persuade you that the Constitution we currently live under is grievously flawed, even in some ways a "clear and present danger" to achieving the laudable and inspiring goals to which this country professes to be committed, including republican self-government.

I believe that the best way to grasp the goals of our common enterprise is to ponder the inspiring words of the Preamble to the Constitution:

> We the People of the United States, in Order to form a more perfect Union, establish Justice, insure domestic tranquility, provide for the common defence, promote the general Welfare, and secure the Blessings of Liberty to ourselves and our Posterity, do ordain and establish this Constitution for the United States of America.

It is regrettable that law professors rarely teach and that courts rarely cite the Preamble, for it is *the single most important part* of the Constitution. The reason is simple: It announces the *point* of the entire enterprise. The 4,500 or so words that followed the Preamble in the original, unamended Constitution were all in effect merely means that were thought to be useful to achieving the great aims set out above. It is indeed the ends articulated in the Preamble that justify the means of our political institutions. And to the extent that the means turn out to be counterproductive, then we should revise them.

It takes no great effort to find elements in the original Constitution that run counter to the Preamble. It is impossible for us today to imagine how its authors squared a commitment to the "Blessings of Liberty" with the toleration and support of chattel slavery that is present in various articles of the Constitution. The most obvious example is the bar placed on Congress's ability to forbid the participation by Americans in the international slave trade until 1808. The most charitable interpretation of the framers, articulated by Frederick Douglass, is that they viewed these compromises with the acknowledged evil of slavery as temporary; the future would see its eradication through peaceful constitutional processes.

One might believe that the Preamble is incomplete because, for example, it lacks a commitment to the notion of equality. Political scientist Mark Graber has suggested that the reference to "*our* Posterity" suggests a potentially unattractive limitation of our concerns *only* to members of the American political community, with no notice taken of the posterity of other societies, whatever their plight. Even if one would prefer a more explicitly cosmopolitan Preamble, I find it hard to imagine rejecting any of the overarching values enunciated there. In any event, I am happy to endorse the Preamble as the equivalent of our creedal summary of America's civil religion.

There are two basic responses to the discovery that ongoing institutional practices are counterproductive with regard to achieving one's announced goals. One is to adjust the practices in ways that would make achievement of the aims more likely. This is, often, when we mean by the very notion of rationality: One does not persist in behaviors that are acknowledged to make more difficult the realization of one's professed hopes. Still, a second response, which has its own rationality, is to adjust the goals to the practices. Sometimes, this makes very good sense if one comes to the justified conclusion that the goals may be utopian. In such cases, it is a sign of maturity to recognize that we will inevitably fall short in our aims and that "the best may be enemy of the good" if we are tempted to throw over quite adequate, albeit imperfect, institutions in an attempt to attain the ideal.

Perhaps one might even wish to defend the framers' compromises with slavery on the ground that they were absolutely necessary to the achievement of the political union of the thirteen states. One must believe that such a union, in turn, was preferable to the likely alternative, which would have been the creation of two or three separate countries along the Atlantic coast. Political scientist David

Hendrickson has demonstrated that many of the framers—and many other theorists as well—viewed history as suggesting a high probability that such separate countries would have gone to war with one another and made impossible any significant measure of "domestic tranquility." Hendrickson well describes the Constitution as a "peace pact" designed to prevent the possibility of war. If there is one thing we know, it is that unhappy compromises must often be made when negotiating such pacts. Of course, American slaves—and their descendants—could scarcely be expected to be so complacently accepting of these compromises, nor, of course, should *any* American who takes seriously the proclamation of the Pledge of Allegiance that ours is a system that takes seriously the duty to provide "liberty and justice for all."

Not only must we restrain ourselves from expecting too much of any government; we must also recognize that the Preamble sets out potentially conflicting goals. It is impossible to maximize the achievement of all of the great ends of the Constitution. To take an obvious example, providing for the "common defence" may require on occasion certain incursions into the "Blessings of Liberty." One need only refer to the military draft, which was upheld in 1918 by the Supreme Court against an attack claiming that it constituted the "involuntary servitude"—that is, slavery—prohibited by the Thirteenth Amendment. We also properly accept certain limitations on the freedom of the press with regard, say, to publishing certain information—the standard example is troop movements within a battle zone—deemed to be vital to American defense interests. The year 2005 ended with the beginning of a great national debate about the propriety of warrantless interceptions of telephone calls and other incursions on traditional civil liberties in order, ostensibly, to protect ourselves against potential terrorists.

Even if one concedes the necessity of adjusting aims in light of practical realities, it should also be readily obvious that one can easily go overboard. At the very least, one should always be vigilant in assessing such adjustments lest one find, at the end of the day, that the aims have been reduced to hollow shells. It is also necessary to ask if a rationale supporting a given adjustment that might well have been convincing at time A necessarily continues to be present at time B. Practical exigencies that required certain political compromises in 1787 no longer obtain today. We have long since realized this about slavery. It is time that we apply the same critical eye to the compromise of 1787 that granted all states an equal vote in the Senate.

To criticize that particular compromise—or any of the other features of the Constitution that I shall examine below—is not necessarily to criticize the Founders themselves. My project—and, therefore, your own vote for a new convention, should you be persuaded by what follows—requires no denigration of the Founders. They were, with some inevitable exceptions, an extraordinary group of men who performed extraordinary deeds, including drafting a Constitution that started a brand-new governmental system. By and large, they deserve the monuments that have been erected in their honor. But they themselves emphasized the importance—indeed, necessity—of learning from experience.

They were, after all, a generation that charted new paths by overturning a centuries-long notion of the British constitutional order because it no longer conformed to their own sense of possibility (and fairness). They also, as it happened, proved ruthlessly willing to ignore the limitations of America's "first constitution," the Articles of Confederation. Although Article XIII of that founding document required unanimous approval by the thirteen state legislatures before any amendment could take effect, Article VII of the Constitution drafted in Philadelphia required the approval of only nine of the thirteen states, and the approval was to be given by state conventions rather than by the legislatures.

The most important legacies handed down by the founding generation were, first, a remarkable willingness to act in bold and daring ways when they believed that the situation demanded it, coupled with the noble visions first of the Declaration of Independence and then of the Preamble. Both are as inspiring—and potentially disruptive—today as when they were written more than two centuries ago. But we should also be inspired by the copious study that Madison and others made of every available history and analysis of political systems ranging from ancient Greece to the Dutch republic and the British constitutional order. We best honor the framers by taking the task of creating a republican political order as seriously as they did and being equally willing to learn from what the history of the past 225 years, both at home and abroad, can teach us about how best to achieve and maintain such an order. At the time of its creation, we could legitimately believe that we were the only country committed to democratic self-governance. That is surely no longer the case, and we might well have lessons to learn from our co-ventures in that enterprise. To the extent that experience teaches us that the Constitution in significant aspects demeans "the consent of the governed" and has become an impediment to achieving the goals of the Preamble, we honor rather than betray the founders by correcting their handiwork.

Overcoming Veneration

* * * I suspect * * * that at least some readers might find it difficult to accept even the possibility that our Constitution is seriously deficient because they venerate the Constitution and find the notion of seriously criticizing it almost sacrilegious.

In an earlier book, *Constitutional Faith*, I noted the tension between the desire of James Madison that Americans "venerate" their Constitution and the distinctly contrasting views of his good friend Thomas Jefferson that, instead, the citizenry regularly subject it to relentless examination. Thus, whatever may have been Jefferson's insistence on respecting what he called the "chains" of the Constitution, he also emphasized that the "Creator has made the earth for the living, not the dead." It should not be surprising, then, that he wrote to Madison in 1789, "No society can make a perpetual constitution, or even a perpetual law."

Jefferson and Madison might have been good friends and political associates, but they disagreed fundamentally with regard to the wisdom of subjecting the Constitution to critical analysis. Jefferson was fully capable of writing that "[w]e may consider each generation as a distinct nation, with a right, by the will of its majority, to bind themselves, but none to bind the succeeding generation, more than the inhabitants of another country." His ultimate optimism about the Constitution lay precisely in its potential for change: "Happily for us, that when we find our constitutions defective and insufficient to secure the happiness of our people, we can assemble with all the coolness of philosophers, and set it to rights, while every other nation on earth must have recourse to arms to amend or restore their constitutions." * * *

Madison, however, would have none of this. He treated 1787 almost as a miraculous and singular event. Had he been a devotee of astrology, he might have said that the stars were peculiarly and uniquely aligned to allow the drafting of the Constitution and then its ratification. Though Madison was surely too tactful to mention this, part of the alignment was the absence of the famously contentious Jefferson and John Adams. Both were 3,000 miles across the sea, where they were serving as the first ambassadors from the new United States to Paris and London, respectively. Moreover, it certainly did not hurt that Rhode Island had refused to send any delegates at all and therefore had no opportunity to make almost inevitable mischief, not to mention being unable to vote in an institutional structure where the vote of one state could make a big difference. And, if pressed, Madison would presumably have agreed that the Constitutional Convention—and the ratifying conventions thereafter—would never have succeeded had the delegates included American slaves, Native Americans, or women in the spirit of Abigail Adams. She had famously—and altogether unsuccessfully—told her husband that leaders of the new nation should "remember the ladies." One need not see the framers in Philadelphia as an entirely homogeneous group—they were not—in order to realize that the room was devoid of those groups in America that were viewed as merely the *objects*, and not the active *subjects*, of governance.

Madison sets out his views most clearly in the *Federalist*, No. 49, where he explicitly takes issue with Jefferson's proposal for rather frequent constitutional conventions that would consider whether "alter[ation]" of the constitution might be desirable. Madison acknowledges the apparent appeal, in a system where "the people are the only legitimate fountain of power," of "appeal[ing] to the people themselves." However, "there appear to be insuperable objections against the proposed recurrence to the people." Perhaps the key objection is that "*frequent appeal to the people would carry an implication of some defect in the government [and] deprive the government of that veneration which time bestows on every thing, and without which perhaps the wisest and freest governments would not possess the requisite stability.*" Only "a nation of philosophers" can forgo this emotion of veneration—and, therefore, feel free of guilt-ridden anxiety about the idea of constitutional change. However, "a nation of philosophers is as little to be expected as the philosophical race of kings wished for by Plato."

Madison is thus fearful of "disturbing the public tranquillity by interesting too strongly the public passions." The success of Americans in replacing a defective Articles of Confederation with a better Constitution does not constitute a precedent for future action. We should "recollect," he says, "that all the existing constitutions were formed in the midst of a danger which repressed the passions most unfriendly to order and concord." Moreover, the people at large possessed "an enthusiastic confidence . . . in their patriotic leaders," which, he says, fortunately "stifled the ordinary diversity of opinions on great national questions." He is extremely skeptical that the "future situations in which we must expect to be usually placed" will "present any equivalent security against the danger" of an excess of public passion, disrespect for leaders, and the full play of diverse opinions. In case there is any doubt, he writes of his fear that the "*passions*, therefore, not the *reasons*, of the public would sit in judgment."

Madison's view of his fellow Americans was far closer to that of Alexander Hamilton, with whom he had coauthored the *Federalist*. One can doubt that Madison expressed any reservations when hearing Hamilton, addressing his fellow delegates to the Philadelphia convention on June 18, 1787, denounce the conceit that "the voice of the people" is "the voice of God." On the contrary, said Hamilton: "The people are turbulent and changing; they seldom judge or determine right." Although Madison was not opposed to constitutional amendment as such, he clearly saw almost no role for a public that would engage in probing questions suggesting that there might be serious "defects" in the Constitution. Only philosophers (like himself?) or, perhaps, "patriotic leaders" could be trusted to engage in dispassionate political dialogue and reasoning. In contrast, the general public should be educated to feel only "veneration" for their Constitution rather than be encouraged to use their critical faculties and actually assess the relationship between the great ends set out in the Preamble and the instruments devised for their realization.

* * *

This is a mistake. To the extent that we continue thoughtlessly to venerate, and therefore not subject to truly critical examination, our Constitution, we are in the position of the battered wife who continues to profess the "essential goodness" of her abusive husband. To stick with the analogy for a moment, it may well be the case that the husband, when sober or not gambling, is a decent, even loving, partner. The problem is that such moments are more than counterbalanced by abusive ones, even if they are relatively rare. And he becomes especially abusive when she suggests the possibility of marital counseling and attendant change. Similarly, that there are good features of our Constitution should not be denied. But there are also significantly abusive ones, and it is time for us to face them rather than remain in a state of denial.

Trapped Inside the Article V Cage

The framers of the Constitution were under no illusion that they had created a perfect document. The best possible proof for this proposition comes from George Washington himself. As he wrote to his nephew Bushrod two months after the conclusion of the Philadelphia convention over which he had presided, "*The warmest friends and the best supporters the Constitution has do not contend that it is free from imperfections*; but they found them unavoidable and are sensible if evil is likely to arise there from, the remedy must come hereafter." Sounding a remarkably Jeffersonian note, Washington noted that the "People (for it is with them to Judge) can, as they will have the advantage of experience on their Side, decide with as much propriety on the alteration[s] and amendment[s] which are necessary." Indeed, wrote the man described as the Father of Our Country, "I do not think we are more inspired, have more wisdom, or possess more virtue, than those who will come after us."

Article V itself is evidence of the recognition of the possibility—and inevitable reality—of imperfection, else they would have adopted John Locke's suggestion in a constitution that he drafted for the Carolina colonies that would have made the document unamendable. It is an unfortunate reality, though, that Article V, practically speaking, brings us all too close to the Lockean dream (or nightmare) of changeless stasis.

As University of Houston political scientist Donald Lutz has conclusively demonstrated, the U.S. Constitution is the most difficult to amend of any constitution currently existing in the world today. Formal amendment of the U.S. Constitution generally requires the approval of two-thirds of each of the two houses of our national Congress, followed by the approval of three-quarters of the states (which today means thirty-eight of the fifty states). Article V does allow the abstract possibility that amendments could be proposed through the aegis of a constitutional convention called by Congress upon the petition of two-thirds of the states; such proposals, though, would still presumably have to be ratified by the state legislatures or, in the alternative, as was done with regard to the Twenty-First Amendment repealing the prohibition of alcohol required by the Eighteenth Amendment, by conventions in each of the states. As a practical matter, though, Article V makes it next to impossible to amend the Constitution with regard to genuinely controversial issues, even if substantial—and intense—majorities advocate amendment.

As I have written elsewhere, some significant change functionally similar to "amendment" has occurred informally, outside of the procedures set out by Article V. One scholar has aptly described this as a process of "constitutional change off-the-books." Yale law professor Bruce Ackerman has written several brilliant books detailing the process of "non-Article V" amendment, and I warmly commend them to the reader. Yet it is difficult to argue that such informal amendment has occurred, or is likely to occur, with regard to the basic *structural* aspects of the American political system with which this book is primarily concerned.

It is one thing to argue, as Ackerman has done, that the New Deal worked as a functional amendment of the Constitution by giving Congress significant new powers to regulate the national economy. Similarly, one could easily argue that the president, for good or for ill, now possesses powers over the use of armed forces that would have been inconceivable to the generation of the framers. Whatever the text of the Constitution may say about the power of Congress to "declare war" or whatever the original understanding of this clause, it is hard to deny that many presidents throughout our history have successfully chosen to take the country to war without seeking a declaration of war (or, in some cases, even prior congressional approval of any kind). Ackerman and David Golove have also persuasively argued that the Treaty Clause, which requires that two-thirds of the Senate assent to any treaty, has been transformed through the use of "executive agreements." Although such agreements are unmentioned in the text of the Constitution, presidents have frequently avoided the strictures of the Treaty Clause by labeling an "agreement" what earlier would have been viewed as a "treaty." Thus, the North American Free Trade Agreement did not have to leap the hurdles erected by the Treaty Clause; instead, it was validated by majority votes of both the House of Representatives and the Senate.

These developments are undoubtedly important, and any complete analysis of our constitutional system should take account of such flexibility. But we should not overemphasize our system's capacity to change, and it is *constitutional stasis* rather than the potential for adaptation that is my focus.

* * *

One cannot, as a practical matter, litigate the obvious inequality attached to Wyoming's having the same voting power in the Senate as California. Nor can we imagine even President George W. Bush, who has certainly not been a shrinking violet with regard to claims of presidential power, announcing that Justice John Paul Stevens—appointed in 1976 and embarking on this fourth decade of service on the Supreme Court at the age of eighty-six—is simply "too old" or has served "long enough," and that he is therefore nominating, and asking the Senate to confirm, a successor to Justice Stevens in spite of the awkward fact that the justice has not submitted his resignation.

In any event, * * * the Constitution makes it unacceptably difficult to achieve the inspiring goals of the Preamble and, therefore, warrants our disapproval. * * *

Although I am asking you to take part in a hypothetical referendum and to vote no with regard to the present Constitution, I am *not* asking you to imagine simply tearing it up and leaping into the unknown of a fanciful "state of nature." All you must commit yourself to is the proposition that the Constitution is sufficiently flawed to justify calling a new convention authorized to scrutinize all aspects of the Constitution and to suggest such changes as are felt to be desirable. The new convention would be no more able to bring its handiwork into being by fiat than were the framers in Philadelphia. All proposals would require popular approval in a further national referendum. This leaves open the possibility that, even after voting to trigger the convention, you could ultimately decide that the "devil you know" (the present Constitution) is preferable to the "devil you don't" (the proposed replacement). But the important thing, from my perspective, is to recognize that there are indeed "devilish" aspects of our present Constitution that should be confronted and, if at all possible, exorcised. To complete this metaphor, one might also remember that "the devil is in the details." * * *

Greg Abbott

Restoring the Rule of Law with States Leading the Way

The Constitution is increasingly eroded with each passing year. That is a tragedy given the volume of blood spilled by patriots to win our country's freedom and repeatedly defend it over the last 240 years. Moreover, the declining relevance of our Nation's governing legal document is dangerous. Thomas Hobbes's observation more than 350 years ago remains applicable today: The only thing that separates a nation from anarchy is its collective willingness to know and obey the law.

But today, most Americans have no idea what our Constitution says. According to a recent poll, one-third of Americans cannot name the three branches of government; one-third cannot name any branch; and one-third thinks that the President has the "final say" about the government's powers. Obviously, the American people cannot hold their government accountable if they do not know what the source of that accountability says.

The Constitution is not just abstract and immaterial to average Americans; it also is increasingly ignored by government officials. Members of Congress used to routinely quote the Constitution while debating whether a particular policy proposal could be squared with Congress's enumerated powers. Such debates rarely happen today. In fact, when asked to identify the source of constitutional authority for Obamacare's individual mandate, the Speaker of the House revealed all too much when she replied with anger and incredulity: "*Are you serious?*" And, while the Supreme Court continues to identify new rights protected by the Constitution's centuries-old text, it is telling that the justices frequently depart from what the document actually says and rely instead on words or concepts that are found nowhere in the document. That is why one scholar observed that "in this day and age, discussing the doctrine of enumerated powers is like discussing the redemption of Imperial Chinese bonds."

Abandoning, ignoring, and eroding the strictures of the Constitution cheapens the entire institution of law. One of the cornerstones of this country was that ours would be a Nation of laws and not of men. The Constitution is the highest such law and the font of all other laws. As long as all Americans uphold the Constitution's authority, the document will continue to provide the ultimate defense of our liberties. But once the Constitution loses its hold on American life, we also lose confidence in the ability of law to protect us. Without the rule of law, the things we treasure can be taken away by an election, by whims of individual leaders, by impulsive social-media campaigns, or by collective apathy.

The Constitution provides a better way—if only we were willing to follow it. The Constitution imposes real limits on Congress and forces its members to do their jobs rather than pass the buck. The Constitution forces the President to work with Congress to accomplish his priorities rather than usurping its powers by circumventing the legislative process with executive orders and administrative fiats. And the Constitution forces the Supreme Court to confront the limits on its powers to transform the country. Although the Constitution provides no assurance that any branch of government will make policy choices you like, the Constitution offers *legitimacy* to those choices and legitimate pathways to override those choices. The people who make those choices would have to stand for election, they would have to work with others who stand for election, and crucially, they would have to play by rules that we all agree to beforehand rather than making them up as they go along.

Of course, the Constitution already does all of this. And thus it bears emphasis at the outset that *the Constitution itself is not broken*. What *is* broken is our Nation's willingness to obey the Constitution and to hold our leaders accountable to it. As explained in the following pages, all three branches of the federal government have wandered far from the roles that the Constitution sets out for them.

For various reasons, "We the People" have allowed all three branches of government to get away with it. And with each power grab the next somehow seems less objectionable. When measured by how far we have strayed from the Constitution we originally agreed to, the government's flagrant and repeated violations of the rule of law amount to a wholesale abdication of the Constitution's design.

That constitutional problem calls for a constitutional solution, just as it did at our Nation's founding. Indeed, a constitutional crisis gave birth to the Constitution we have today. The Articles of Confederation, which we adopted after the Revolutionary War, proved insufficient to protect and defend our fledgling country. So the States assembled to devise what we now know as our Constitution. At that assembly, various States stepped up to offer their leadership visions for what the new Constitution should say. Virginia's delegates offered the "Virginia Plan," New Jersey's delegates offered the "New Jersey Plan," and Connecticut's delegates brokered a compromise called the "Connecticut Plan." Without those States' plans, there would be no Constitution and probably no United States of America at all.

Now it is Texas's turn. The Texas Plan is not so much a vision to alter the Constitution as it is a call to restore the rule of our current one. The problem is that we have forgotten what our Constitution means, and with that amnesia, we also have forgotten what it means to be governed by laws instead of men. The solution is to restore the rule of law by ensuring that our government abides by the Constitution's limits. Our courts are supposed to play that role, but today, we have judges who actively subvert the Constitution's original design rather than uphold it. Yet even though we can no longer rely on our Nation's leaders to enforce the Constitution that "We the People" agreed to, the Constitution provides another way forward. Acting through the States, the people can amend their Constitution to force their leaders in all three branches of government to recognize renewed limits on federal power. Without the consent of any politicians in Washington, D.C., "We the People" can rein in the federal government and restore the balance of power between the States and the United States. The Texas Plan accomplishes this by offering nine constitutional amendments:

I. Prohibit Congress from regulating activity that occurs wholly within one State.

II. Require Congress to balance its budget.

III. Prohibit administrative agencies—and the unelected bureaucrats that staff them—from creating federal law.

IV. Prohibit administrative agencies—and the unelected bureaucrats that staff them—from preempting state law.

V. Allow a two-thirds majority of the States to override a U.S. Supreme Court decision.

VI. Require a seven-justice super-majority vote for U.S. Supreme Court decisions that invalidate a democratically enacted law.

VII. Restore the balance of power between the federal and state governments by limiting the former to the powers expressly delegated to it in the Constitution.

VIII. Give state officials the power to sue in federal court when federal officials overstep their bounds.

IX. Allow a two-thirds majority of the States to override a federal law or regulation.

* * *

Objections to an Article V Convention Lack Merit

The framers intended for States to call for conventions to propose constitutional amendments when, as now, the federal government has overstepped its bounds. And over the last 200 or so years, there have been hundreds of applications calling for such a convention spread out among virtually every state legislature. Yet no application has reached the critical two-thirds threshold to require the convention.

The States' previous failures to reach the two-thirds threshold for a convention could stem from the fact that, before now, circumstances did not demand it. But it is also possible that the States' efforts have been thwarted by counterarguments that surely will surface again in response to the Texas Plan. Whatever influence such counterarguments may have in previous contexts and other state legislatures' applications for constitutional conventions, they lack merit here.

* * *

Nor can critics credibly claim that a convention is "scary" or that it somehow threatens valuable tenets of the Constitution. That is so for at least two reasons. First, whatever happens at the convention, no amendments will be made to the Constitution unless and until they are approved by an overwhelming majority (three-fourths) of the States. That is an extraordinary super-majority requirement that ensures, in James Iredell's words, that "[i]t is highly probable that amendments agreed to in either of [Article V's] methods would be conducive to the public welfare, when so large a majority of the states consented to them." It takes only 13 States to block any measure from becoming a constitutional amendment.

* * * [It] is not as if the three-fourths approval requirement is the Constitution's only failsafe against imprudent amendments. The Constitution also leaves it to the States to limit the scope of the convention itself. In fact, four States already have applied for constitutional conventions that include some portion of the Texas Plan, and all of them limit their applications to specific issues. Likewise, the Texas Legislature can limit its application for a convention—or its participation in a convention—to the specific issues included in the Texas Plan and discussed above. To the extent the convention strayed from those issues, Texas's consent to the convention's activities would automatically dissolve. State legislatures could even command in their laws authorizing participation in a convention that the state must vote against any constitutional convention provision not authorized by the state.

Some nonetheless argue that the Constitution does not allow state legislatures to limit the scope of a convention. The critics seize on this argument to raise the specter of a "runaway convention," in which the States propose a convention to debate limited amendments, but in which the delegates end up throwing the entire Constitution in the trashcan. Even if that happened, none of the delegates' efforts would become law without approval from three-fourths of the States. But even on its own terms, the criticism lacks merit.

The specter of a "runaway convention" goes like this. First, the critics argue, the Constitution says state legislatures "shall call a Convention for proposing Amendments," not for *confirming* a pre-written amendment that the state legislatures included in their applications for a convention. That means, the critics say, that States must call general, open-ended conventions; the convention delegates then perform the work of drafting the amendments; and the States' only option is to give a thumbs-up or thumbs-down at the end of the convention process. If the framers of Article V wanted to authorize conventions limited to particular issues, the critics conclude, they would have said so.

It is true that Article V does not expressly authorize States to limit conventions to particular issues—but the problem for would-be critics of the Texas Plan is that Article V *also* does not require general and open-ended conventions. Indeed, that is by design. As noted above, the whole point of the second path for proposing amendments was to *empower* States to propose amendments to the Constitution. In adopting that second path, the framers agreed with George Mason that the States should have constitutional redress when the federal government overstepped its bounds. And nothing that Mason (or his fellow framers) said would suggest that the States were somehow limited in *how* they exercised that power to defend their prerogatives against a federal government. To the contrary, James Madison specifically noted that the Constitution was silent on the issue, and he argued that that silence was good and necessary to preserve the States' flexibility. In Madison's words, "Constitutional regulations [of such matters] ought to be as much as possible avoided."

While the Constitution's text is silent on the topic, the framers themselves were not. To take just one example, George Nicholas pointed out during Virginia's ratification debates that conventions called by the States could—indeed, *would*— be limited to particular issues: "The conventions which shall be so called will have their deliberations confined to a few points; no local interest to divert their attention; nothing but the necessary alterations." And because the States would limit their applications for conventions to particular issues, "[i]t is natural to conclude that those states who apply for calling the convention will concur in the ratification of the proposed amendments." Of course, it would not be natural to assume that the States would support the results of the convention they called if—as the critics argue—the States could have zero assurances regarding what the convention delegates would do at that convention.

The very thing that belies any allegation of radicalism in the Texas Plan— namely, the super-majority requirements for proposing and ratifying amendments—arguably undermines its efficacy as a check on federal overreach. The latter was the principal point of Patrick Henry, one of the greatest orators of the eighteenth century and a ferocious Anti-Federalist. He argued that the States' power to amend the Constitution did not go nearly far enough to protect the people from an overbearing federal government. In particular, he bemoaned Article V's super-majority requirements:

> This, Sir, is the language of democracy; that a majority of the community have a right to alter their Government when found to be oppressive: But how different is the genius of your new Constitution from this! How different from the sentiments of freemen, that a contemptible minority can prevent the good of the majority! . . . If, Sir, amendments are left to the twentieth or tenth part of the people of America, your liberty is gone forever. . . . It will be easily contrived to procure the opposition of one tenth of the people to any alteration, however judicious. The Honorable Gentleman who presides, told us, that to prevent abuses in our Government, we will assemble in Conven-

tion, recall our delegated powers, and punish our servants for abusing the trust reposed in them. Oh, Sir, we should have fine times indeed, if to punish tyrants, it were only sufficient to assemble the people!

Patrick Henry might be right that even an assembly of the people will be insufficient to restore the rule of law and to bring the federal government to heel. And it is true that Article V allows a minority to oppose any amendment that the overwhelming majority of Americans support.

But far from dissuading the effort to amend our Constitution, Henry's words should encourage it. The benefits of the Texas Plan are many because any change effectuated by an assembly of the people will force the federal government—whether in big ways or small—to take the Constitution seriously again. And the downsides of such an assembly are virtually nonexistent, given that any change to our Constitution's text requires such overwhelming nationwide support. The only true downside comes from doing nothing and allowing the federal government to continue ignoring the very document that created it.

Walter Olson

An Article V Constitutional Convention?
Wrong Idea, Wrong Time

In his quest to catch the Road Runner, the Coyote in the old Warner Brothers cartoons would always order supplies from the ACME Corporation, but they never performed as advertised. Either they didn't work at all, or they blew up in his face.

Which brings us to the idea of a so-called Article V convention assembled for the purpose of proposing amendments to the U.S. Constitution, an idea enjoying some vogue at both ends of the political spectrum.

On the left, a group founded by liberal TV host Cenk Uygur is pushing a convention aimed at overturning the Supreme Court's hated *Citizens United* decision and declaring that from now on corporations should stop having rights, or at least not a right to spend money spreading political opinions. Four liberal states—California, Vermont, Illinois, and New Jersey—have signed on to this idea.

On the right, the longstanding proposal for a convention to draft a balanced budget amendment has at times come within striking distance of the requisite two-thirds of state legislatures needed to trigger the idea. And for the past few years, talk-show host Mark Levin has been campaigning for a convention with broader conservative goals, an idea that got a boost when Florida Senator Marco Rubio recently endorsed it, citing "Washington's refusal to place restrictions on itself."

Rubio's specifics are still sketchy—term limits for members of Congress and Supreme Court justices would be part of it—but Texas Republican Governor Greg Abbott has now jumped in with a detailed "Texas Plan" of nine constitutional amendments mostly aimed at wresting various powers back from the federal government to the states.

Some of these ideas are better than others—Governor Abbott's 92-page report is rather erudite, and lays out its arguments skillfully even if I do not find all of them sound—but every such scheme to stage an Article V convention should come with a giant ACME brand stenciled on its side. If it doesn't just sit there doing nothing, it's apt to blow up on the spot.

The detonation that skeptics most fear is what's called a runaway convention, in which the delegates called together to, say, install term limits or revamp campaign finance, decide to venture into other areas as well, and perhaps start proposing whatever new amendments they think might be a good idea. Hence [the late] Justice Antonin Scalia's brusque dismissal: "I certainly would not want a constitutional convention. Whoa! Who knows what would come out of it?"

Some respected scholars who favor a convention argue that strict instructions would deter the assembled delegates from venturing beyond the velvet rope. But if that cannot be made a legal requirement, it winds up more like an honor code. "Congress might try to limit the agenda to one amendment or to one issue, but there is no way to assure that the Convention would obey," wrote the late Chief Justice Warren Burger.

Don't believe Scalia or Burger? Go ahead and read the instruction kit for a convention, such as it is, in Article V of the U.S. Constitution. It's quite brief. Here's the full relevant text:

> The Congress, whenever two-thirds of both houses shall deem it necessary, shall propose amendments to this Constitution, or, on the application of the legislatures of two-thirds of the several states, shall call a convention for proposing amendments, which, in either case, shall be valid to all intents

and purposes, as part of this Constitution, when ratified by the legislatures of three-fourths of the several states, or by conventions in three-fourths thereof, as the one or the other mode of ratification may be proposed by the Congress . . .

Note what this does *not* say. It says not a word expressly authorizing the states, Congress, or some combination of the two to confine the subject matter of a convention. It says not a word about whether Congress, in calculating whether the requisite 34 states have called for a convention, must (or must not) aggregate calls for a convention on, say, a balanced budget, with differently worded calls arising from related or perhaps even unrelated topics. It says not a word prescribing that the makeup of a convention, as many conservatives imagine, will be one-state-one-vote (as Alaska and Wyoming might hope) or whether states with larger populations should be given larger delegations (as California and New York would surely argue).

Does Congress, or perhaps the Supreme Court, get to resolve these questions—the same Congress and Supreme Court that the process is aimed at doing an end run around? If the Supreme Court resolves them, does it do so only at the very end of the process, after years of national debate have been spent in devising amendments that we find out after the fact were not generated in proper form?

Justice Burger described the whole process as "a grand waste of time." One reason is that after advocates get the process rolling by convincing two-thirds of states—or 34, itself a fairly demanding number—the amendments that emerge from a convention do not get ratified unless three-quarters of states ratify—or 38, a quite demanding number.

Put differently, it takes only 13 states to refuse to act to kill any of these ideas, bad or good, in the end. Sorry, Cenk and Marco, but so long as we have a nation fairly closely divided between Blue and Red sentiment, there will be at least 13 states skeptical of some systemic change so big that you had to go around the backs of both Congress and the Supreme Court to pull it off. If you're a progressive who thinks the populist winds blow only in your favor, reflect for a moment on the success of Donald Trump. If you're a conservative to whom radio call-ins resound as the voice of the people, consider that state legislatures confronted with the hard legal issues a convention would raise might turn for advice and assistance to elite lawyers (yikes) or even law professors (double yikes).

Finally, we shouldn't assume—as do some of Governor Abbott's co-thinkers—that most state governments are as eager as Texas to curtail the powers of the feds. One of the most significant conservative books on federalism lately, George Mason University professor Michael Greve's *The Upside-Down Constitution*, sheds light on this. Conservatives tell a campfire story of how the federal government got big by taking power away from the states. But in his (admittedly long and complicated) book, Greve argues that the truth is closer to the opposite.

Whether in spending programs, regulations, subsidies, you name it, almost every big expansion of federal power has been skillfully designed as a deal that cuts state political elites into some of the resulting flow of power and money—consider, for example, how state education, police, road, and environmental departments have come to depend on Washington's largesse. And while many states may join Texas in sincerely griping at the bad end of the deal—the endless paperwork, the unfunded mandates—that doesn't mean they'd actually join Governor Abbott in risking the connection.

Yes, the federal government has slipped its constitutional bounds, and yes, that's infuriating. Just don't confuse a plan for talking, which is what these amount to, with a plan for actually changing things, and always beware of a cure that might kill the patient.

DISCUSSION QUESTIONS

1. Most of the time, people become critical of the Constitution when they don't get the policy results they want. When Congress fails to pass legislation because of the power of small-state senators, when the Supreme Court issues a ruling they oppose, or when the president makes a decision regarding the use of force that they oppose, the immediate impulse is to blame the system and call for change that would make their preferred policies more likely. Is this a valid reason for wanting the system to change?

2. The Constitution was written more than 230 years ago by a group of white men who had very "unmodern" views about democracy and equality. On what basis should we be bound by the decisions that they made? What would be the result if each generation were permitted to remake the rules, as Abbott suggests? Do you agree with Olson's concerns about the constitutional convention?

3. Often, opinions about the Constitution divide along philosophical lines. On one side are people who believe that the most important purpose of a constitution is to limit government size and power. On the other are people who believe that the Constitution must protect rights and promote equality, which almost always involves expanding the size and power of government. Who has the better case? Why?

3

Federalism: Immigration Reform—More Power to the States?

The election of Donald Trump as president would seem to indicate that a radical shift in immigration policy is imminent. He started his campaign by claiming that undocumented immigrants from Mexico were rapists and criminals, and by promising to build a wall along the entire Mexican border while making the Mexican government pay for it. Later in the campaign, Trump called for the deportation of an estimated 11–12 million undocumented workers in the first 18 months of his presidency and said that he would bar all Muslims from entering the country. After the election, there was no talk of making Mexico pay for a wall and President Trump said that deportation efforts would focus on those who had committed crimes. As the article from *The Economist* points out, this would be much like President Obama's policy.

Even with this more narrow focus, *The Economist* points out that President Trump would have a difficult time deporting 2–3 million illegal residents for two reasons. First, the federal agencies that would carry out the deportations are already facing a huge backlog of cases (more than 500,000 cases are in immigrations court) and it would be difficult to more than double their efforts. Second, states and cities are serving as "sanctuaries" by resisting deportation efforts, which would also complicate efforts to step up the pace of deportations.

While it is unlikely that the extreme measures proposed by Donald Trump during the 2016 presidential election will be implemented, it is even less likely that comprehensive immigration reform will become law any time soon. Favored by both Presidents George W. Bush and Barack Obama, comprehensive reform would have provided a "path to citizenship" for the United States' 11–12 million undocumented residents. Given the absence of significant change at the national level, Gulasekaram and Ramakrishnan argue that state and local governments will be the source of innovation in immigration policy in the next few years. They point out that while the national government still sets the main direction of immigration policy, state and local governments have a great deal of power over how those policies are implemented. These governments may choose a more restrictive approach, as pioneered in Arizona, or a more immigrant-friendly approach, as in California. Given the broad range of state-based policies, it would be difficult for the national government to impose a uniform approach.

Shikha Dalmia takes this state-based argument to the next level, proposing that states be given the power to grant work visas to meet local needs. She argues that agricultural states have been forced to shift jobs to Mexico because of a lack of workers, and the tech industry in California, Washington, and Massachusetts is losing highly skilled people because of a shortage of H-1B visas. Dalmia suggests that states be allowed to follow the lead of Canada, which allows its provinces to establish their own guest worker programs. This seems to be an immigration reform proposal that could attract bipartisan support.

The Economist

Hamilton's Heirs: If He Wins a Second Term, the President-Elect Could Realistically Expel around 4 Million People in Total

When she was seven Greisa Martinez moved illegally from Hidalgo, in Mexico, to Dallas with her parents. Now aged 28, Ms. Martinez works for United We Dream, an immigration advocacy group. Following the election of Donald Trump she has been busy. In case of an immigration raid, she instructs her charges not to open their doors to immigration officials unless they have a court-ordered warrant, and to remain silent until speaking with a lawyer. Ms. Martinez is one of around 740,000 beneficiaries of the Deferred Action for Childhood Arrivals

(DACA) policy that Barack Obama implemented in 2012 by executive action. In his 100-day plan published in October, Mr. Trump vowed to reverse every one of Mr. Obama's executive actions. He could kill DACA on his first day in the Oval Office.

He could also opt to let it die a slower, gentler death by refusing to renew DACA permits, which expire every two years. Either way DACA's beneficiaries would lose their right to work legally. DACA grants undocumented immigrants who arrived in America before the age of 16, and who meet several other requirements, temporary amnesty from deportation, and eligibility to work. Applicants must not have criminal histories and they must either be enrolled in or have finished high school or have been honorably discharged from the armed forces.

In his earlier stump speeches, Mr. Trump repeatedly pledged to rid the country of all 11 million unauthorized undocumented migrants living within its borders, the bulk of whom arrived before 2004 (see [Figure 1]). He has picked the Senate's most enthusiastic deporter, Jeff Sessions, as his attorney-general. This has alarmed DACA recipients. "When we applied for DACA, we identified ourselves as undocumented. We gave our addresses. The government now has this information and can come after us or our families," says Perla Salgado from Arizona, who arrived to America at age six and has not once returned to Mexico.

Since winning the election, Mr. Trump has said he will focus on illegal immigrants with criminal records—not unlike President Obama, whose administration has deported more people than any other president's. He has also made some sympathetic noises about those who arrived in the country as children. In an interview on *60 Minutes*, a television program, Mr. Trump estimated the number of criminal immigrants to be between 2 million and 3 million. The Migration Policy Institute, a think-tank, says it is closer to 820,000.

Even if Mr. Trump's administration aims for the top end of the range, it will be hard for him to keep all his campaign promises related to immigration. To gather funding for his proposed wall along America's border with Mexico, for example, Mr. Trump would need congressional approval. The president requires no such authorization to change the Department of Homeland Security's (DHS) deportation priorities, though. From his first day in the White House, Mr. Trump will have discretion over what groups should be targeted for removal. "He could easily expand the definition for what constitutes criminality to meet the 2 million to 3 million goal he set," says Ms. Martinez, the activist.

Two factors will limit the size of the deportation dragnet. The first is capacity. The federal government already spends more on enforcing immigration laws

Figure 1. The 9/11 Effect
United States, Adult Unauthorized Immigrants by Years of Residence

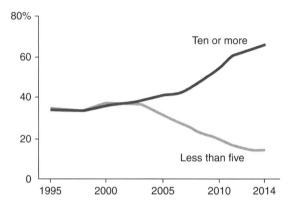

SOURCE: Pew Research Center

than on the FBI, Drug Enforcement Agency, U.S. Marshals service and Bureau of Alcohol, Tobacco and Firearms combined. Finding people to deport is also getting ever harder. That is partly because the number of border apprehensions has declined markedly in recent years as the flow of Mexicans into the United States has also ebbed. Immigrants captured within two weeks and 100 miles of the border are the easiest to deport because they do not have to be granted a court hearing. Those further from the country's edges do get a hearing and so are much harder to remove. Deportation hearings can take years to complete; in July, the backlog of cases in immigration court surpassed 500,000.

The second variable is cooperation from cities and states. California has been the busiest state in preparing for the Trump administration's immigration policies. Over 3 million undocumented immigrants reside in the Golden State; Texas, the second most popular home for undocumented foreigners, hosts half that number. A 2014 study by the University of Southern California estimated that workers who are in the state illegally make up 10 percent of the workforce and contribute $130 billion of California's $2.5 trillion gross domestic product.

On December 5th, California lawmakers introduced a package of bills to obstruct mass deportation. These measures include a state program to fund legal representation for immigrants in deportation hearings; a ban on immigration enforcement in public schools, in hospitals and on courthouse premises. "California will be your wall of justice," declared the president of the state senate in a statement. "We will not stand by and let the federal government use our state and local agencies to separate mothers from their children." According to a study by the University of Pennsylvania in 2015, only 37 percent of immigrants and 14 percent of detained immigrants in deportation proceedings secured lawyers to defend them in court. The same study found that immigrants with representation had five-and-a-half times better odds of avoiding deportation than their peers who represented themselves.

Some Place to Hide

The policies of so-called "sanctuary cities" such as Los Angeles, New York, San Francisco and Chicago will further hinder any plans Mr. Trump might have for a huge increase in the rate of deportation. There is no specific legal definition for what constitutes a sanctuary jurisdiction, but it is widely used to refer to areas that limit cooperation with federal immigration authorities. The Immigrant Legal Resource Center counted 4 states, 39 cities, and 364 counties that qualify as sanctuary jurisdictions. Some prohibit local police from asking people they arrest about their immigration status. Others refuse to obey immigration officers unless they have a warrant. Such policies can be mandated expressly by law or merely become customary. Supporters of these approaches say they help guarantee that fear of deportation does not dissuade undocumented immigrants from reporting crimes, visiting hospitals or enrolling in schools.

Scrutiny of sanctuary cities ramped up in July this year after a young American woman was killed in a touristy area of San Francisco by a man who was in the country illegally, had seven previous felony convictions, and had already been deported five times. Mr. Trump has since vowed to block federal funding to areas deemed uncooperative. Such cuts would be painful, but several mayors have cast doubt on whether they will actually happen, reasoning that it would be counterproductive to hurt the economies of America's biggest cities. Jayashri Srikantiah of Stanford Law School argues that there is case law that validates sanctuary policies and there are constitutional problems with coercing states into action with financial threats.

Even so, between 2009 and 2015 the Obama administration deported an average of about 360,000 people a year. Muzaffar Chishti, a lawyer at the Migration Policy Institute, believes that unless ample resources are poured into recruiting and training new immigration officers and expanding the pool of immigration courts, the Trump administration will struggle to remove more than half a million people a year. Over eight years that would still add up to 4 million people.

Pratheepan Gulasekaram and Karthick Ramakrishnan

Forget Border Walls and Mass Deportations: The Real Changes in Immigration Policy Are Happening in the States

Arguments over the proper relationship between federal and state governments have been looming in the presidential campaign. The GOP candidates recently brought the issue of federalism front and center when discussing marijuana. For instance, in the second Republican primary debate, Rand Paul strongly defended the rights of states like Colorado to pass laws that legalize marijuana; Jeb Bush and Chris Christie came down on the side of strong federal enforcement.

Curiously, the candidates did not discuss the role of states in regulating immigration, which featured prominently in the 2012 election. So far, GOP presidential hopefuls have offered controversial statements and proposals for national reform that would be difficult to implement, ranging from ending birthright citizenship to building more walls and deporting millions of undocumented residents.

But these proposals for federal immigration reform face little chance of becoming law. Congress will almost certainly be strongly partisan and divided through at least 2020. Federal immigration legislation, whether permissive or restrictive, appears highly unlikely. And states and localities have stepped into the breach.

States and Localities Are Setting Immigration Policy

* * * [S]tate and local immigration regulation has now become a central feature of our national policy landscape. The decade following 9/11 saw a sharp increase in state and local immigration regulation. Until 2012, the weight of that trend was restrictionist, highlighted by high profile enactments like Arizona's SB 1070 that sought to create new state-level penalties for being in the country illegally. Since 2012, however, the state and local tide has turned largely integrationist.

This reality upends the long-held notion that immigration is solely a federal responsibility. To be sure, visas, national citizenship, and deportation remain squarely under federal control, as the U.S. Supreme Court made clear in its landmark 2012 decision *Arizona v. United States*. But state and local policies affect the daily lives of immigrants profoundly on everything from access to public higher education to health insurance coverage to driver's licenses. Such state-level changes will be difficult to undo, no matter who becomes president in 2017.

For example, California, New York, and Illinois have enacted a suite of policies that confer meaningful membership to all residents, including the undocumented. The "California Package" of immigrant-friendly laws is popular in a state that accounts for a quarter of all undocumented immigrants in the United States. A few states and localities have already passed important components of the "California Package," and we can expect a widening and deepening of state and local policy adoption, especially in places with Democratic majorities and a sizeable proportion of Latino voters.

By contrast, Republican-controlled states have passed aspects of the "Arizona Package" that include penalties on employers who don't comply with *e-Verify*, bans on city "sanctuary laws," and denial of in-state tuition. Given this variegated state policy landscape and its strong correlation with partisanship, it will be very difficult for Congress and the president to pass federal laws that run roughshod over these state and local enactments.

The Federal Government Relies on the States to Help Carry Out Its Immigration Policy

In addition, the federal government leans on state systems to administer key parts of immigration policy. For instance, the federal Priority Enforcement Program (PEP) relies on local police to send fingerprints and other information to Immigration and Customs Enforcement (ICE) so that ICE can decide who to deport. This reliance on the informational advantages available to local police continues to be critical in fashioning federal enforcement policy.

Indeed, the Secure Communities Program, the predecessor federal enforcement program to PEP, more robustly conscripted local police, with ICE issuing "detainers" or "hold requests" that directed local police to hold an individual so that ICE could pick them up. In dismantling Secure Communities and replacing it with PEP, DHS Secretary Jeh Johnson specifically noted the state and local resistance to these detainers as motivation for reimagining the way in which federal authorities would interact with them.

Similarly, federal law gives state welfare systems some control over whether noncitizens are eligible for public assistance. While some states have exercised that authority to restrict the public assistance only to those required by federal law, others have chosen to provide broader welfare coverage. Five states with high-immigrant populations—California, Illinois, Massachusetts, New York, and Washington—provide immigrant children access to health insurance regardless of legal status. Other states have expanded pregnancy and low-income health insurance coverage in ways that benefit immigrant populations.

And even when the White House declared undocumented immigrants who arrived here as children are free to stay and to work, as it did with its Deferred Action for Child Arrivals (DACA) program, states have to decide whether or not to help those recipients maximize their opportunities. The ability to attend school or seek work is meaningful only if state laws also provide in-state tuition, financial aid, driver's licenses, and access to health insurance.

Immigration is going to continue being a hot and provocative topic throughout the presidential primaries. But the heat is unlikely to come with any light. Donald Trump and others may energize some potential voters with extreme proposals, but that's not what leads to national change. For now and for the foreseeable future, the United States' most significant changes on immigration will be happening in the states. Those who want to reform immigration may well do better to push for piecemeal changes at the state level than to chase comprehensive reform federally.

Shikha Dalmia

A States' Rights Approach to Immigration Reform

Over the last decade, neither Republican president George W. Bush nor Democratic Barack Obama has succeeded in prodding Congress to enact immigration reform. That's because Congress can't find a way to balance the contradictory demands of labor, business, and talk-radio restrictionists. Meanwhile, as the economy gathers steam, industries in many states are facing a paucity of workers at all skill levels.

But there might be a way out of this logjam. How? By embracing a more federalist approach that gives states flexibility to craft their own immigration policies. This might sound radical but the under-reported story is that states have already been trying to do this and Canada did it 18 years ago. Even Sen. Jeff Sessions (R-Alabama), who has torpedoed many a reform effort, praised Canada's provincial program at a Heritage Foundation event last year as a model for America because it allows an orderly matching between foreign workers and local labor needs.

Thanks to an improving Mexican economy and aggressive immigration enforcement, net illegal migration from Mexico to America has dropped to zero, according to the Pew Hispanic Center. The upshot is crucial gaps in the construction, cleaning, landscaping, farming, crab fishing, hotel, tourism, restaurant, and many other local industries that have been relying on undocumented labor since existing visa programs for low-skilled foreign workers are either woefully inadequate or unusable.

The National Restaurant Association expects to add 1.8 million positions in the next decade—a 14 percent boost in its workforce. But the 16–24 [year-old] native-born U.S. workforce that fills these jobs isn't expected to grow at all—so either restaurants hire foreigners or the industry faces retrenchment. Similar labor shortages have forced American growers in California, Idaho and many other states to move to Mexico. Direct U.S. investment in Mexican agriculture has increased seven-fold in recent years.

Industries relying on low-skilled labor aren't the only ones suffering. A shallow STEM-worker pool is stymying high-tech companies in California and Washington. Massachusetts' start-up sector has been facing an exodus of highly qualified foreign students graduating from the Bay State's world-class universities because they are unable to obtain H-1B visas.

To deal with the problem, Massachusetts last year implemented the ingenious Global Entrepreneur In Residence programs. Startups, where the employee is also the founder of a company, have nowhere to go for visas because H-1Bs don't apply to them. But under the GEIR program, these students are placed in participating universities where they can incubate their businesses. Universities then sponsor them for H-1B visas as university employees, something that is especially clever since they are exempt from the annual H-1B quota that other employers face.

Nor is Massachusetts alone in pushing state solutions. Fed up with Uncle Sam's insensitivity to their labor needs, lawmakers in about eight states in recent years have pushed resolutions or bills demanding permission from the federal government to craft their own immigration programs. These include not just blue states like California and New Mexico but also arch-red ones like Texas, Utah, Oklahoma, Kansas, Georgia, and even Arizona.

Utah, New Mexico, California, and Kansas have all flirted with guest worker programs for undocumented aliens to both protect mixed-status Hispanic families in their states and to avoid labor disruptions for local businesses. Utah's conservative legislature overwhelmingly approved legislation in 2011 that would allow undocumented workers who meet certain requirements to obtain a two-year guest worker visa to live in the state. The program was supposed to have been implemented two years ago but was postponed till 2017. Why? Because immigration is constitutionally a federal function and the state needs a federal waiver or permission. But the Obama administration has been dragging its feet, maybe because letting a conservative state implement pro-immigration policies won't have a political upside like unilateral executive action.

Likewise, the Texas legislature has three bills pending that would let Texas employers hire foreign workers from abroad on temporary work visas. But this program too will need federal authorization.

One way to release states from the political whims of sitting administrations would be for Congress to pass a law giving states statutory authority to create their own guest worker programs just as Canada has done through its highly successful Provincial Nominee Program (PNP).

Under the PNP, each of Canada's 13 provinces gets a quota based on its population to hand out permanent residencies or green cards, as I've written. They can sponsor foreigners for almost any reason but most use the program to fill labor gaps. Some provinces have even lured foreign techies stuck in America's green card labyrinth.

Ottawa's role is confined to conducting security or health checks on those sponsored—leaving the planning of local labor markets to the provinces. This divides central and provincial authority based on each side's primary interest, as behooves a federalist system. But the big advantage of this approach in times of heightened concern for national security is that it'll allow Uncle Sam to concentrate on conducting thorough background checks on prospective workers rather than dissipating its energy on redundant regulations.

However, notes Niskanen Center's David Bier, who has drafted a federal bill to create a pilot program along the lines of the PNP in the United States, America can begin by letting states hand out an average of 5,000 work visas—not green cards—to recruit foreign workers of their choice. These visas could be renewed indefinitely and their holders would be eventually eligible for green cards, just as H-1Bs currently are.

Although these workers would be confined to employment in the sponsoring state, they would have far more labor mobility than under the current system where visas tether them to a single employer. Moreover, it would be possible under this scheme, notes Bier, for participating states to form compacts allowing foreign workers to take jobs anywhere in the consortium.

The beauty of the program is not just that it would cut an enormous amount of red tape by letting states—instead of Uncle Sam—perform (or not) a labor certification to ensure that foreigners are not displacing native workers. By giving states more control over immigration flows, the program would change the incentive of states to treat foreigners like assets—not liabilities.

States could eschew participation if they fear a strain on their public services—eliminating a major restrictionist objection that has stymied national reform. But they'd pay an economic price as businesses—and tax revenues—moved to states with plentiful labor.

Some might worry that immigrants would use a state visa to enter the country but then relocate to another state or overstay. But immigrants have little incentive to live illegally when usable legal options are available, especially since illegals earn 22 percent less for the same job than legals, according to Princeton University's Douglas Massey's research. What's more, even though foreigners admitted through Canada's PNP are free to relocate immediately, the average three-year retention rate of provinces is close to 80 percent, as a Cato Institute study notes. The main reason is that the program allows such a granular matching between immigrant skills and local jobs that few need to leave for job opportunities elsewhere.

But to placate worries about foreigners skipping town or overstaying, Bier's proposal would set a 97 percent compliance target for participating states. States that miss this target would face a 50 percent decrease in their visa allocation for each year of non-compliance. Conversely, those that meet them would get a 10 percent increase. This would give states an incentive to enforce their own programs.

The immigration debate in America has become distressingly focused on militarizing the border and draconian interior enforcement. But a federalist solution that lets states experiment with different immigration strategies offers a realistic compromise in line with conservative principles. It is something that all

Republicans—even restrictionists—should not just embrace but champion. This will turn them from cranky, naysaying obstructionists to innovative, yay-saying reformers and let them steal an issue from Democrats.

DISCUSSION QUESTIONS

1. Who do you think should control immigration policy, the national government or the states? What if the executive branch under-enforces federal laws? Should states be able to step in and enforce congressional law?

2. Do you agree with several of the authors that significant change in immigration policy at the national level is unlikely?

3. What do you see as the advantages and disadvantages of allowing states to run their own guest worker programs? Do you think this is a proposal that President Trump and the Republican Congress would support?

4

The Constitutional Framework and the Individual: Civil Liberties and Civil Rights— Should There Be a Religious Exemption to Nondiscrimination Laws?

The Supreme Court settled the legal debate over same-sex marriage in 2015, when in *Obergefell v. Hodges* it held that same sex-couples had a constitutional right to marry. As the readings in this section show, however, that decision did not resolve every dispute that has arisen over the issue, but rather shifted the debate to a new terrain. Now, a key question is whether a person who objects to same-sex marriage on religious grounds can be compelled to recognize or participate in it. Can a person object to a law by claiming that it burdens their religious belief? The theoretical dispute has concrete expression: in 2015, bakery owners in Oregon were fined $135,000 for refusing to bake a wedding cake for a gay couple. A Colorado bakery was ordered to provide cakes to same-sex couples, train its staff, and provide reports to a state agency showing it was complying with the order. A County Clerk in Kentucky claimed that issuing marriage licenses to gay couples violated her religious belief; she was jailed after refusing a federal judge's order to issue them.

These are the latest examples of longer debate over balancing individuals' religious freedom (which is a core constitutional right) with laws that individuals claim burden that freedom. Earlier disputes have involved Native Americans who claimed the right to take peyote as part of their religious celebrations, business owners who objected to federal law requiring them to offer birth control in their health plans, Amish who objected to a state law mandating education through the eighth grade, or a private university that cited a religious basis for its policy banning interracial dating. Sometimes the government wins these legal disputes, and sometimes the private actors win.

The legal doctrines are complicated, reflecting the fact that governments may not prohibit the free exercise of religion, but neither can they favor one religion over another, or even favor religion over non-religion.

The readings in this section approach the debate by examining Religious Freedom Restoration Acts (RFRAs) passed by the federal government and 21 states, many of them as it became clear that the *Obergefell* case was going to turn out as it did. These laws take many forms, but typically specify that the government must accommodate religious objections to laws unless the government has a "compelling interest" in an area, and has chosen the "least restrictive means" of enacting a policy. The first such law was enacted by the federal government in 1993, in part as a reaction to a 1990 Supreme Court decision that held an individual may not defy a law of "general applicability" because it burdens their religious belief.

Both authors wrote shortly before *Obergefell* was decided. Cole argues that the RFRAs are inconsistent with Supreme Court doctrine, but considers the question from a policy perspective. *Should* states allow religious exemptions to state anti-discrimination laws in ways that would permit a baker (or florist, or caterer) to refuse service to a same-sex wedding? While such laws are likely constitutional under current Supreme Court doctrine, Cole argues that they impose important symbolic harms by denying the dignity and equality of same-sex couples. And, in his view, they impose "a strong presumption that individual religious claims take precedence over democratically chosen collective goals," such as anti-discrimination. "The freedom to exercise one's religion," Cole concludes, "is a fundamental value, but like other values, it has its limits."

Helfman discusses the controversy of Indiana's Religious Freedom Restoration Act in March 2015. Critics insisted that the law was a thinly veiled attempt to legalize antigay discrimination (Indiana did not have a general law that prohibited discrimination on the basis of sexual orientation), and its enactment triggered widespread condemnation and boycotts.

Helfman argues that these claims are exaggerated, and that the law merely sought "to stabilize an unsteady line of judicial precedent against how judges should treat laws that impair the First Amendment right to the free exercise of religion." When religious freedom and government action conflict, she concludes that the government *should* face a heavy burden in justifying its laws: "The right of free exercise *is* a civil right, and the First Amendment places very real demands on government."

David Cole

The Angry New Frontier: Gay Rights vs. Religious Liberty

1.

At the end of June, the Supreme Court will likely declare that the Constitution requires states to recognize same-sex marriages on the same terms that they recognize marriages between a man and a woman. If it does, the decision will mark a radical transformation in both constitutional law and public values. Twenty-five years ago, the very idea of same-sex marriage was unthinkable to most Americans; the notion that the Constitution somehow guaranteed the right to it was nothing short of delusional.

One sign of how far we have come is that the principal ground of political contention these days is not whether same-sex marriages should be recognized, but whether persons who object to such marriages on religious grounds should have the right to deny their services to couples celebrating same-sex weddings. Opponents of same-sex marriage can read the shift in public opinion as well as anyone else: a 2014 Gallup poll reported that, nationwide, 55 percent of all Americans, and nearly 80 percent of those between eighteen and twenty-nine, favor recognition of same-sex marriage. Today, same-sex couples have the right to marry in thirty-seven states and the District of Columbia. And come June, most legal experts expect the Supreme Court to require the remainder to follow suit.

Having lost that war, opponents of same-sex marriage have opened up a new battlefield—claiming that people with sincere religious objections to it should not be compelled to participate in any acts that are said to validate or celebrate same-sex marriage. There is an obvious strategic reason for this. One of the problems for opponents of same-sex marriage was that they could not credibly point to anyone who was harmed by it. Proponents, by contrast, could point to many sympathetic victims—couples who had lived in stable, committed relationships for years, but were denied the freedom to express their commitment in a state-recognized marriage, and who were therefore also denied many tangible benefits associated with marriage, including parental rights, health insurance, survivor's benefits, and hospital visitation privileges. Claims that "traditional marriage" would suffer were, by contrast, abstract and wholly unsubstantiated.

Focusing on religiously based objectors puts a human face on the opposition to same-sex marriage. Should the fundamentalist Christian florist who believes that same-sex marriage is a sin be required to sell flowers for a same-sex wedding ceremony, if she claims that to do so would violate her religious tenets? There are plenty of florists, the accommodationists argue, so surely the same-sex couple can go elsewhere, and thereby respect the florist's sincerely held religious beliefs. Should a religious nonprofit organization that makes its property available to the general public for a fee be required to rent it for a same-sex wedding? Should a religious employer be compelled to provide spousal benefits to the same-sex spouse of its employee? Should Catholic Charities' adoption service have to refer children to otherwise suitable homes of married same-sex couples? At its most general level, the question is whether religious principles justify discrimination against same-sex couples.

2.

In late March, Indiana Governor Mike Pence signed into law the Indiana Religious Freedom Restoration Act (RFRA), a state law that requires officials to exempt those with religious objections from any legal obligation that is not "essential" and the "least restrictive means" to serve "a compelling state interest." Arkansas enacted a similar law at the beginning of April. Georgia and North Carolina are considering doing so. And nineteen other states already have such laws, which could permit individuals to cite religious objections as a basis for refusing to abide by prohibitions on discrimination in public accommodations, employment, housing, and the like.

The Indiana and Arkansas laws prompted strong objections from gay rights advocates and leaders of the business community, including Apple, the NCAA, Walmart, and Eli Lilly. They see the laws as thinly veiled efforts to establish a religious excuse for discrimination against gay men and lesbians. Governor Pence initially dismissed these objections as unfounded, but as criticism mounted, Indiana legislators passed an amendment specifying that the law does not authorize a provider to refuse to offer or provide services, facilities, use of public accommodations, goods, employment, or housing . . . on the basis of race, color, religion, ancestry, age, national origin, disability, sex, sexual orientation, gender identity, or United States military service.

Most of the other state RFRAs, however, have no such anti-discrimination language. In Arkansas, Governor Asa Hutchinson responded to criticism by getting the legislature to tailor the law more closely to the federal Religious Freedom Restoration Act, but that law has no anti-discrimination language, and for reasons discussed below, it is far from clear that this revision will stop the law from being invoked to authorize religiously motivated discrimination.

In addition, still other state laws that have received far less attention specifically grant religious exemptions from a variety of legal obligations regarding same-sex marriage. In fact, to date every state except Delaware that has adopted same-sex marriage by legislation has included a religious exemption of some kind. They vary in their details, but among other things, they allow clergy to opt out of conducting marriage ceremonies; permit religiously affiliated nonprofit organizations to deny goods and services to same-sex weddings; and allow religiously affiliated adoption agencies freedom to deny child placements with same-sex married couples. Most were enacted as part of a political bargain, designed to ease passage of laws recognizing same-sex marriage.

At bottom, all of these laws pose the same question: How should we balance the rights of gay and lesbian couples to equal treatment with the free exercise rights of religious objectors?

Under the U.S. Constitution, the answer to this question is clear. The state violates no constitutionally protected religious liberty by imposing laws of general applicability—such as anti-discrimination mandates—on the religious and nonreligious alike. In 1990, the Supreme Court ruled, in a decision written by Justice Antonin Scalia, that being subjected to a general rule, neutrally applied to all, does not raise a valid claim under the First Amendment's free exercise of religion clause, even if the rule burdens the exercise of one's religion.

The case, *Employment Division v. Smith*, involved a Native American tribe that sought an exemption from a criminal law banning the possession and distribution of peyote; the tribe argued that the drug was an integral part of its religious ceremonies. The Court rejected the claim. Justice Scalia reasoned that to allow religious objectors to opt out of generally applicable laws would, quoting an 1878 Supreme Court precedent, "make the professed doctrines of religious belief superior to the law of the land, and in effect . . . permit every citizen to become a law unto himself." The Court accordingly ruled that laws implicate the free exercise clause only if they specifically target or disfavor religion, not if they merely impose general obligations on all that some religiously scrupled individuals find burdensome.

Even before the Court in *Employment Division v. Smith* adopted this general rule, it rejected a claim that religious convictions should trump anti-discrimination laws. The IRS had denied tax-exempt status to Bob Jones University, a religious institution that banned interracial dating, and to Goldsboro Christian Schools, Inc., which interpreted the Bible as compelling it to admit only white students. The religious schools sued, asserting that the IRS's denial violated their free exercise rights. In *Bob Jones University v. United States*, the Court in 1983 summarily rejected that contention, asserting that the state's compelling interest in eradicating racial discrimination "outweigh[ed] whatever burden denial of tax benefits places on petitioners' exercise of their religious beliefs." If the state seeks to eradicate discrimination, the reasoning goes, it cannot simultaneously tolerate discrimination.

Under these precedents, the Constitution plainly does not compel states to grant religious exemptions to laws requiring the equal treatment of same-sex marriages. Laws recognizing same-sex marriages impose a general obligation, do not single out any religion for disfavored treatment, and in any event further the state's compelling interest in eradicating discrimination against gay men and lesbians.

But can or should states adopt such exemptions as a policy matter? In some instances, to be sure, it seems appropriate to accommodate religious scruples. Everyone agrees, for example, that a priest should not be required to perform a wedding that violates his religious tenets. But it is not at all clear that those who otherwise provide goods and services to the general public should be able to cite religion as an excuse to discriminate.

Take the fundamentalist florist. Proponents of an exemption insist that the same-sex couple denied flowers can find another florist, while the florist would either have to violate her religious tenets or lose some of her business. But this argument fails to take seriously the commitment to equality that underlies the recognition of same-sex marriage—and the harm to personal dignity inflicted by unequal treatment. Just as the eradication of race discrimination in education could not tolerate the granting of tax-exempt status to Bob Jones University, even though plenty of nondiscriminatory schools remained available, so the eradication of discrimination in the recognition of marriage cannot tolerate discrimination against same-sex marriages.

Justice Robert Jackson got the balance right when he stated, in 1944, that limits on religious freedom "begin to operate whenever [religious] activities begin to affect or collide with liberties of others or of the public." James Madison struck the same balance, noting that religion should be free of regulation only "where it does not trespass on private rights or the public peace." When a religious principle is cited to deny same-sex couples equal treatment, it collides with the liberties of others and trespasses on private rights, and should not prevail.

The fact that many of the state laws specifically single out religious objections to same-sex marriage for favorable treatment may itself pose constitutional issues under the First Amendment's clause prohibiting the establishment of religion. While states are permitted some leeway to accommodate religion, the establishment clause forbids states from favoring specific religions over others, or religion over nonreligion. And when states accommodate a religious believer by simply shifting burdens to third parties, such as when religiously motivated employers are permitted to deny benefits to same-sex spouses of their employees, the state impermissibly takes sides, favoring religion. In *Estate of Thornton v. Calder* (1984), for example, the Supreme Court held that the establishment clause invalidated a state requirement that businesses accommodate all employees' observations of the Sabbath, regardless of the impact on other workers or the business itself. State laws granting exemptions for religious objectors to same-sex marriage both give preference to religious over other conscientious objections and shift burdens to same-sex couples. Such favoritism is not only not warranted by the free exercise clause, but may be prohibited by the establishment clause.

3.

The "religious freedom restoration" laws that Indiana, Arkansas, and nineteen other states have adopted do not single out same-sex marriage as such, but they also have serious flaws. These statutes are almost certainly constitutional under existing doctrine, since they are modeled on the federal Religious Freedom Restoration Act, enacted in 1993 in response to the *Smith* decision. That's the statute the Supreme Court relied upon last year in *Burwell v. Hobby Lobby* to rule that the Department of Health and Human Services must accommodate for-profit corporations that object on religious grounds to providing insurance coverage to their employees for certain kinds of contraception. (Significantly, the Court in *Hobby Lobby* found that the religious corporations' objections could be accommodated without imposing any cost on their female employees, by extending to those for-profit businesses an existing HHS accommodation that required insurance providers to provide contraception at no cost to the employees of objecting nonprofit organizations).

The federal and state RFRAs provide, as a statutory matter, what the Court refused to provide as a matter of constitutional law in the *Smith* decision. They require the government to meet a very demanding standard to justify any law, no matter how neutral and generally applicable, that imposes a "substantial burden" on anyone's exercise of religion. Because the courts are reluctant to second-guess individual religious commitments, the "substantial burden" threshold is often easily met: an individual need only articulate a plausible claim that the law requires him to do something that violates his religious principles. Religious objections could be raised to anti-discrimination laws, criminal laws, taxes, environmental and business regulations, you name it; the only limit is the creativity of religious objectors.

Once a religious objection is raised, the RFRA laws require the state to show not only that it has a "compelling" reason for denying a religious exemption, but that no more narrowly tailored way to achieve its ends is possible. This language appears to direct courts to apply the same skeptical standard—called "strict scrutiny"—applied to laws that explicitly discriminate on the basis of race, or that censor speech because of its content. This standard is so difficult to satisfy that it has been described as "strict in theory, but fatal in fact." If the RFRAs were literally enforced, many state laws would not survive that standard of review. They appear to give religious objectors what the Court in *Smith* properly refused—"a private right to ignore generally applicable laws."

Perhaps for this reason, courts have not interpreted state RFRAs literally, but have instead generally construed them to uphold laws that impose a burden on religion as long as the state has a reasonable justification for doing so. They have looked to the purpose of the RFRAs rather than to their literal language; the laws were designed, after all, to "restore" the constitutional protection of religious free exercise that existed prior to the *Smith* decision, and while the Supreme Court before *Smith* sometimes spoke in terms of compelling interests and least restrictive means, its actual application of the free exercise clause was much more measured.

Thus, there have been relatively few successful RFRA lawsuits in the state or federal courts.

The courts have resisted applying strict scrutiny to religious freedom claims for good reason. Strict scrutiny is triggered by regulations of speech only where the state censors speech because of its content, such as when a state bans labor picketing or regulates political campaign advocacy. In equal protection cases, the Court applies strict scrutiny only to those rare laws that intentionally draw distinctions based on race, ethnicity, national origin, or religion, such as race-based affirmative action. By contrast, as Justice Scalia noted in *Smith*, a religious objection can be raised to virtually any law. Applying the same scrutiny to claims of religious freedom would therefore have few meaningful limits, and would give religious objectors a presumptive veto over any law they claimed infringed their religious views.

But there is reason to believe that judicial interpretation of RFRAs may change. The Supreme Court in *Hobby Lobby* interpreted the federal RFRA to impose a much more demanding, pro-religion standard of review than had ever been imposed before. Encouraged by this development, over one hundred lawsuits have been filed under the federal RFRA challenging the Affordable Care Act's requirement that health insurance plans cover contraception. Some state courts may well follow the Supreme Court's lead and apply their state RFRAs more aggressively. And now that many states have been required by federal courts to recognize same-sex marriage, some state judges may be inclined to push back through interpretation of state RFRAs permitting religious exemptions.

When *Smith* was decided, the prohibition of the peyote ceremony seemed to many an unfair deprivation of the religious rights of Native Americans. Religious groups across the spectrum condemned the decision, and a coalition of liberals and conservatives joined together to endorse the enactment of the federal RFRA. The law was supported by the ACLU, the American Jewish Congress, and the National Association of Evangelicals, among many others; it passed the House unanimously, and passed 97–3 in the Senate. Many argued, with justification, that the Court's approach in *Smith* was insensitive to religious minorities. As the peyote case illustrated, minority religions are unlikely to have their concerns taken seriously by the majority through the ordinary democratic process. And if a generally applicable law does interfere with the exercise of religion, the bill's proponents asked, shouldn't the state bear a burden of justification?

The problem is not so much that RFRAs create a presumption in favor of religious accommodation, but that the presumption is at once so easily triggered and so difficult to overcome. Advocates for religious liberty and marriage equality might find common ground were they to support modified RFRAs that would impose a less demanding standard of justification, requiring states to show that permitting a religious exemption would undermine important collective interests or impose harm on others.

The stringent standard imposed by RFRAs, by contrast, means that anytime anyone objects on religious grounds to any law, he or she is entitled to an exemption unless the state can show that it is absolutely necessary to deny the exemption in order to further a compelling end. Because these laws impose such a heavy burden of justification, they effectively transfer a great deal of decision-making authority from the democratic process to religious objectors and the courts.

Instead of the polity deciding when to grant particular religious exemptions from a specific law, RFRAs transfer to courts the power to decide that question—subject to a strong presumption that individual religious claims take precedence over democratically chosen collective goals. Religious liberty has an important place in American society, to be sure. Accommodation of religious practices is a sign of a tolerant multicultural society—so long as the accommodation does not simply shift burdens from one minority to another. The freedom to exercise one's religion is a fundamental value, but like other values, it has its limits. It is not a right to ignore collective obligations, nor is it a right to discriminate. Those who oppose same-sex marriage should be free to express their opposition in speech to their heart's (and religion's) content, but not to engage in acts of discrimination. As Oliver Wendell Holmes Jr. is said to have remarked: "The right to swing my fist ends where the other man's nose begins."

Tara Helfman
The Religious-Liberty War

When the curtain opens on Sophocles's *Antigone*, Thebes is reeling from a fratricidal war. The rivals for the crown have killed each other in battle, and the new king has ordered that no one may bury the body of the rebel leader. The play's heroine confronts a tragic choice: Should she obey divine commandment and offer her slain brother funeral rites? Or should she obey the king's command and defy the will of the gods?

The Religious Freedom Restoration Act, which became law at the federal level in 1993 and has been followed by 20 state-level versions in the decades since, attempts to shield Americans from the sort of choice Antigone had to make between the state's command and her faith's calling. In general, the RFRA statutes ensure that government cannot compel an individual to act against her faith unless (1) a compelling government interest demands it, and (2) the measure is narrowly tailored to serve those interests. But when Indiana Governor Mike Pence became the 20th governor to sign a state-level RFRA into law in March, legal tragedy degenerated into political farce as the statute became the latest staging ground in the ongoing national debate on gay rights.

Gay-rights activists charged that the Indiana law amounted to a license to discriminate on religious pretexts. The American Civil Liberties Union, originally one of the key supporters of the federal RFRA, denounced the statute as "a terrible and dangerous mistake," and Hillary Clinton, whose husband signed the original act into law in 1993, lamented on Twitter: "Sad this new Indiana law can happen in America today. We shouldn't discriminate against [people because] of who they love." Everyone from the CEO of Angie's List to the president of the NCAA had something to say about the Indiana statute, and none of it was good. When a similar backlash arose in response to the Arkansas religious-freedom bill, that state's governor, Asa Hutchinson, quickly withdrew his support, musing that his own son had signed a petition against it and stating his concerns that it would have "a negative impact on our state's image."

Lost in all this fury was the simple purpose of these RFRAs: They are designed to stabilize an unsteady line of judicial precedent regarding how judges should treat laws that impair the First Amendment right to the free exercise of religion.

The tension between the public interest and private faith is written into the very text of the Constitution, which safeguards religious liberty and guarantees the equal protection of laws. The First Amendment provides that Congress shall make no law prohibiting the free exercise of religion. But sometimes laws of general application—laws that are designed to apply equally to *all* Americans—impair the religious practice of *some* Americans.

Justice William Brennan, celebrated as a liberal lion of the Supreme Court, first formulated the test later codified by the federal RFRA in *Sherbert v. Verner*. The 1963 case involved a claim by a Seventh-Day Adventist who had been denied unemployment benefits by the state of South Carolina because she refused to work on the Sabbath. The Court held that forcing the claimant to choose between abandoning a precept of her faith and forgoing her unemployment benefits was tantamount to fining her for practicing her religion. The government would henceforth have to show that any law impairing the free exercise of religion was narrowly tailored to serve a compelling government interest. This came to be known as the Sherbert Test.

In *Wisconsin v. Yoder* (1972), the Court reaffirmed the Sherbert Test, striking down a state statute establishing compulsory eighth-grade education on the ground that it violated the First Amendment rights of Wisconsin's Amish community. In so doing, the Court was mindful of the potential danger that religious exemptions posed to the equal protection of laws. It explained:

> Although a determination of what is a "religious" belief or practice entitled to constitutional protection may present a most delicate question, the very concept of ordered liberty precludes allowing every person to make his own standards on matters of conduct in which society as a whole has important interests. Thus, if the Amish asserted their claims because of their subjective evaluation and rejection of the contemporary secular values accepted by the majority, much as Thoreau rejected the social values of his time and isolated himself at Walden Pond, their claims would not rest on a religious basis. Thoreau's choice was philosophical and personal rather than religious, and such belief does not rise to the demands of the Religion Clauses.

In short, the Court found, faith enjoys a higher degree of protection under the Constitution than philosophy, and that is by constitutional design.

Then, in the 1989 case *Employment Division v. Smith*, the Court revisited the Sherbert Test. At issue was whether two Native Americans had been unlawfully denied unemployment benefits under Oregon law because they took peyote as part of a religious sacrament. The claimants argued they should be granted a religious exemption because state drug law placed an undue burden on their First Amendment right to free exercise of religion. Writing for the Court, Justice Antonin Scalia rejected the argument: "To make an individual's obligation to obey such a law contingent upon the law's coincidence with his religious beliefs, except where the State's interest is 'compelling'—permitting him, by virtue of his beliefs, to become a law unto himself—contradicts both constitutional tradition and common sense." The majority ruled that the answer to the problem of generally applicable laws that encroach upon religious liberty is not to carve out constitutional exemptions but for legislative bodies to carve out *statutory* exemptions.

Congress stepped into the breach. In 1993, it enacted the Religious Freedom Restoration Act, whose stated purpose was "to restore the compelling interest test as set forth in [*Sherbert* and *Yoder*] and to guarantee its application in all cases where free exercise of religion is substantially burdened." As initially enacted, the RFRA prohibited *any* government—federal, state, or local—from substantially burdening a person's exercise of religion unless the government could demonstrate that the burden furthered a compelling government interest. In a 1997 case, the Supreme Court invalidated the statute's applicability to state and local law. Congress then revised the RFRA to apply only to federal measures.

Since there were no longer protections below the federal level, states began passing their own versions of the federal RFRA, to ensure that religious liberty enjoyed the same standard of protection from state and local law as it did from federal law.

In many respects, the problems underlying the RFRA are representative of the broader challenge that the growth of government poses to the liberties enshrined in the Bill of Rights. As public regulation grows increasingly pervasive, the risk that it will encroach upon individual liberty grows correspondingly greater.

States are not passing RFRAs to protect the faithful from laws that specifically target the practices of religious groups or institutions. Such statutes are few and far between, and have been dispensed with in short order by the courts under existing First Amendment jurisprudence. Rather, RFRAs seek to protect First Amendment rights from the sort of ubiquitous regulatory creep that has come to define American government in the twenty-first century. For example, state laws requiring autopsies might conflict with the religious beliefs of the deceased and their survivors. Local zoning regulations might prevent homeowners from displaying emblems of their faith on private property. Rules establishing dress and uniform requirements might exclude Jews who wear yarmulkes from military service. And prison regulations may bar observant Muslims from having beards. It would be wrong to suggest that government lacks a compelling interest in any of these cases, all of which have been argued before courts; to take one example, the demand that there be exceptions to military dress creates a potential disciplinary hazard for the armed forces. Rather, the injury that such measures might cause to the individual's right of free exercise is all the *more* reason to require that the government show that a law's means are narrowly tailored to compelling government ends.

The judicial standards established by RFRAs are moderate and measured; the debate provoked by the Indiana law has been anything but. Presented a matter of weeks before the Supreme Court was due to hear oral arguments on the constitutionality of state bans on gay marriage, the statute unleashed a frenzy of public outcry and political posturing that has bordered at times on the surreal. Critics from Al Sharpton to the CEO of Apple Computers have denounced the Indiana law as a modern-day Jim Crow measure designed to relegate gays to a constitutional underclass. A #boycottIndiana campaign sprang up on social media, and Angie's List announced that it was canceling a $40-million expansion project in the state on account of the law.

The governors of Connecticut, Washington, and New York banned state-funded travel to Indiana. Connecticut Governor Dannel P. Malloy went so far as to call Indiana's law "disturbing, disgraceful, and outright discriminatory," notwithstanding the fact that his state was the first to pass its own RFRA in 1993. (In fact, the Connecticut RFRA establishes a less exacting standard for religious exemptions than Indiana's: A law must "burden" rather than "substantially burden" a person's free exercise of religion.) And New York State lawmakers denounced the law as "legalized discrimination and injustice against LGBT people."

Then, amid all the histrionics and hyperbole, a small-town pizzeria became Ground Zero in the broader culture war. When the owner of Memories Pizza in Walkerton told a local news reporter she would not cater a gay wedding because doing so would violate her religious beliefs, social media exploded with outrage. The business's Yelp page was inundated with slurs, and threats poured in via social media. The pizzeria had to shut its doors temporarily because of the outcry.

Neither the federal RFRA nor its state counterparts sanction discrimination. The Indiana RFRA, like the federal statute, requires that courts apply the very same standard to laws that impair free exercise as they do to laws that discriminate against racial minorities. What is more, RFRAs stand against a broad backdrop of federal and state anti-discrimination law, not least of which is the Civil Rights Act of 1964. Its Title II prohibits discrimination in public accommodation on the basis of race, color, religion, or national origin. Thus a restaurant owner may not invoke his religious beliefs in refusing service to an interracial couple. Nor, for that matter, could he refuse to cater an interracial wedding.

Same-sex weddings are a different matter, but this has less to do with the RFRAs than it does with the unsettled position of gay rights under state and federal law. Some states, such as New Mexico and Connecticut, have passed local variants on Title II that require businesses offering their services to the general public to do so without regard to the sex or sexual orientation of patrons. In fact, in response to the backlash over the Indiana law, that state's statute was amended to prohibit providers of public accommodations from denying goods and services to individuals on the basis of sexual orientation. Where such local anti-discrimination laws serve a compelling interest by the least restrictive means, gay rights must prevail over First Amendment claims under state RFRAs.

But where such protections are not in place, the right of free exercise of religion must prevail. The Supreme Court may well bring this debate to a close next summer, when it decides whether state prohibitions of same-sex marriage are constitutional. Whatever the outcome of that case, both state and federal courts will be bound to apply RFRAs accordingly. In the meantime, it is at best a benign mistake—at worst, cynical opportunism—to condemn RFRAs as mere pretexts for the violation of civil rights.

The right of free exercise *is* a civil right, and the First Amendment places very real demands on government. Not only do the Establishment and Free Exercise clauses require that government not interfere in religious *belief*, they also limit the government's power to burden religious *practice*. RFRAs establish a clear test against which to balance the rights of the individual and the interests of the state. If the history of religious practice in this nation is anything to go by, the constitutional debate on faith will continue long after the constitutional debate on gay marriage is settled. And for as long as that is the case, these Religious Freedom Restoration Acts are likely to be the most reliable shield individuals have against government encroachments on religious liberty. It is the shield Antigone needed.

DISCUSSION QUESTIONS

1. What do you make of the slippery slope argument that if a business owner or local government official claims the right to refuse service to a same-sex couple (by, for example, refusing to bake a wedding cake or issue a marriage license) on the grounds that it violates their religion, could they also refuse to serve, or hire, an African American, a Muslim, a woman, a Jew, or a Born Again Christian, based on a claim of religious belief?

2. Now think about the argument from the other side. If the government can force a caterer to violate her religious belief by, say, fining her if she refuses to serve dinner at a same-sex marriage reception, what else could government mandate? Could the government punish an evangelical Christian computer programmer who refused to design a website for the Freedom from Religion

Foundation? An Orthodox Jewish restaurant owner who refused to host a wedding dinner because the bride and groom insisted on having pork served? How would you draw the line?

3. Can you articulate a general rule that resolves questions of when government action should outweigh individual religious beliefs and when individual religious beliefs should prevail?

5

Congress: Checks and Balances—Too Many Checks, or Not Enough Balance?

For the past decade there has been a growing public perception that Congress can't govern. Battles over raising the debt ceiling, repealing Obamacare, shutting down the government, and refusing to act on President Obama's nomination of Merrick Garland to the Supreme Court in 2016 are indicators of the gridlock that has gripped Washington. President Obama responded by trying to act on his own through executive orders and the regulatory process, which produced a backlash from conservatives against "executive branch overreach."

With the election of Donald Trump and a Republican Congress, gridlock is less of a concern as unified government should allow Republicans to pass much of their policy agenda. However, fear of executive overreach is now coming from the other side of the ideological spectrum. Liberals hope that Congress will prevent some of Trump's more extreme policy proposals from the 2016 presidential campaign (such as deporting 12 million Mexican Americans, building a wall along the Mexican border, preventing all Muslims from entering the country, and starting a trade war with China). Trump's critics take great comfort in our system of checks and balances, arguing that "The Founders anticipated Trump. We can handle this," as a *Los Angeles Times* op-ed said shortly after the election.

Yoni Appelbaum isn't so sure, arguing that our Constitution is more fragile that we might think. He says that our Founders' debates over institutional structures were between those who feared legislative tyranny (the "royalists") and those who feared executive tyranny (the "parliamentarians"). Appelbaum claims the royalists won and created a "mixed monarchy" in which the president had more power than King George III. However, the fragility of our presidential system of separated powers comes from the fact that our president cannot run the show by himself. "Neither Congress nor the president has the capacity to govern alone," Appelbaum points out, "but either can refuse to compromise, and prevent the other from governing." In many other nations that have our system of government, such impasses often lead to military coups or the collapse of the political system. Indeed, the United States' longevity is unique among nations that share our constitutional form of government. Unless we recognize our system's fragility, we may not persist for another 200 years.

Matthew Spalding places the blame for our recent problems more squarely at the feet of Congress. By abdicating its law-making responsibilities, Congress has given too much authority to the bureaucratic executive—a problem that has been 100 years in the making. Congress has slowly allowed its control over lawmaking to slip away as it engages in limited oversight of the bureaucracy and allows the president to dominate through executive orders. The only solution, Spalding argues, "is for Congress to strengthen its constitutional muscles as a co-equal branch of government" by reestablishing its legislative authority and "relearn[ing] the art of lawmaking." The clear means to do this is the power of the purse, which Congress must use with more authority. While this critique was written in the context of President Obama's overreach, Spalding makes it clear that the analysis applies to the new president as well.

Yoni Appelbaum
America's Fragile Constitution

Over the past few decades, many of the unwritten rules of American political life have been discarded. Presidential appointees, once routinely confirmed by the Senate, now spend months in limbo. Signing statements have increased in frequency and scope, as presidents announce which aspects of a law they intend to enforce, and which they intend to ignore. Annual spending bills stall in Congress, requiring short-term extensions or triggering shutdowns.

The system isn't working. But even as the two parties agree on little else, both still venerate the Constitution. Politicians sing its praises. Public officials and military officers swear their allegiance. Members of Congress keep miniature copies in their pockets. The growing dysfunction of the government seems only to have increased reverence for the document; leading figures on both sides of the aisle routinely call for a return to constitutional principles.

What if this gridlock is not the result of abandoning the Constitution, but the product of flaws inherent in its design?

The history recounted in a recent book on the Constitution's origins, by Eric Nelson, a political theorist at Harvard, raises that disturbing possibility. In *The Royalist Revolution*, Nelson argues that the standard narrative of the American Revolution—overthrowing a tyrannical king and replacing him with a representative democracy—is mistaken. Many leaders of the patriot cause actually wanted George III to intervene in their disputes with parliament, to veto the bills it passed, even to assert that he alone had the right to govern the American colonies. In short, they wanted him to rule like a king. When he declined, they revolted.

As they framed their appeals to the king, Nelson demonstrates, the patriots reached back to the debate leading up to the English civil wars. In the 1620s, the Stuart monarch Charles I feuded with his parliament, which feared that he would usurp its authority to approve taxes, and reign as an absolute monarch. Both sides claimed to be working for the common good. The parliamentarians insisted that only a legislature—a miniature version of the people as a whole—could represent the people's interests. Royalists responded that legislators were mere creatures of their constituencies, bound to cater to voters' whims instead of tending to the kingdom's needs. Only a monarch, they argued, could counterbalance legislative parochialism and look to the long term.

Charles required revenues, but parliament was determined not to authorize taxes on his terms. So from 1629 to 1640, he ruled without calling parliament into session, scraping together funds by reviving moribund fines and fees, and creatively reinterpreting his royal prerogatives. The deadlock led to a series of civil wars from 1642 to 1651, to Charles's execution, and to the ultimate triumph of parliament, which absorbed almost all executive authority, leaving England's monarchs to reign in name alone.

While the wars raged, the early settlers of New England sided squarely with parliament, decrying monarchical tyranny and celebrating its replacement by parliamentary democracy. A century later, however, many of their descendants were nostalgic for Stuart royalism. By the 1760s, parliament was imposing taxes on the colonists without their consent. Patriot leaders like John Adams expressed longing for George III to restrain the legislative tyranny of parliament.

Generations of historians have largely regarded such statements as insincere rhetorical ploys—as arguments of convenience lodged and then quickly forgotten. Nelson makes a convincing case that in so doing, historians have overlooked an important part of the political philosophy that impelled the American Revolution. By citing the king's refusal to act like a king, he writes, the patriots justified taking matters into their own hands.

Once the war was over, Nelson shows, many of the patriot leaders who had previously argued for royal prerogatives proceeded to push for an executive empowered to do what George III would not. At the Constitutional Convention, the Pennsylvania delegate James Wilson stepped forward and moved "that the Executive consist of a single person." This was a loaded phrase with which to introduce a controversial idea: When, in 1649, shortly after executing Charles I, parliament abolished the monarchy, it famously declared, "The office of a King . . . shall not henceforth . . . be exercised by any one single person." Wilson was not just proposing that the United States have a president. He was attempting, in the horrified view of the Virginia delegate Edmund Randolph, to insert into the Constitution "the foetus of monarchy."

Wilson and Randolph, and their respective allies in Philadelphia, revived the old debate between the royalists and the parliamentarians: Which posed the greater threat, legislative tyranny or monarchy? Had America revolted against a king, or against his parliament? In the end, Nelson argues persuasively, the royalists won.

In this telling, the Constitution created not a radical democracy, but a very traditional mixed monarchy. At its head stood a king—an uncrowned one called a president—with sweeping powers, whose steadying hand would hopefully check the factionalism of the Congress. The two houses of the legislature, elected by the people, would make laws, but the president—whom the Founders regarded as a third branch of the legislature—could veto them. He could also appoint his own Cabinet, command the Army, and make treaties.

The Convention placed limits on the president's powers, to be sure: Some of his actions would be contingent on approval by the Senate, or subject to overrides.

But these hedges on presidential authority did not make the office a creature of Congress. Having defeated the armies of George III, the framers seized upon a most unlikely model for their nascent democracy—the very Stuart monarchy whose catastrophic failure had produced the parliamentary system—and proceeded to install an executive whose authority King George could only envy.

Since the American Revolution, many new democracies have taken inspiration from the U.S. Constitution. Around much of the world, parliamentary systems became prevalent, but some countries, particularly in Latin America, adopted the presidential model, splitting power between an executive and a legislative branch.

When, in 1985, a Yale political scientist named Juan Linz compared the records of presidential and parliamentary democracies, the results were decisive. Not every parliamentary system endured, but hardly any presidential ones proved stable. "The only presidential democracy with a long history of constitutional continuity is the United States," Linz wrote in 1990. This is quite an uncomfortable form of American exceptionalism.

Linz's findings suggest that presidential systems suffer from a large, potentially fatal flaw. In parliamentary systems, governmental deadlock is relatively rare; when prime ministers can no longer command legislative support, the impasse is generally resolved by new elections. In presidential systems, however, contending parties must eventually strike a deal. Except sometimes, they don't. Latin America's presidential democracies have tended to oscillate between authoritarianism and dysfunction.

In the 30 years since Linz published these findings, his ideas have enjoyed wide currency among political scientists and seized the imagination of pundits, but gained little purchase among U.S. politicians or the American public at large. America has, after all, defied the odds, through the rise and demise of political parties, through depressions and wars, to the present day. Why would that change? Linz's critics, moreover, suggest that trying to infer immutable laws of politics from a handful of Latin American governments is a pointless exercise.

Even if we discount the failures of other presidential democracies, though, we should not dismiss the fact that the U.S. Constitution was modeled on a system that collapsed into civil war, and that it is inherently fragile. "This is a system that requires a particular set of political norms," Eric Nelson told me, "and it can be very dangerous and dysfunctional where those norms are not present." Once those norms have been discarded, the president or either house of

Congress can simply go on strike, refusing to fulfill their responsibilities. Nothing can compel them to act.

Until recently, American politicians have generally made the compromises necessary to govern. The trouble is that cultures evolve. As American politics grows increasingly polarized, the goodwill that oiled the system and helped it function smoothly disappears. In 2013, fights over the debt ceiling and funding for the Affordable Care Act very nearly produced a constitutional crisis. Congress and the president each refused to yield, and the government shut down for 16 days. In November 2014, claiming that he was "acting where Congress has failed," President Obama announced a series of executive actions on immigration. House Republicans denounced him as "threatening to unravel our system of checks and balances" and warned that they would cut off funding for the Department of Homeland Security unless Obama's actions were rolled back. For months, the two sides faced off, pledging fealty to the Constitution even as they exposed its flaws. Only at the eleventh hour did the House pull back from the edge.

Strikingly, in these and other recent crises, public opinion has tended to favor the president. As governments deadlock, executives are inclined to act unilaterally, thereby deepening crises. When parliament refused to provide Charles I with funds unless he met its demands, he moved to circumvent the legislators, and they in turn deposed him. Other presidential systems have collapsed in much the same way.

The framers do not seem to have understood this particular flaw of mixed monarchy. But then, neither did they express absolute faith in their own wisdom. "They were incredibly conscious of the fragility of what they were creating," Nelson says, "that it depends on forbearance." The Constitution was an experiment, and its signers believed that its success was contingent on the willingness of varied constituencies to work together.

When politicians today praise America's system of checks and balances, they seem to understand it as a self-correcting mechanism: When one branch pushes too hard, the other branches must push back, preserving equilibrium. That understanding actually encourages politicians to overreact, in the belief that they are playing a vital constitutional role. It also encourages complacency, because a system that rights itself requires no painful compromises to preserve.

Neither Congress nor the president has the capacity to govern alone, but either can refuse to compromise, and prevent the other from governing. If the system is thought to be indestructible, the temptation to take stands becomes overwhelming. Filibusters, shutdowns, and executive orders multiply. The veneration of the Constitution becomes its undoing.

This is the paradox of America's mixed monarchy, a system that operates best when politicians and the public remain skeptical of its ability to operate at all. Blind faith in the wisdom of the Constitution, and in its capacity to withstand the poor behavior of politicians, will eventually destroy it.

But a constant fear that the entire system will collapse absent frenzied efforts to save it might just help the country continue to defy the odds, and last another 200 years.

Matthew Spalding

Congress' Constitutional Prerogative vs. Executive Branch Overreach

"In framing a government which is to be administered by men over men, the great difficulty lies in this," Madison writes in *Federalist* 51, "you must first enable the government to control the governed; and in the next place oblige it to control itself."

That meant that, in addition to performing its proper constitutional functions, there needed to be an internal check to further limit the powers of government. For that purpose, the Founders not only divided power, but also set it against itself.

This separation of powers is the defining structural mechanism of the Constitution. It divides the powers of government among three branches and vests each with independent powers and responsibilities.

"The accumulation of all powers," Madison notes in *Federalist* 47, "legislative, executive and judiciary, in the same hands, whether of one, a few, or many, and whether hereditary, self-appointed, or elective, may justly be pronounced the very definition of tyranny." Thus, for "the preservation of liberty," each branch has only those powers granted to it, and can do only what its particular grant of power authorizes it to do.

The Founders were acutely aware that each branch of government would be tempted to encroach upon the powers of the other, and sought to grant each branch of government the means to preserve its rightful powers from encroachments by the others.

The separation of powers and legislative checks and balances discourage the concentration of power and frustrate tyranny. At the same time, they require the branches of government to collaborate and cooperate, limiting conflict and strengthening consensus.

The Rise of Central Administration

The United States has been moving down the path of administrative government in fits and starts from the initial Progressive Era reforms through the New Deal's interventions in the economy. But the most significant expansion occurred more recently, under the Great Society and its progeny.

The expansion of regulatory activities on a society-wide scale in the 1960s and 1970s led to vast new centralizing authority in the federal government and a vast expansion of federal regulatory authority.

When administration is nationalized, though, it does not easily or naturally fall under the authority of one branch or another. As we've seen, bureaucracy and its control created a new source of conflict between the executive and legislative branches.

During the first part of our bureaucratic history, Congress had the upper hand. Congress, after all, had been creating these regulatory agencies to carry out its wishes and delegating its legislative powers to them in the form of broad regulatory authority.

Congress was the first to adapt to the administrative state, continuously reorganizing itself since 1970 by committees and subcommittees to oversee and interact with the day-to-day operations of the bureaucratic apparatus as it expanded.

Rather than control or diminish the bureaucracy through lawmaking or budget control, Congress has settled mostly on "oversight" of the bureaucracy.

Today, when Congress writes legislation, it uses very broad language that turns extensive power over to agencies, which are also given the authority of executing and usually adjudicating violations of their regulations in particular cases. The result is that most of the actual decisions of lawmaking and public policy—decisions previously the constitutional responsibility of elected legislators—are delegated to bureaucrats whose "rules" have the full force and effect of laws.

In 2014, about 220 pieces of legislation became law, amounting to a little more than 3,000 pages of law, while federal bureaucrats issued 79,066 pages of new and updated regulations. The modern Congress is almost exclusively a supervisory body exercising post-legislative oversight of administrative policymakers.

Modern administrative bureaucracies consolidate the powers of government by exercising the lawmaking power, executing their own rules and then judging their application in administrative courts, binding individuals not through legislative law or judicial decision, but through case-by-case rulemaking based on increasingly broad and undefined mandates, all the while less apparent and accountable to the political process and popular consent.

The consequences of the administrative state's lack of accountability have been made much more severe by Congress' current inclination to deal with every policy issue through "comprehensive" legislation.

Congress has ceased to tackle distinct problems with simple laws that can be deliberated upon and then made known to the public. Instead, for everything from health care to financial restructuring to immigration reform, Congress proposes labyrinthine bills that extend to every corner of civil society and impose an ever more complicated and expansive administrative apparatus upon a public that has no way to understand the laws it will be held accountable for.

The Affordable Care Act is a perfect example. This law transferred massive regulatory authority over most health-care decision making to a collection of more than 100 federal agencies, bureaus and commissions.

Likewise, the Dodd-Frank Wall Street Reform and Consumer Protection Act requires administrative rulemakings reaching not only to every financial institution, but well into every corner of the American economy. Its new bureaucracies, like the Consumer Financial Protection Bureau and the Financial Stability Oversight Council, operate outside of the public eye and are subject to virtually none of the traditional checks.

The Consumer Financial Protection Bureau is literally outside the rule of law. It has an independent source of revenue, insulation from legislative or executive oversight and the broad latitude and discretion to determine and enforce its own rulings.

The rise of the new imperial presidency—acting by executive orders more than legislative direction—should come as no surprise, then, given the overwhelming amount of authority that has been delegated to decision-making actors and bodies largely under executive control.

Modern executives can command the bureaucracy to implement new policies without the cooperation of Congress by abusing executive discretion, by exploiting the vagaries of poorly written laws, and by willfully neglecting and disregarding even laws that are clear and well-crafted.

By acting unilaterally without or even against the authority of Congress, the executive assumes a degree of legislative powers without legislative accountability.

Once it has been established that the president with "a pen and a phone" can govern by executive orders and regulations without Congress, it will prove difficult and perhaps impossible to prevent future executives from following this lawless path.

Rebuilding Congress

It may be a prudent option at this point to assert checks and balances through litigation.

A successful lawsuit could prevent things from getting worse, but the legislative branch's going to the judicial branch to solve its disagreements with the executive branch is not going to solve the problem.

If Congress' turning to litigation to assert its constitutional prerogative becomes the norm, it would have the perverse (and unintended) effect of further nullifying the institutional powers of Congress.

The only way to reverse the trend of a diminishing legislature and the continued expansion of the bureaucratic executive is for Congress to strengthen its constitutional muscles as a co-equal branch of government.

Thus, the first step toward restoring the structural integrity of the Constitution is for Congress to reassert its legislative authority and, as much as possible, to cease delegating what amounts to the power to make laws to administrative agencies.

Congress needs to relearn the art of lawmaking. It must regain legislative control over today's labyrinthine state through better lawmaking up front and better oversight after the fact.

Regular legislative order, especially the day-to-day, back-and-forth of authorizing, appropriating and overseeing the operations of government, will do more than anything else to restore the Article I powers of Congress and restore legislative control over today's unlimited government.

The one place where the power of Congress is not entirely lost—and where there's opportunity for gaining leverage over an unchecked executive—is Congress' power of the purse.

Used well, it would also prevent Congress from continually getting cornered in fights over incomprehensible omnibus budgets at the end of every fiscal year, the settlement of which advantages the executive.

Strategically controlling and using the budget process will turn the advantage back to Congress, forcing the executive to engage with the legislative branch and get back into the habit of executing the laws enacted by Congress.

If Congress does not act to correct the growing tilt toward executive-bureaucratic power, the structure of our government will be fundamentally—and perhaps permanently—altered.

It's still possible for Congress to restore its legislative powers, and to correct this structural imbalance. But Congress needs to act as a constitutional institution—indeed, the primary branch of constitutional government.

It must do so by putting down clear markers and drawing enforceable institutional lines before the inauguration of the next president—whoever that may be, and regardless of his or her political party.

DISCUSSION QUESTIONS

1. If Appelbaum is correct that our constitutional system is fragile because it depends on informal norms of cooperation to work, is congressional abdication as analyzed by Spalding actually a good thing rather than something to be worried about? That is, by deferring to the bureaucracy and executive action, does Congress allow the government to function even when the president and Congress cannot agree?

2. What problems do you see with Spalding's argument about Congress reasserting its lawmaking authority? Why do you think Congress delegates so much power to the bureaucracy in the first place?

3. Do either of these authors' arguments seem to depend on whether we have unified or divided government?

6

The Presidency: Should the Electoral College Be Replaced with a Direct Popular Vote for President?

Donald Trump won the 2016 presidential election by winning a majority of the Electoral College votes (306, 36 more than the 270 required to win), even though he lost the popular vote to Hillary Clinton by nearly 3 million votes (roughly 63 million to her 65.8 million). It was the fifth time in U.S. history, and the second in sixteen years, that a president was elected without receiving the most votes. To a modern observer of democratic systems, the election of a popular vote loser seems inconsistent with the majoritarian principle of representative government.

At the time of the Constitution's ratification, the Electoral College was a compromise designed to address concerns of small states worried about being overwhelmed by the power of large states, to respect the importance of states in a federal system, to insulate the presidential election from strong public passions, and to provide the executive a degree of independence from the legislature. It also was designed to require candidates to gain support from across the country: as Alexander Hamilton argued in *Federalist* 68, the indirect process would filter out individuals whose "talents for low intrigue, and the little arts of popularity" might be enough to win the support of one state, and would "require other talents, and a different kind of merit, to establish [an individual] in the esteem and confidence of the whole Union, or of so considerable a portion of it as would be necessary to make him a successful candidate."

But given that our concepts of representation, and the vast differences between how we think of legitimacy now and how the framers thought of it then, does the Electoral College still deserve our deference? Should it be abolished and be replaced with a simple national popular vote?

The three readings in this section provide competing perspectives. In "Democracy Denied," John Nichols, a progressive writer, argues that the Electoral College is an absurd anachronism than violates the fundamental notion that a government founded on "the will of the people" must itself be based on "the premise that the popular vote defines who wins and who loses." While we have corrected other errors in the original compromises that produced the Constitution—by adopting the direct election of Senators and abolishing slavery—he writes that "the most anti-democratic of the founding constructs—an elite Electoral College created to thwart the will of the great mass of voters—remains." Nichols supports the National Popular Vote Compact, in which states have changed their laws to award their Electoral College votes to the winner of the national popular vote, and sees reform as part of a broader move to protect voting rights nationwide.

Richard Posner, a retired federal judge, wrote in 2012 that the Electoral College has five crucial advantages: it ensures a definitive outcome, requires a candidate to have national appeal, gives swing state voters an incentive to pay close attention to candidates, gives large states due importance, and ensures that the winner has an absolute majority of votes. Posner dismisses the criticism that the Electoral College is undemocratic: "No form of representative democracy . . . is or aspires to be perfectly democratic." The entire federal judiciary, for example, (appointed to life terms) is manifestly undemocratic.

Guelzo (a professor of history) and Hulme (an attorney in Washington, D.C.) defend the Electoral College in the context of the 2016 results. They stress the importance of the institution to our federal system, and argue that "the Electoral College is preeminently both a symbol and a practical implementation of that federalism." They specifically contest the notion that the Electoral College was connected to the protection of slavery (as Nichols argues), and maintain that the claim is "more of a rhetorical posture than a serious argument."

John Nichols

Democracy Denied

In the mid-1980s, shortly after Ronald Reagan won a forty-nine-state landslide victory in his campaign for a second term, David Bowie had a top-forty hit with a haunting song from the soundtrack to the spy drama *The Falcon and the Snowman*. The song resonated with people who felt disconnected from their nation. It was titled "This Is Not America."

Sometimes, of course, an election result *is* America: a Franklin Roosevelt or a Dwight Eisenhower or a Lyndon Johnson wins so decisively that the President can claim a genuine mandate. As frustrating as it may have been for a lot of us, Ronald Reagan won big in 1984—the year George Orwell had warned about.

But what about those times when the "winner" is not the winner at all? What about those years when the finish of a long campaign is in conflict with itself?

There is always a tendency on the part of major media outlets and political insiders to suggest that the United States is defined by the prominent men and women who take office after elections. Too frequently, even those of us who dissent from the conventional wisdom of American politics fall into the trap of imagining that the headlines declaring who has won define our times. But when that is not the case, there is a duty to speak the truth: "This is not America."

Such is our circumstance today.

The Washington Post's post-election headline declared, "Trump Triumphs." The *New York Post* trumpeted, "President Trump: They Said It Couldn't Happen."

But it didn't actually happen in the way that so much of the media imagines. Trump's America is not America. In order to imagine that Trump's presidency has a triumphant mandate, or even the barest measure of democratic legitimacy, Americans must surrender to the hoax that media branding is reality.

The reality, as Michael Moore noted in caps, is that "HILLARY CLINTON WON THE POPULAR VOTE!" "If you woke up this morning thinking you live in an effed-up country, you don't," the filmmaker explained on the day after the election, stating what the headlines did not: "Your fellow Americans wanted Hillary, not Trump."

Democracies and democratic republics that take seriously the notion that governing extends from the will of the people begin with the premise that the popular vote defines who wins and who loses. In other countries that elect presidents, Hillary Clinton's popular-vote victory would have her preparing for an inauguration. In America, it had her walking her dogs on the day after her concession speech.

On election night, Clinton's win was a narrow one. But the United States has archaic systems for casting and counting ballots, which means that the tabulation process stretches out for weeks, even months, after the polls close. One week after the election, Clinton's lead had grown to more than one million votes. The Democratic advantage will just keep expanding, as the longest counts tend to be in West Coast states such as California, where Clinton is leading Trump by an almost 2-to-1 margin. Nate Cohn argues that Clinton could end up winning by two million votes and more than 1.5 percent of the total; others suggest the margin could go higher.

Even as the count progressed, Clinton's winning margin grew greater than Richard Nixon's in 1968. It was greater than John F. Kennedy's in 1960. In fact, it was greater than the winning margin in more than twenty of the presidential elections the United States has held since its founding. Of course, the elections of the distant past had smaller overall turnouts. But Kennedy and Nixon were elected in high turnout elections in relatively recent times.

And there's an even more recent election that offers an even more relevant comparison. In 2000, Democrat Al Gore beat Republican George W. Bush by 543,895 votes. At the time, that was the biggest ever popular-vote victory for someone who lost the presidency. But Hillary Clinton's popular-vote victory over Donald Trump is already dramatically greater than Gore's.

At the same time, the final 2016 count will give Trump a substantially lower percentage of the overall vote than Republican Mitt Romney received in his losing 2012 challenge to Democratic President Barack Obama.

But none of this matters, we are told, because Trump will prevail by a narrow margin in the December vote by the 538 members of the Electoral College.

So how do 538 electors trump—apologies—the choice of the more than 120,000,000 actual voters for the presidency? Because they represent a relic of the same set of founding compromises that permitted human bondage in a land where the Declaration of Independence announced "all men are created equal." The Electoral College is, constitutional scholars say, a "vestige of slavery," and was created to help protect that institution. The goal, history reminds us, was to keep the more populous northern states from overruling the South.

"It's embarrassing," argues Paul Finkelman, a law professor who has studied the institution. "I think if most Americans knew what the origins of the Electoral College is, they would be disgusted."

The Constitution has been amended frequently to correct the errors of the past. The franchise has been extended to African Americans and women; the poll tax has been banned; the voting age has been lowered. The old practice of choosing Senators via backroom deals has been replaced with an elected Senate. Yet the most anti-democratic of the founding constructs—an elite Electoral College created to thwart the will of the great mass of voters—remains.

The Electoral College warps and diminishes American democracy at every turn. As George C. Edwards III, a political science professor at Texas A&M University who edits the *Presidential Studies Quarterly*, tells us: "The Electoral College . . . has the potential to undo the people's will at many points in the long journey from the selection of electors to counting their votes in Congress."

Consider this: In Wyoming, each elector represents roughly 160,000 eligible voters, compared with the more than 600,000 eligible voters represented by an elector from California.

Often this warping and diminishment is obscured when the Electoral College's choice mirrors that of the national popular vote. The Electoral College only gets major attention when the college's choice diverges from the national popular vote.

What Americans need to recognize is that such major malfunctions are becoming more common.

For the second time in sixteen years, the national popular vote decision is going to be overridden by the Electoral College. Trump has a narrow advantage in the Electoral College (so narrow that a shift of just 57,000 votes would have made Clinton the winner in the three states she needed—Michigan, Pennsylvania and Wisconsin—to gain the 270 electors required to prevail). But that advantage is definitional under the current system.

This is a problem.

To be fair, it is a problem that has been flagged since 1787.

The group FairVote tells us that more than 700 constitutional amendments have been proposed to modify or abolish the Electoral College, "making it the subject of more attempted reforms than any other subject." A proposal to replace the current allocation of state electors on a winner-take-all basis with a proportional electoral vote gained the endorsement of the Senate in the 1950s but failed in the House. A proposal to abolish the Electoral College won the support of the House in 1969 but was blocked by a Senate filibuster led by southern Senators who had opposed civil rights legislation.

Even Donald Trump griped that "the Electoral College is a disaster for a democracy"—but that was in 2012, not 2016.

The trouble with historic attempts to replace or reform the Electoral College is that they tended to be based on frustrations and fears extending from a particular election result, and thus absorbed in the closed circle of Congress.

The aftermath of the 2016 election, in which the Electoral College has again proven to be a disaster for democracy, can and must be different. There are many proper reactions to this election, including solidarity movements to defend those most threatened by the combination of a Trump presidency and a fiercely right-wing Congress. But if ever an election demanded a mass movement for reform, this is it.

Yes, this Congress is disinclined toward reform. But FairVote and other groups are advancing a credible vehicle for getting around Congress, and it has already gained considerable traction. Activists want state legislatures to endorse a National Popular Vote compact, which requires states to "choose to allocate their electoral votes to the candidate who wins the most popular votes in all fifty states and the District of Columbia."

Ten states and the District of Columbia—with a combined total of 165 electoral votes—have passed legislation to enter the compact. And the idea has been proposed in the legislatures of the remaining states. This is a real reform plan. But it does not need to be the only one. What is necessary now is for Americans to organize on behalf of a constitutional amendment to abolish the Electoral College, or at the least to reform it with a proportional representation plan. We can sort out the specifics later. But this moment cannot be lost to frustration at a rigged system, or hopelessness about prospects for reform.

This should be a moment of radical urgency. Activism to abolish the Electoral College should be combined with advocacy to end the corrupt practice of gerrymandering, which allows incumbent politicians and their allies to draw maps of voting districts that are skewed to prevent competition. (Since 2010, these have been used to lock in Republican control of the U.S. House of Representatives. In 2012, for instance, GOP House candidates won 49 percent of the votes and 54 percent of the seats.)

Any movement for real democracy must also address voter suppression, which played a profound role in the 2016 election. Restrictive voter ID laws, complex registration procedures, limits on early voting, and cuts in the number of polling places undermined democracy in jurisdictions across the country and, voting rights activists argue, contributed to declines in turnout that benefited Trump and his allies.

This was the first national election in fifty years that was not conducted under the full protection of the Voting Rights Act of 1965. That is a travesty, yet there is little chance that a Congress led by House Speaker Paul Ryan and Senate Majority Leader Mitch McConnell will renew the act's protections, especially under a President who has dismissed efforts to make voting easy and efficient as the "rigging" of elections.

The time really has come to embrace the proposal by Democratic Congressmen Keith Ellison of Minnesota and Mark Pocan of Wisconsin to amend the Constitution to declare: "Every citizen of the United States, who is of legal voting age, shall have the fundamental right to vote in any public election."

The same goes for the amendment proposed by Vermont Senator Bernie Sanders to overturn the U.S. Supreme Court's anti-democratic rulings in cases including the 2010 *Citizens United* decision. Only an amendment will address the flow of billionaire and corporate money into our politics, which in 2016 Senate races proved decisive.

Yes, it requires hard work to amend the Constitution. But the document has been updated twenty-seven times since 1787, often in moments as difficult and divisive and challenging as these. And the American people are ready to make the change. * * *

The anger, the frustration, the fear and loathing that extends from the 2016 presidential race is real. It will find many expressions. One of them must be a bold and unapologetic call for democracy—a call grounded in the recognition that Donald Trump did not win a mandate. He did not even win the popular vote. And a system that allows the loser to win is not sufficient for a nation that proposes to be of, by, and for the people. * * *

It will not be easy. But if the 2016 election has taught us anything, it is that radical reform is necessary. We renew ourselves not with bitterness, but with a commitment to make the change that brings democracy to the United States of America.

Richard A. Posner

In Defense of the Electoral College

The Electoral College is widely regarded as an anachronism, a nondemocratic method of selecting a president that ought to be superseded by declaring the candidate who receives the most popular votes the winner. The advocates of this position are correct in arguing that the Electoral College method is not democratic in a modern sense. The Constitution provides that "Each State shall appoint, in such Manner as the Legislature thereof may direct, a Number of Electors, equal to the whole Number of Senators and Representatives to which the State may be entitled in the Congress." And it is the electors who elect the president, not the people. When you vote for a presidential candidate you're actually voting for a slate of electors.

But each party selects a slate of electors trusted to vote for the party's nominee (and that trust is rarely betrayed). Because virtually all states award all their electoral votes to the winner of the popular vote in the state, and because the Electoral College weights the less populous states more heavily along the lines of the Senate (two Senators and two Electoral College votes for every state, and then more electoral votes added for each state based on population), it is entirely possible that the winner of the electoral vote will not win the national popular vote. Yet that has happened very rarely. It happened in 2000, when Gore had more popular votes than Bush yet fewer electoral votes, but that was the first time since 1888.

There are five reasons for retaining the Electoral College despite its lack of democratic pedigree; all are practical reasons, not liberal or conservative reasons.

1) Certainty of Outcome

A dispute over the outcome of an Electoral College vote is possible—it happened in 2000—but it's less likely than a dispute over the popular vote. The reason is that the winning candidate's share of the Electoral College invariably exceeds his share of the popular vote. In last week's election, for example, Obama received 61.7 percent of the electoral vote compared to only 51.3 percent of the popular votes cast for him and Romney. (I ignore the scattering of votes not counted for either candidate.) Because almost all states award electoral votes on a winner-take-all basis, even a very slight plurality in a state creates a landslide electoral-vote victory in that state. A tie in the nationwide electoral vote is possible because the total number of votes—538—is an even number, but it is highly unlikely.

Of course a tie in the number of popular votes in a national election in which tens of millions of votes are cast is even more unlikely. But if the difference in the popular vote is small, then if the winner of the popular vote were deemed the winner of the presidential election, candidates would have an incentive to seek a recount in any state (plus the District of Columbia) in which they thought the recount would give them more additional votes than their opponent. The lawyers would go to work in state after state to have the votes recounted, and the result would be debilitating uncertainty, delay, and conflict—look at the turmoil that a dispute limited to one state, Florida, engendered in 2000.

2) Everyone's President

The Electoral College requires a presidential candidate to have transregional appeal. No region (South, Northeast, etc.) has enough electoral votes to elect a president. So a solid regional favorite, such as Romney was in the South, has no incentive to campaign heavily in those states, for he gains no electoral votes by increasing his plurality in states that he knows he will win. This is a desirable result because a candidate with only regional appeal is unlikely to be a successful president. The residents of the other regions are likely to feel disfranchised— to feel that their votes do not count, that the new president will have no regard for their interests, that he really isn't their president.

3) Swing States

The winner-take-all method of awarding electoral votes induces the candidates— as we saw in last week's election—to focus their campaign efforts on the toss-up states; that follows directly from the candidates' lack of inducement to campaign in states they are sure to win. Voters in toss-up states are more likely to pay close attention to the campaign—to really *listen* to the competing candidates— knowing that they are going to decide the election. They are likely to be the most thoughtful voters, on average (and for the further reason that they will have received the most information and attention from the candidates), and the most thoughtful voters should be the ones to decide the election.

4) Big States

The Electoral College restores some of the weight in the political balance that large states (by population) lose by virtue of the malapportionment of the Senate decreed in the Constitution. This may seem paradoxical, given that electoral votes are weighted in favor of less populous states. Wyoming, the least populous state, contains only about one-sixth of 1 percent of the U.S. population, but its three electors (of whom two are awarded only because Wyoming has two senators like every other state) give it slightly more than one-half of 1 percent of total electoral votes. But winner-take-all makes a slight increase in the popular vote have a much bigger electoral-vote payoff in a large state than in a small one. The popular vote was very close in Florida; nevertheless Obama, who won that vote, got 29 electoral votes. A victory by the same margin in Wyoming would net the winner only 3 electoral votes. So, other things being equal, a large state gets more attention from presidential candidates in a campaign than a small states does. And since presidents and senators are often presidential candidates, large states are likely to get additional consideration in appropriations and appointments from presidents and senators before as well as during campaigns, offsetting to some extent the effects of the malapportioned Senate on the political influence of less populous states.

5) Avoid Run-Off Elections

The Electoral College avoids the problem of elections in which no candidate receives a majority of the votes cast. For example, Nixon in 1968 and Clinton in 1992 both had only a 43 percent plurality of the popular votes, while winning a majority in the Electoral College (301 and 370 electoral votes, respectively). There is pressure for run-off elections when no candidate wins a majority of the votes cast; that pressure, which would greatly complicate the presidential election process, is reduced by the Electoral College, which invariably produces a clear winner.

Against these reasons to retain the Electoral College the argument that it is undemocratic falls flat. No form of representative democracy, as distinct from direct democracy, is or aspires to be perfectly democratic. Certainly not our federal government. In the entire executive and judicial branches, only two officials are elected—the president and vice president. All the rest are appointed—federal Article III judges for life.

It can be argued that the Electoral College method of selecting the president may turn off potential voters for a candidate who has no hope of carrying their state—Democrats in Texas, for example, or Republicans in California. Knowing their vote will have no effect, they have less incentive to pay attention to the campaign than they would have if the president were picked by popular vote, for then the state of a voter's residence would be irrelevant to the weight of his vote. But of course no voter's vote swings a national election, and in spite of that, about one-half the eligible American population did vote in last week's election. Voters in presidential elections are people who want to express a political preference rather than people who think that a single vote may decide an election. Even in one-sided states, there are plenty of votes in favor of the candidate who is sure not to carry the state. So I doubt that the Electoral College has much of a turn-off effect. And if it does, that is outweighed by the reasons for retaining this seemingly archaic institution.

Allen Guelzo and James Hulme

In Defense of the Electoral College

There is hardly anything in the Constitution harder to explain, or easier to misunderstand, than the Electoral College. And when a presidential election hands the palm to a candidate who comes in second in the popular vote but first in the Electoral College tally, something deep in our democratic viscera balks and asks why the Electoral College shouldn't be dumped as a useless relic of eighteenth-century white, gentry privilege.

Actually, there have been only five occasions when a closely divided popular vote and the electoral vote have failed to point in the same direction. No matter. After last week's results, we're hearing a litany of complaints: the Electoral College is undemocratic, the Electoral College is unnecessary, the Electoral College was invented to protect slavery—and the demand to push it down the memory hole.

All of which is strange because the Electoral College is at the core of our system of federalism. The Founders who sat in the 1787 Constitutional Convention lavished an extraordinary amount of argument on the Electoral College, and it was by no means one-sided. The great Pennsylvania jurist James Wilson believed that "if we are to establish a national Government," the president should be chosen by a direct, national vote of the people. But wise old Roger Sherman of Connecticut replied that the president ought to be elected by Congress, since he feared that direct election of presidents by the people would lead to the creation of a monarchy. "An independence of the Executive [from] the supreme Legislature, was in his opinion the very essence of tyranny if there was any such thing." Sherman was not trying to undermine the popular will, but to keep it from being distorted by a president who mistook popular election as a mandate for dictatorship.

Quarrels like this flared all through the convention, until, at almost the last minute, James Madison "took out a Pen and Paper, and sketched out a mode of Electing the President" by a "college" of "Electors . . . chosen by those of the people in each State, who shall have the Qualifications requisite."

The Founders also designed the operation of the Electoral College with unusual care. The portion of Article 2, Section 1, describing the Electoral College is longer and descends to more detail than any other single issue the Constitution addresses. More than the federal judiciary—more than the war powers—more than taxation and representation. It prescribes in precise detail how "Each State shall appoint . . . a Number of Electors, equal to the whole Number of Senators and Representatives to which the State may be entitled in the Congress"; how these electors "shall vote by Ballot" for a president and vice president; how they "shall sign and certify, and transmit sealed to the Seat of the Government of the United States, directed to the President of the Senate" the results of their balloting; how a tie vote must be resolved; what schedule the balloting should follow; and on and on.

Above all, the Electoral College had nothing to do with slavery. Some historians have branded the Electoral College this way because each state's electoral votes are based on that "whole Number of Senators and Representatives" from each State, and in 1787 the number of those representatives was calculated on the basis of the infamous 3/5ths clause. But the Electoral College merely reflected the numbers, not any bias about slavery (and in any case, the 3/5ths clause was not quite as proslavery a compromise as it seems, since Southern slaveholders wanted their slaves counted as 5/5ths for determining representation in Congress, and had to settle for a whittled-down fraction). As much as the abolitionists before the Civil War liked to talk about the "proslavery Constitution," this was more of a rhetorical posture than a serious historical argument. And the simple fact remains, from the record of the Constitutional Convention's proceedings (James Madison's famous Notes), that the discussions of the Electoral College and the method of electing a president never occur in the context of any of the convention's two climactic debates over slavery.

If anything, it was the Electoral College that made it possible to end slavery, since Abraham Lincoln earned only 39 percent of the popular vote in the election of 1860, but won a crushing victory in the Electoral College. This, in large measure, was why Southern slaveholders stampeded to secession in 1860–61. They could do the numbers as well as anyone, and realized that the Electoral College would only produce more anti-slavery Northern presidents.

Yet, even on those terms, it is hard for Americans to escape the uncomfortable sense that, by inserting an extra layer of "electors" between the people and the president, the Electoral College is something less than democratic. But even if we are a democratic nation, that is not all we are. The Constitution also makes us a federal union, and the Electoral College is preeminently both the symbol and a practical implementation of that federalism.

The states of the union existed before the Constitution, and in a practical sense, existed long before the revolution. Nothing guaranteed that, in 1776, the states would all act together, and nothing guaranteed that after the Revolution they might not go their separate and quarrelsome ways, much like the German states of the eighteenth century or the South American republics in the nineteenth century. The genius of the Constitutional Convention was its ability to entice the American states into a "more perfect union." But it was still a union of states, and we probably wouldn't have had a constitution or a country at all unless the route we took was federalism.

The Electoral College was an integral part of that federal plan. It made a place for the states as well as the people in electing the president by giving them a say at different points in a federal process and preventing big-city populations from dominating the election of a president.

Abolishing the Electoral College now might satisfy an irritated yearning for direct democracy, but it would also mean dismantling federalism. After that, there would be no sense in having a Senate (which, after all, represents the interests of the states), and further along, no sense even in having states, except as administrative departments of the central government. Those who wish to abolish the Electoral College ought to go the distance, and do away with the entire federal system and perhaps even retire the Constitution, since the federalism it was designed to embody would have disappeared.

None of that, ironically, is liable to produce a more democratic election system. There are plenty of democracies, like Great Britain, where no one ever votes directly for a head of the government. But more important, the Electoral College actually keeps presidential elections from going undemocratically awry because it makes unlikely the possibility that third-party candidates will garner enough votes to make it onto the electoral scoreboard.

Without the Electoral College, there would be no effective brake on the number of "viable" presidential candidates. Abolish it, and it would not be difficult to imagine a scenario where, in a field of a dozen micro-candidates, the "winner" only needs 10 percent of the vote, and represents less than 5 percent of the electorate. And presidents elected with smaller and smaller pluralities will only aggravate the sense that an elected president is governing without a real electoral mandate.

The Electoral College has been a major, even if poorly comprehended, mechanism for stability in a democracy, something which democracies are sometimes too flighty to appreciate. It may appear inefficient. But the Founders were not interested in efficiency; they were interested in securing "the blessings of liberty." The Electoral College is, in the end, not a bad device for securing that.

DISCUSSION QUESTIONS

1. One other argument in favor of the Electoral College is that it "contains" electoral disputes: there is no reason for the losing candidate to contest the election in a state unless that state is pivotal in getting past the 270 vote threshold (as was the case in Florida in 2000). Is there merit in this argument? Would a national popular vote be more likely to produce a disputed result?

2. Defenders of the Electoral College often claim (as Posner, Guelto, and Hulme do here) that it discourages multiple candidacies and third parties. But is that an advantage or a disadvantage?

3. How would a national popular vote be tabulated? There actually is no official national vote total: the result is simply the sum of all state vote totals. Would a national popular vote require a new mechanism for computing official results? How would that affect the role of states in the election system?

7

Bureaucracy: Should Government Functions Be Outsourced to Private Contractors?

Public organizations (meaning governments) have different incentives and performance measures than private organizations (meaning, in this context, private sector businesses). Another way to say this is that governments tend to be much less efficient than businesses, but this does not mean that government can be run like a business.

Nevertheless, governments today at all levels face pressure to transfer functions to the private sector, either by spinning off government functions entirely (privatization) or by contracting with private firms to provide services once provided by government employees (outsourcing). Turning over the air traffic control system or the postal service to private companies—leaving them to provide services and collect fees in a profitmaking venture—would be examples of privatization. Using contractors to replace government personnel or carry out public functions—food service at national museums or military bases; private security forces instead of military personnel in Iraq—are examples of outsourcing.

Privatization has its risks. For example, in 2006, the state of Indiana sold the rights to its major highway to a Spanish and Australian consortium for $3.8 billion: in return for the rights to all tolls, the companies took the responsibility for maintenance. But lower than expected traffic and high debt led to bankruptcy in 2011, and led to a takeover by another corporation in 2015. Other private toll road operators in

Alabama, California, Michigan, and Virginia have also gone through bankruptcy proceedings. Proponents of privatization argue that this process has had no impact on states, since private companies have assumed all of the risk. But critics respond that infrastructure is a basic governmental function that should not be farmed out as a profit-making enterprise.

Both outsourcing and privatization have advantages, at least as far as proponents see it: smaller government or more efficient government. Yet both practices also have some disadvantages compared to using government agencies to provide services. Compared to private firms, governments are more sensitive to problems of equity and accountability. For example, one reason the Postal Service is inefficient is that legislators created laws that require it to serve remote areas of the country and maintain post offices in small towns. A private company (say, FedEx or UPS) may not find it profitable to do the same thing, and would either not provide service or charge more for it. We would purchase efficiency at the cost of equity. Your view of whether that tradeoff is worth making probably depends heavily on whether you are a beneficiary of those inefficient services.

But disputes over whether the government does something well or not are often policy disputes about whether the government should be doing something at all. The debate here involves some of the same issues. "Options for Federal Privatization and Reform Lessons from Abroad" was written by Chris Edwards of the Cato Institute, a libertarian think-tank that supports a significantly smaller government. Here, the author proposes privatizing a wide range of government functions: the post office, air traffic control, airports, public lands, etc. He argues that privatization increases efficiency, spurs capital investment, rewards entrepreneurship, leads to more transparency, and removes "politics" from the entire process.

Not so fast, argues Janine Wedel, who is critical of contracting out government functions. Wedel argues that using contractors to provide crucial government functions—intelligence, security, information technology—has a number of negative consequences, including reduced accountability, loss of vital institutional expertise, and poor supervision. The result is that the federal government has abdicated responsibility for important functions, and has substituted profit-seeking for the more difficult (but still vital) task of allocating resources in a way that meets public demands.

Chris Edwards

Options for Federal Privatization and Reform Lessons from Abroad

A privatization revolution has swept the world since the 1980s. Governments in more than 100 countries have moved thousands of state-owned businesses and other assets to the private sector. Airports, airlines, railroads, energy companies, postal services, and other businesses valued at about $3.3 trillion have been privatized over the past three decades.

Privatization has improved government finances by raising revenues and reducing spending. More important, it has spurred economic growth and improved services because privatized businesses have cut costs, increased quality, and pursued innovation.

In a 1969 essay, management expert Peter Drucker said that politicians in the twentieth century had been "hypnotized by government . . . in love with it and saw no limits to its abilities." But he said that the love affair was coming to an end as the mismanagement of state-owned businesses was becoming more apparent everywhere. In his essay, Drucker called for a "reprivatization" of government activities, but he was a bit ahead of his time.

The privatization revolution was launched by Margaret Thatcher's government in the United Kingdom, which came to power in 1979. Prime Minister Thatcher popularized the word *privatization*, and her successful reforms were copied around the globe. She was determined to revive the stagnant British economy, and her government privatized dozens of major businesses, including British Airways, British Telecom, British Steel, and British Gas. Other nations followed the British lead because of a "disillusionment with the generally poor performance of state-owned enterprises and the desire to improve efficiency of bloated and often failing companies," noted a report on privatization by the Organisation for Economic Cooperation and Development (OECD).

Privatization swept through other developed countries in the 1980s and 1990s, with major reforms in Australia, Canada, France, Italy, New Zealand, Portugal, Spain, Sweden, and other nations. A Labour government elected in New Zealand in 1984 privatized dozens of state-owned companies, including airports, banks, energy companies, forests, and the national airline and telecommunications companies. Australia privatized dozens of companies between the mid-1990s and mid-2000s, generating proceeds of more than $100 billion. * * *

Privatization has gained support from both the political right and left. Left-of-center governments in Australia, the United Kingdom, France, Canada, and New Zealand all pursued privatization. Privatization has attracted opposition from the public in many countries, but very rarely have reforms been reversed once put in place. Privatization works, and so the reforms have lasted.

Privatization has "massively increased the size and efficiency of the world's capital markets," one finance expert found. As of 2005, the 10 largest share offerings in world history were privatizations. By 2010, about half of the global stock market capitalization outside of the United States was from companies that had been privatized in recent years. Privatization has had a huge effect on the global economy.

Today, many countries have privatized the "lowest hanging fruit." But there is much left to sell, and global privatization is continuing at a robust pace. Over the past four years, governments worldwide have sold an average $203 billion of state-owned businesses annually. China is now the largest privatizer, but Western nations continue to pursue reforms. The British government, for example, sold a majority stake in Royal Mail in 2013 and then unloaded the final block of shares in 2015.

Privatization has been a very successful reform. An OECD report reviewed the research and found "overwhelming support for the notion that privatization brings about a significant increase in the profitability, real output and efficiency of privatized companies." And a review of academic studies in the *Journal of Economic Literature* concluded that privatization "appears to improve performance measured in many different ways, in many different countries."

Despite the success of privatization, reforms have largely bypassed our own federal government. President Ronald Reagan's administration explored selling the U.S. Postal Service, Amtrak, the Tennessee Valley Authority, the air traffic control system, and federal land, but those efforts stalled. President Bill Clinton had more success. His administration oversaw the privatization of the Alaska Power Administration, the Elk Hills Naval Petroleum Reserve, the U.S. Enrichment Corporation, and Intelsat.

Little action on federal privatization has been pursued since then, but there are many federal activities that should be turned over to the private sector. The United States has a government postal system, but European countries are privatizing their systems and opening them to competition. The United States has a government air traffic control system, but Canada and the United Kingdom have privatized their systems. Our federal government owns electric utilities and a passenger rail service, but other countries have privatized those businesses.

The first section of this study examines the path-breaking British privatizations of recent decades. The second section discusses 12 advantages of privatization. The third section describes six businesses and assets that federal policymakers should privatize: the U.S. Postal Service, Amtrak, the Tennessee Valley Authority, the air traffic control system, land, and buildings. That section also highlights other businesses and assets to sell.

This study mainly uses *privatization* in a narrow sense to mean fully moving ownership of businesses and assets to the private sector. The term is often used more broadly to include government contracting, public-private partnerships, vouchers, and other forms of partial privatization. Those are all worthy reforms, but they are not the focus here.

When the next president comes into office in 2017, the time will be ripe for privatization reforms. Privatization would help spur growth in our underperforming economy and modestly reduce rising budget deficits. Privatization would also create qualitative benefits, such as increasing transparency and improving environmental stewardship.

* * *

Advantages of Privatization

* * *

1. Promotes Efficiency and Innovation

Private businesses in competitive markets have strong incentives to increase efficiency—to produce more and better products at lower costs. Businesses seek profits, which are a measure of net value creation. If a business performs poorly, it will lose money and have to change course, or ultimately face bankruptcy or a takeover.

By contrast, government entities are usually not penalized for excess costs, misjudging public needs, or other failures. They can deliver bad results year after year and still receive funding. Government workers are rarely fired, and there is no imperative for managers to generate net value.

The superiority of private enterprise is not just a static efficiency advantage. Instead, businesses in competitive markets must pursue continuous improvements. They learn by doing and adjust to changes in society, a process called adaptive efficiency. By contrast, governments get ossified by bureaucracy and are slow to adapt.

Businesses routinely abandon low-value activities, but "the moment government undertakes anything, it becomes entrenched and permanent," noted management expert Peter Drucker. As an example, the demand for mail has plunged and the U.S. Postal Service (USPS) is losing billions of dollars a year, but Congress has blocked obvious reforms, such as ending Saturday delivery. Private businesses make such adjustments all the time as demand for their products fluctuates.

Government organizations undermine growth by keeping resources employed in low-value activities, even as tastes and technologies change. That is why Drucker said, "[T]he strongest argument for private enterprise is not the function of profit. The strongest argument is the function of loss." Losses encourage private businesses to drop less-valuable activities and move resources to more promising ones.

In the twentieth century, many economists supported government ownership because they thought that expert planners could efficiently organize production. But they ignored the dynamic role of businesses in continuously improving products and production techniques. In a *Journal of Economic Perspectives* article, Andrei Shleifer said that many economists did not foresee the "grotesque failure" of government ownership, and they did not appreciate the private-sector role in generating innovation.

✳ ✳ ✳

[2.] Improves Capital Investment

In the private sector, businesses have incentives to maintain their facilities in good repair and to invest to meet rising demands. To fund expansions, they reinvest their profits and raise financing on debt and equity markets.

By contrast, government organizations often consume their funding on bureaucratic bloat and have little left over for repairs and upgrades. Government infrastructure is often old, congested, and poorly maintained. Capital investment falls short and tends to be misallocated. This was a common experience with British industries before they were privatized, and access to private funding to increase capital investment was an important factor in the Thatcher government's privatization drive.

The same problems of run-down public infrastructure are apparent in the United States today. The National Park Service has many poorly maintained facilities and billions of dollars of deferred maintenance. Urban subway and light rail systems across the nation have tens of billions of dollars of maintenance backlogs. Politicians enjoy launching new parks and rail systems, but they put little effort into maintaining what the government already owns.

Federal agencies cannot count on Congress for funding. Consider the air traffic control system, which is run by the Federal Aviation Administration (FAA). The system needs billions of dollars in investment to meet rising passenger demands, but the FAA has not secured stable long-term funding from Congress. Furthermore, the FAA mismanages its capital investment projects, which often experience delays and cost overruns.

Amtrak's investment budget is also mismanaged. Because of politics, the company invests in rural routes that have few passengers instead of higher-demand routes in the Northeast. In his book on Amtrak, rail expert Joseph Vranich argued, "Congressional requirements that Amtrak spend money on capital improvements to lightly used routes are outrageous. . . . Throughout Amtrak's history, it has devoted too much of its budget to where it is not needed, and not enough to where it is."

Privatization solves these sorts of problems. Privatized businesses use customer revenues and capital markets to finance upgrades. They do not have to lobby Congress to receive needed funding. And they have strong incentives to invest where the actual demand is, free from political pressures that plague government-owned businesses.

[3.] Expands Entrepreneurship and Competition

When the government produces goods and services, it tends to squelch competition, either directly by enforcing a monopoly, or indirectly by deterring entrants unwilling to compete with a subsidized government producer.

Devoid of competition, government organizations resist change and are slow to adopt better ways of doing things. The FAA runs the air traffic control system with outdated technology. The USPS is being undermined by email, but it does not have the flexibility to adapt. Airlines and intercity buses have improved their efficiencies and reduced costs under competitive pressures, but Amtrak's costs remain high.

In the economy, major innovations often come from upstarts, not industry-dominant firms. Big advances in industries, from computers to retail, have come from new firms doing things in new ways. So economic progress depends on open entry, on the ability of entrepreneurs to challenge existing providers. That is hard to do when the existing provider is the government.

Privatization abroad has often been paired with the removal of entry barriers. The European Union has urged member countries to open their markets as they privatize their airline, energy, telecommunications, transportation, and postal companies. British postal markets were opened for competition, and then Royal Mail was privatized. The privatization of British Telecom was followed by deregulation and then the rise of competitors such as Vodaphone, which is now one of the largest telecommunications firms in the world.

U.S. policymakers should use privatization as a catalyst for pro-competition reforms. The government should privatize USPS, Amtrak, and other companies, and at the same time open industries to new entrants. Open entry attracts people with new ideas and encourages the dissemination of new production techniques. The best and the brightest do not want to work for moribund bureaucracies such as the USPS and Amtrak. As a result, those companies today are essentially closed to external know-how and global best practices.

The American economy is rapidly evolving, driven by globalization and new technologies. We can keep up with all the changes by making our economy as flexible and open to new ideas as possible, and privatization and competition are the best ways to do that. If America opened its postal industry to competition, there would likely be many entrepreneurs ready to revolutionize it.

[4.] Increases Transparency

Citizens have difficulty monitoring the activities of government agencies. The goals of agencies are often vague, and their finances are difficult to understand. Government officials are protected by civil service rules and can be secretive in their activities. Even members of Congress have difficulty squeezing information out of agency leaders, as we often see at congressional hearings.

By contrast, private companies have clear goals such as earning profits and expanding sales. Performance is monitored by auditors, shareholders, and creditors. And consumers monitor companies in the marketplace, giving feedback with their purchasing behavior.

Moving government activities to the private sector would make them more "public." Economist John Blundell said that, where he grew up in England, a government water facility had posted a sign, Public Property: Keep Out. But after the facility was privatized, a new sign went up: Private Property: Public Welcome. Private businesses have an incentive to be transparent and promote good community relations.

British privatizations revealed problems that had been hidden inside government businesses, such as unknown debts, pension liabilities, and performance issues. With the privatization of the British nuclear industry, the large size of its financial problems was revealed. In preparing British Telecom for privatization, the Thatcher government found that the company "had not the faintest idea which of its activities were profitable and which were not." For British Airways, the government found undisclosed losses of hundreds of millions of British pounds as the company was being readied for privatization.

In the U.S. government, the National Park Service provides few public details about the budgets of its individual parks and sites. By contrast, the private, non-profit Mount Vernon estate in Virginia—home of George Washington—publishes audited financial statements showing how money is raised and spent.

Or consider the USPS's accounting. The postal company provides some services in its legal monopoly and other services in competitive markets, but its financial statements make it difficult to determine how much it earns or loses on each. The company attributes a large share of costs to overhead, which hides internal cross-subsidies. Economist Robert Shapiro found that the USPS manipulates its accounting to raise prices on letters, and then uses the extra revenues to subsidize its express mail and package delivery.

Amtrak similarly hides cross-subsidies behind its opaque accounting, so it is difficult to determine the profits or losses on each of its routes. Amtrak also has a history of hiding information from investigators and of presenting unrealistic projections to Congress.

The Tennessee Valley Authority (TVA) has long been a secretive organization and immune from outside criticism, particularly with respect to its safety and environmental record. Failures at its Kingston Fossil Plant in 2008 led to the largest coal ash spill in U.S. history. The TVA had been aware of the risk but failed to take needed steps to avert it. Why? Federal auditors blamed TVA's management culture, which focuses on covering up mistakes. At the TVA, a "litigation strategy seems to have prevailed over transparency and accountability," said the auditors.

A final transparency issue is that federal agencies that operate services are often the same agencies that regulate them. The FAA operates air traffic control and regulates aviation safety. The Transportation Security Administration operates airport security and also regulates it. In such cases, privatizing the operations would eliminate the conflict of interest, and agency decisions that are now made internally would be made externally and publicly. This transparency issue is one reason the Thatcher government figured that—even if an industry had monopoly elements—privatizing that industry would improve it because the government regulator would be split off from the entity being regulated. Privatization and transparency go hand in hand.

* * *

[5.] Enhances Customer Service

Governments are often the butt of jokes for their poor customer service. Not all government agencies provide poor service, and people have bad experiences with private companies, of course. But public polling shows that Americans have a dim view of the service they receive from federal agencies. One poll found that just one-third of the public thinks that the government gives competent service. And an annual survey of the public's "customer satisfaction" with various public and private services found that satisfaction with federal services is lower than with virtually all private services.

The problem is one of incentives. Government employees usually receive no tips, promotions, or other benefits for providing good service. Unlike sales people in private companies, they do not have to compete to find customers, so they have free rein to be unfriendly and slow.

A British Treasury study found that "most indicators of service quality have improved" in the privatized industries in that nation. When British Telecom was privatized and opened to competition, the wait time for a new phone line fell from many months to two weeks.

With British passenger rail privatization, on-time performance improved and customer satisfaction has been quite high, despite a huge increase in ridership. With Japanese rail privatization, fares dipped modestly, accident rates plunged, and ridership increased.

In the United Kingdom's privatized water industry, supply interruptions are down, the number of customers with low water pressure has fallen, and water quality has improved. Privatization is not just about efficiency, it is also about better serving public needs.

[6.] Removes Politics from Decision Making

Decisions in government organizations often reflect political factors that raise costs and misallocate spending. Comparing government and private ownership in the *Journal of Economic Perspectives*, economist Andrei Shleifer argued, "Elimination of politically motivated resource allocation has unquestionably been the principal benefit of privatization around the world."

A British finance expert said that in the years before Thatcher, "there had been frequent interference in running the nationalized industries," with politicians often making conflicting demands of companies, such as favoring higher prices one day and lower prices the next. Before Thatcher, many coal mines were kept open, not because they made economic or environmental sense, but because the coal mining unions had political power.

In America, federal businesses are unable to end unneeded spending because members of Congress defend activities in their districts. To please politicians, Amtrak runs low-value routes that lose hundreds of dollars per passenger. And Congress blocks the USPS from consolidating mail processing centers and closing low-volume post offices. The agency's least-used 4,500 rural post offices average just 4.4 customer visits a day.

The story of the FAA is similar. Politicians prevent the agency from closing unneeded air traffic control (ATC) facilities, and they prevent the elimination of jobs in FAA facilities in their districts. They have even required the FAA "to procure certain hardware and encouraged it to select certain contractors." Then there is the problem of "zombie" ATC towers:

> More than 100 U.S. airport towers and radar rooms have so few flights that they should be shut down late at night under the government's own guidelines, a move that would save taxpayers $10 million a year. Air-traffic controllers, who make a median $108,000 annual wage, have little to do overnight at those locations, which remain open because of pressure from lawmakers who control the Federal Aviation Administration's budget. Members of Congress from both parties have blocked attempts to cut tower hours or merge radar rooms, according to interviews and documents.

Such pork barrel politics make us all poorer by raising the costs of services. The environment also suffers because it is wasteful to run low-value trains and to keep open low-value ATC facilities and post offices.

* * *

Opportunities for Federal Privatization

President Ronald Reagan started a discussion on federal privatization in the 1980s. His administration explored privatizing the postal service, railroads, electric utilities, the air traffic control system, and federal land. A Reagan-appointed commission issued a major report in 1988 proposing various privatization options, but the administration's efforts mainly stalled. The administration did oversee the privatization of the National Consumer Cooperative Bank in 1981 and the freight railroad, Conrail, in 1987 for $1.7 billion. Following Reagan, President George H. W. Bush issued an executive order supporting privatization, but he made little progress on reforms.

President Bill Clinton had more success. During his administration, the Alaska Power Administration was sold in 1996 for $87 million; the Elk Hills Naval Petroleum Reserve was sold in 1998 for $3.7 billion; and the U.S. Enrichment Corporation was sold in 1998 for $3.1 billion. In 2000, Congress passed legislation putting Intelsat (owned by a consortium of governments) on the road to privatization.

The George W. Bush administration proposed partly privatizing the Social Security retirement system, but that effort was blocked in Congress. On the other side of the ledger, Bush signed into law a bill nationalizing security screening at U.S. airports.

President Barack Obama's budget for 2014 proposed privatizing the Tennessee Valley Authority. The administration also pursued the sale of excess federal buildings.

Recent decades have seen more of a focus on partial privatization. Under Presidents Bill Clinton and George W. Bush, for example, the Pentagon moved a large number of military families to 187,000 private housing units. That program has been very successful: housing quality has improved and costs are down. Also, recent administrations have encouraged private involvement in the U.S. space program, and a number of firms have won contracts to resupply the International Space Station.

Privatization will likely be on the agenda in coming years. Budget deficits are here to stay, so policymakers will be looking for ways to reduce spending and raise revenues. Policymakers will also be looking for ways to boost America's sluggish economic growth. As time passes, policymakers will be able to draw on ever more foreign privatization successes. We know that postal services, air traffic control, passenger railroads, and other activities can be successfully moved to the private sector because other countries have now done it.

Any activity that can be supported by customer charges, advertising, voluntary contributions, or other sorts of private support can be privatized. Government activities may be privatized as either for-profit businesses or nonprofit organizations, depending on the circumstances. The important thing is to move activities to the private sector, where they can grow, change, and be an organic part of society connected to the actual needs of citizens.

* * *

Janine R. Wedel

Federalist No. 70: Where Does the Public Service Begin and End?

Without revolution, public debate, or even much public awareness, a giant work-force has invaded Washington, D.C.—one that can undermine the public and national interest from the inside. This workforce consists of government contrac-tors, specifically those who perform "inherently governmental" functions that the government deems so integral to its work that only federal employees should carry them out. Today, many federal government functions are conducted, and many public priorities and decisions are driven, by private companies and play-ers instead of government agencies and officials who are duty-bound to answer to citizens and sworn to uphold the national interest.

It is hard to imagine that the founding fathers would have embraced this state of affairs. Acting as a nation—defending its security and providing for the safety of its citizens—is a bedrock concept in some of the *Federalist Papers*. For instance, John Jay writes in *Federalist* No. 2,

> As a nation we have made peace and war; as a nation we have vanquished our common enemies; as a nation we have formed alliances, and made trea-ties, and entered into various compacts and conventions with foreign states.
>
> A strong sense of the value and blessings of union induced the people, at a very early period, to institute a federal government to preserve and per-petuate it.

James Madison lays out a forceful case for the separation and distribution of government powers. He cautions against "a tyrannical concentration of all the powers of government in the same hands" and outlines the importance of main-taining boundaries among the divisions of government (see *Federalist* No. 47, 48, 51). I argue that the considerable contracting out of government functions is counter to the vision espoused by these statesmen. Such contracting out potentially erodes the government's ability to operate in the public and national interest. It also creates the conditions for the intertwining of state and private power and the concentration of power in just a few hands—about which Madison warned.

The Indispensable Hand

Once, government contractors primarily sold military parts, prepared food, or printed government reports. Today, contractors routinely perform "inherently governmental" functions—activities that involve "the exercise of sovereign government authority or the establishment of procedures and processes related to the oversight of monetary transactions or entitlements." The 20 "inherently governmental" functions on the books include "command of military forces, especially the leadership of military personnel who are members of the combat, combat support, or combat service support role"; "the conduct of foreign relations and the determination of foreign policy"; "the determination of agency policy, such as determining the content and application of regulations"; "the determination of Federal program priorities or budget requests"; "the direction and control of Federal employees"; "the direction and control of intelligence and counter-intelligence operations; the selection or nonselection of individuals for Federal Government employment, including the interviewing of individuals for employment"; and "the approval of position descriptions and performance standards for Federal employees."

Government contractors are involved in many, if not all, of these arenas of government work. Consider, for instance, that contractors perform the following tasks:

- Run intelligence operations: Contractors from private security companies have been hired to help track and kill suspected militants in Afghanistan and Pakistan. At the National Security Agency (NSA), the number of contractor facilities approved for classified work jumped from 41 in 2002 to 1,265 in 2006. A full 95 percent of the workers at the very secret National Reconnaissance Office (one of the 16 intelligence agencies), which runs U.S. spy satellites and analyzes the information that they produce, are full-time contractors. In more than half of the 117 contracts let by three big agencies of the

U.S. Department of Homeland Security (DHS)—the Coast Guard, Transportation Security Administration, and Office of Procurement Operations—the Government Accountability Office (GAO) found that contractors did inherently governmental work. One company, for instance, was awarded $42.4 million to develop budget and policies for the DHS, as well as to support its information analysis, procurement operations, and infrastructure protection.

- Manage—and more—federal taxpayer monies doled out under the stimulus plans and bailouts: The government enlisted money manager BlackRock to help advise it and manage the unsuccessful attempt to rescue Bear Stearns, as well as to save AIG and Citigroup. BlackRock also won a bid to help the Federal Reserve evaluate hard-to-price assets of Freddie Mac and Fannie Mae. * * * With regard to the $700 billion bailout in the fall of 2008, known as the Troubled Asset Relief Program, the U.S. Treasury Department hired several contractors to set up a process to disburse the funds.

- Control crucial databases: In a mega-contract awarded by the DHS in 2004, Accenture LLP was granted up to $10 billion to supervise and enlarge a mammoth U.S. government project to track citizens of foreign countries as they enter and exit the United States. As the undersecretary for border and transportation security at the DHS at the time remarked, "I don't think you could overstate the impact of this responsibility in terms of the security of our nation."

- Choose other contractors: The Pentagon has employed contractors to counsel it on selecting other contractors. The General Services Administration enlisted CACI, a company based in Arlington, Virginia—some of whose employees were among those allegedly involved in the Abu Ghraib prisoner abuse scandal in Iraq, according to U.S. Department of the Army—to help the government suspend and debar other contractors. . . . (CACI itself later became the subject of possible suspension or debarment from federal contracts.)

- Oversee other contractors: The DHS is among the federal agencies that have hired contractors to select and supervise other contractors. Some of these contractors set policy and business goals and plan reorganizations. And, in the National Clandestine Service, an integral part of the Central Intelligence Agency (CIA), contractors are sometimes in charge of other contractors.

- Execute military and occupying operations: The Department of Defense is ever more dependent on contractors to supply a host of "mission-critical services," including "information technology systems, interpreters, intelligence analysts, as well as weapons system maintenance and base operation support."

U.S. efforts in Afghanistan and Iraq illustrate this reliance. As of September 2009, U.S.-paid contractors far outnumbered U.S. military personnel in Afghanistan, composing nearly two-thirds of the combined contractor and military personnel workforce (approximately 104,000 Defense Department contractors compared with 64,000 uniformed personnel). In Iraq, contractors made up nearly half of the combined contractor and military personnel workforce (roughly 114,000 Defense Department contractors compared with 130,000 uniformed personnel). These proportions are in sharp contrast to the 1991 Persian Gulf War: The 540,000 military personnel deployed in that effort greatly outnumbered the 9,200 contractors on the scene.

• Draft official documents: Contractors have prepared congressional testimony for the secretary of energy. Websites of contractors working for the Department of Defense also have posted announcements of job openings for analysts to perform functions such as preparing the defense budget. One contractor boasted of having written the U.S. Army's Field Manual on "Contractors on the Battlefield."

In short, the outsourcing of many inherently governmental functions is now routine. The government is utterly dependent on private contractors to carry out many such functions. As the Acquisition Advisory Panel, a government-mandated, typically contractor-friendly task force made up of representatives from industry, government, and academe, acknowledged in a 2007 report that "[m]any federal agencies rely extensively on contractors in the performance of their basic missions. In some cases, contractors are solely or predominantly responsible for the performance of mission-critical functions that were traditionally performed by civil servants." This trend, the report concluded, "poses a threat to the government's long-term ability to perform its mission" and could "undermine the integrity of the government's decision making."

Contractor officials and employees are interdependent with government, involved in all aspects of governing and negotiating "over policy making, implementation, and enforcement," as one legal scholar has noted. Contractor and government employees work side by side in what has come to be called the "blended" or "embedded" workforce, often sitting next to each other in cubicles or sharing an office and doing the same or similar work (but typically with markedly different pay). When the GAO looked into the setup of Defense Department offices, its investigation established that, in some, the percentage of contractors was in the 80s.

Yet contractors' imperatives are not necessarily the same as the government's imperatives. Contractor companies are responsible for making a profit for their shareholders; government is supposedly answerable to the public in a democracy.

Amid this environment, which is complicated by mixed motives, contractors are positioned to influence policy to their liking on even the most sensitive, mission-critical government functions, such as fighting wars, guarding against terrorism, and shaping economic policy. Government investigators looking into intelligence, defense, homeland security, energy, and other arenas have raised questions about who drives policy—government or contractors—and whether government has the information, expertise, institutional memory, and personnel to manage contractors—or is it the other way around? And in three government agencies that the GAO investigated, including the DOD and DHS, the GAO found that "sensitive information is not fully safeguarded and thus may remain at risk of unauthorized disclosure or misuse." The result of all of this is that the nation's safety, security, and sovereignty may be jeopardized, along with the very core of democratic society—citizens' ability to hold their government accountable and have a say in public decisions. This seems far afield from the concept of the nation expressed by, say, John Jay.

Enabling Big Government

How did this state of affairs come to be?

Ironically, the perennial American predilection to rail against "big government" is partly to blame for the creation of still bigger government—the "shadow government" of companies, consulting firms, nonprofits, think tanks, and other nongovernmental entities that contract with the government to do so much of its work. This is government for sure, but often of a less visible and accountable kind.

The necessity of making government *look* small—or at least contained—has fueled the rise of this shadow government. In an ostensible effort to limit government, caps have been put on how many civil servants government can hire. But citizens still expect government to supply all manner of services—from Medicare and Social Security to interstate highways to national defense. To avoid this conundrum, both Democratic and Republican administrations over the years have been busily enlisting more and more contractors (who, in turn, often hire subcontractors) to do the work of government. Because they are not counted as part of the federal workforce, it can appear as if the size of government is being kept in check.

Like the Potemkin village of Russia, constructed to make the ruler or the foreigner think that things are rosy, the public is led to believe they have something they do not.

* * *

Where federal employees once executed most government work, today, upwards of three-quarters of the work of federal government, measured in terms of jobs, is contracted out. Many of the most dramatic alterations have occurred since the end of the Cold War. Contracting out accelerated and assumed new incarnations during and after the Bill Clinton administration. The advent of ever more complex technologies, which gave birth to information technologies on which society now relies and which the U.S. government largely outsources, tipped the balance even further. The shadow government, which devises and implements so much policy and forms the core of governance, is the elephant in the room.

The shadow government encompasses all of the entities that swell the ranks of contractors and entire bastions of outsourcing—neighborhoods whose highrise office buildings house an army of contractors and "Beltway Bandits." Largely out of sight except to Washington-area dwellers, contractors and the companies they work for do not appear in government phone books. They are less likely to be dragged before congressional committees for hostile questioning. They function with less visibility and scrutiny on a regular basis than government employees would face. Most important, they are not counted as government employees, and so the fiction of limited government can be upheld, while the reality is an expanding sprawl of entities that are the government in practice.

The Elephant in the Room

While it may be the elephant in the room, we know little about the nature of the beast. A key barometer of the growth of the shadow government, driven in part by an increase in demand for military, nation-building, and homeland security services after 9/11, is the number of government employees versus contractors. Government scholar Paul C. Light has compiled the most reliable figures on contractors. The number of contract workers—compared with civil servants, uniformed military personnel, and postal service employees—increased steadily over the last two decades. In 1990, roughly three out of every five employees in the total federal labor force worked indirectly for government—in jobs created by contracts and grants, as opposed to jobs performed by civil servants, uniformed military personnel, and postal service workers. By 2002, two out of every three employees in the federal labor force worked indirectly for government, and, by 2008, the number was three out of four.

In the DHS—the mega-bureaucracy established in 2003 through the merger of 180,000 employees and 22 agencies, the creation of which entailed the largest reorganization of the federal government in more than half a century—contractors are more numerous than federal employees. The DHS estimates that it employs 188,000 workers, compared with 200,000 contractors.

In some arenas of government, contractors virtually *are* the government. The DHS, which includes the Customs Service, Coast Guard, and Transportation Security Administration, has relied substantially on contractors to fill new security needs and shore up gaps. In nine cases examined by the GAO, "decisions to contract for . . . services were largely driven by the need for staff and expertise to get DHS programs and operations up and running quickly."

※　※　※

Meanwhile, about 70 percent of the budget of the U.S. intelligence community is devoted to contracts, according to the Office of the Director of National Intelligence, which was created in 2005 and supervises 16 federal agencies. Contract employees make up an estimated one-quarter of the country's core intelligence workforce, according to the same office. The director both heads the U.S. intelligence community and serves as the main advisor to the president on national security matters.

Contractors are plentiful in other arenas of government that directly affect national and homeland security, not only the departments of defense and homeland security. For instance, nearly 90 percent of the budgets of the Department of Energy and NASA go to contracts.

Information technology (IT), which touches practically every area of government operations, is largely contracted out. Upwards of three-quarters of governmental IT is estimated to have been outsourced even before the major Iraq War-related push to contract out. For companies in search of federal business, IT is the "the new frontier," according to Thomas Burlin, who is in charge of IBM Business Consulting Services' federal practice. With ever more complex technologies always on the horizon, the outsourcing of IT only stands to grow. Although contracting out computer network services may be unproblematic or even desirable, many IT functions cannot be separated from vital operations such as logistics that are integral to an agency's mission. ※ ※ ※

Contractors are so integrated into the federal workforce that proponents of insourcing acknowledge that they face an uphill battle. Yet the proliferation of contracting widens the de facto base of government in which new forms of unaccountable governance can flourish. It makes government more vulnerable to operations that fall short of the public and national interest.

Swiss-Cheese Government

In theory, contracts and contractors are overseen by government employees who would guard against abuse. But that has become less and less true as the capacity of government oversight has diminished—a lessening that seems to flow directly from the need to maintain the facade of small government. A look at trend lines is illuminating. The number of civil servants who potentially could oversee contractors fell during the Clinton administration and continued to drop during the George W. Bush administration. The contracting business boomed under Bush, while the acquisition workforce—government workers charged with the conceptualization, design, awarding, use, or quality control of contracts and contractors—remained virtually constant. * * *

The result is that government sometimes lacks the information it needs to monitor the entities that work for it. A top GAO official reported that in many cases, government decision makers scarcely supervise the companies on their payrolls. As a result, she observed, they are unable to answer simple questions about what the firms are doing, whether they have performed well or not, and whether their performance has been cost-effective.

* * *

A paucity of oversight is one factor that has led the GAO to identify large procurement operations as "high risk" because of "their greater susceptibility to fraud, waste, abuse, and mismanagement." The list of high-risk areas has, since 1990 or 1992 (depending on the specific area), included the large procurement operations of the Departments of Defense and Energy, as well as NASA. The DHS has been on the high-risk list since its creation in 2003, and it has been faulted for a lack of oversight in procurement. As comptroller general of the United States, David M. Walker (2003) said that he is "not confident that [high-risk] agencies have the ability to effectively manage cost, quality, and performance in contracts." He added that the current challenges to contract oversight are "unprecedented."

* * *

When the number of civil servants available to supervise government contracts and contractors proportionately falls, thus decreasing the government's oversight capacity, and when crucial governmental functions are outsourced, government begins to resemble Swiss cheese—full of holes. Contractors are plugging these holes. As a consequence, contractors have become the home for much information, legitimacy, expertise, institutional memory, and leadership that once resided in government.

* * *

Concentrating Powers

Swiss-cheese government lends itself to the kind of concentration of powers that Madison warned about. Over the past decade and a half, new institutional forms of governing have gathered force as contractors perform inherently governmental functions beyond the capacity of government to manage them; as government and contractor officials interact (or do not) in the course of projects; as chains of command among contractors and the agencies they supposedly work for have become ever more convoluted; and as contractors standing in for government are not subject to the same rules that apply to government officials. The result is that new forms of governing join the state and the private, often most visibly in intelligence, defense, and homeland security enterprises, where so much has taken place since 9/11.

Incentive structures that encourage government executives (notably intelligence and military professionals) to move to the private sector, as well as new contracting practices and a limited number of government contracting firms, are among the factors that facilitate the intertwining of state and private power. With regard to the former, not only are salaries and perks for comparable jobs typically greater in the private sector, but often, so is prestige. Many government executives, retirees, and other employees follow the money by moving to the private sector. But the landing spots that supply the big bucks—and with them, influence and stature—are often those held by former government executives. Although there are rules to address the revolving door syndrome, companies with significant government contracts often are headed by former senior officials of intelligence- and defense-related government agencies. * * *

When government contractors hire former directors of intelligence- and defense-related government agencies, they are banking on "coincidences" of interest between their hires and their hires' former (government) employers. (A coincidence of interest occurs when a player crafts an array of overlapping roles across organizations to serve his own agenda—or that of his network— above that of those of the organizations for which he works.) The result of such coincidences in the intelligence arena is that "the Intelligence Community and the contractors are so tightly intertwined at the leadership level that their interests, practically speaking, are identical," as one intelligence expert said.

Also potentially facilitating the fusion of state and private power are changes in contracting practices and the dearth of competition among and consolidation of government contracting firms, which has led to government dependence on a limited number of firms. The Clinton administration transformed contracting rules with regard to oversight, competition, and transparency under the rubric of "reinventing government." As a result, small contracts often have been replaced by bigger, and frequently open-ended, multiyear, multimillion- and even billion-dollar and potentially much more lucrative contracts with a "limited pool of contractors," as the Acquisition Advisory Panel put it. Today, most federal procurement contracts are conferred either without competition or to a limited set of contractors. A Barack Obama White House memo noted the "significant increase in the dollars awarded without full and open competition" during the period 2001–2008. Moreover, industry consolidation (defense is a case in point) has produced fewer and larger firms. * * *

The routine outsourcing of government functions, the structures of incentives, and new contracting rules and practices encourage new forms of governing in which state and private power are joined. These forms seem very far afield indeed from Madison's vision of a nation in which government powers cannot be concentrated.

Reclaiming the Soul of Government

Some authorities have sounded alarm bells about the present state of affairs. In 2007, David M. Walker, the comptroller general of the United States and long-time head of the GAO, called for "a fundamental reexamination of when and under what circumstances we should use contractors versus civil servants or military personnel," And President Obama acknowledged the problem. Early in his term, Obama announced plans to "insource" certain jobs—transferring work back to the government—and expressed concern about the outsourcing of inherently governmental functions. While the administration has proposed some insourcing and efforts to push back or review the ever upward spiral of outsourcing, the current state of affairs cannot simply be rolled back.

It is not just that government is utterly dependent on private companies to do much of its work. The United States faces an entrenched problem that cannot be fixed simply by insourcing jobs or by hiring more government employees to oversee contractors, as some observers have suggested. A top-to-bottom rethinking of how government makes use of contractors is necessary. One particularly important issue that deserves attention is how to rebuild capacity that has been lost with the privatization of information, expertise, and institutional memory. Another set of challenges lies in reforming the contract laws and regulations that have been changed over the past decade and a half—and that have made the contracting system less transparent and accountable and more vulnerable to the influence of private and corporate agendas.

The changes that have taken place are so systemic and sweeping that a new system, in effect, is now in place. It is the ground on which any future changes will occur. A fundamental redesign of the system is necessary. In that redesign, we would do well to pay attention to the vision of the founding fathers regarding the security of the nation and safety of its citizens, as well as the dangers inherent in the consolidation of powers.

But reclaiming government is not merely a design challenge. Government must take its soul back. While it may be strange to mention "soul" and government in the same breath, linking the quintessentially personal with the quintessentially bureaucratic and impersonal, a government procurement lawyer described the current state of affairs as the "ebbing away of the soul of government." When an institution is drained of expertise, information, and institutional memory, it not only loses its edge, but also its essence.

* * *

DISCUSSION QUESTIONS

1. What is an "inherently governmental function?" The current definition in federal law is "a function so intimately related to the public interest as to require performance by Federal Government employees." But this actually provides very

little useful guidance, since it is a tautology: work that must be performed by federal government employees is defined as work so important that it must be performed by federal employees. Is there an alternative definition that is both meaningful and precise? What might that be?

2. One criticism is that privatization can actually *increase* costs, since private actors will require a profit which governments do not need. One common example is Medicare, which has far lower administrative expenses (around 2 percent of total costs) than private health insurance companies (which are estimated at around 17 percent of total costs). The bankruptcies of toll road operators show what can happen when private actors can't generate sufficient profits. Is this an argument against privatization in general, in the sense that government responsibilities are by their very nature not profit-generating functions?

8

The Judiciary: Interpreting the Constitution— Originalism or Living Constitution?

Debates over the federal judiciary's role in the political process often focus on the question of how judges should interpret the Constitution. Should judges apply the document's original meaning as stated by the Framers, or should they use a framework that incorporates shifting interpretations across time? This debate intensified during Earl Warren's tenure as Chief Justice (1953–69) because of Court decisions that expanded the scope of civil liberties and criminal rights far beyond what "originalists" thought the Constitution's language authorized. The debate continues in the current, more conservative Court. The two readings in this section offer contrasting viewpoints from one sitting Supreme Court justice (Stephen Breyer) and Justice Antonin Scalia, who died in 2016.

Scalia was the intellectual force behind the conservative wing of the Court, and argued that justices must be bound by the original meaning of the document, because that is the only neutral principle that allows the judiciary to function as a legal body instead of a political one. The alternative is to embrace an evolving or "Living Constitution," which Scalia criticized as allowing judges to decide cases on the basis of what seems right at the moment. He said that this "evolutionary" approach does not have any overall guiding principle and therefore "is simply not a practicable constitutional philosophy." He provided several examples of how the

Living Constitution approach had produced decisions that stray from the meaning of the Constitution in the areas of abortion rights, gay rights, the right to counsel, and the right to confront one's accuser. This last example is especially provocative, given that it concerned the right of an accused child molester to confront the child who accused him of the crime. Scalia argues that there is no coherent alternative to originalism and forcefully concludes, "The worst thing about the Living Constitution is that it will destroy the Constitution."

Stephen Breyer argues for the Living Constitution approach, and places it within a broader constitutional and theoretical framework. He argues for a "consequentialist" approach that is rooted in basic constitutional purposes, the most important of which is "active liberty," which he defines as "an active and constant participation in collective power." Breyer applies this framework to a range of difficult constitutional issues, including freedom of speech in the context of campaign finance and privacy rights in the context of rapidly evolving technology. He argues that the plain language of the Constitution does not provide enough guidance to answer these difficult questions. He turns the tables on Scalia, arguing that it is the literalist or originalist position that will, ironically, lead justices to rely too heavily on their own personal views, whereas his consequentialist position is actually the view that is more likely to produce judicial restraint. Breyer goes on to criticize the originalist position as fraught with inconsistencies. It is inherently subjective, despite its attempt to emphasize the "objective" words of the Constitution. By relying on the consequentialist perspective, which emphasizes democratic participation and active liberty, justices are more likely to reach limited conclusions that apply to the facts at hand, while maximizing the positive implications for democracy.

Linda Greenhouse, an observer of the Supreme Court, summarized the debate between Scalia and Breyer in these terms: "It is a debate over text versus context. For Justice Scalia, who focuses on text, language is supreme, and the court's job is to derive and apply rules from the words chosen by the Constitution's framers or a statute's drafters. For Justice Breyer, who looks to context, language is only a starting point to an inquiry in which a law's purpose and a decision's likely consequences are the more important elements."

Antonin Scalia

Constitutional Interpretation the Old-Fashioned Way

It's a pizzazzy topic: Constitutional Interpretation. It is, however, an important one. I was vividly reminded how important it was last week when the Court came out with a controversial decision in the *Roper* case. And I watched one television commentary on the case in which the host had one person defending the opinion on the ground that people should not be subjected to capital punishment for crimes they commit when they are younger than eighteen, and the other person attacked the opinion on the ground that a jury should be able to decide that a person, despite the fact he was under eighteen, given the crime, given the person involved, should be subjected to capital punishment. And it struck me how irrelevant it was, how much the point had been missed. The question wasn't whether the call was right or wrong. The important question was who should make the call. And that is essentially what I am addressing today.

I am one of a small number of judges, small number of anybody—judges, professors, lawyers—who are known as originalists. Our manner of interpreting the Constitution is to begin with the text, and to give that text the meaning that it bore when it was adopted by the people. I'm not a "strict constructionist," despite the introduction. I don't like the term "strict construction." I do not think the Constitution, or any text, should be interpreted either strictly or sloppily; it should be interpreted reasonably. Many of my interpretations do not deserve the description "strict." I do believe, however, that you give the text the meaning it had when it was adopted.

This is such a minority position in modern academia and in modern legal circles that on occasion I'm asked when I've given a talk like this a question from the back of the room—"Justice Scalia, when did you first become an originalist?"—as though it is some kind of weird affliction that seizes some people—"When did you first start eating human flesh?"

Although it is a minority view now, the reality is that, not very long ago, originalism was orthodoxy. Everybody at least *purported* to be an originalist. If you go back and read the commentaries on the Constitution by Joseph Story, he didn't think the Constitution evolved or changed. He said it means and will always mean what it meant when it was adopted.

Or consider the opinions of John Marshall in the Federal Bank case, where he says, we must not, we must always remember it is a constitution we are expounding. And since it's a constitution, he says, you have to give its provisions expansive meaning so that they will accommodate events that you do not know of which will happen in the future.

Well, if it is a constitution that changes, you wouldn't have to give it an expansive meaning. You can give it whatever meaning you want and, when future necessity arises, you simply change the meaning. But anyway, that is no longer the orthodoxy.

Oh, one other example about how not just the judges and scholars believed in originalism, but even the American people. Consider the 19th Amendment, which is the amendment that gave women the vote. It was adopted by the American people in 1920. Why did we adopt a constitutional amendment for that purpose? The Equal Protection Clause existed in 1920; it was adopted right after the Civil War. And you know that if the issue of the franchise for women came up today, we would not have to have a constitutional amendment. Someone would come to the Supreme Court and say, "Your Honors, in a democracy, what could be a greater denial of equal protection than denial of the franchise?" And the Court would say, "Yes! Even though it never meant it before, the Equal Protection Clause means that women have to have the vote." But that's not how the American people thought in 1920. In 1920, they looked at the Equal Protection Clause and said, "What does it mean?" Well, it clearly doesn't mean that you can't discriminate in the franchise—not only on the basis of sex, but on the basis of property ownership, on the basis of literacy. None of that is unconstitutional. And therefore, since it wasn't unconstitutional, and we wanted it to be, we did things the good old-fashioned way and adopted an amendment.

Now, in asserting that originalism used to be orthodoxy, I do not mean to imply that judges did not distort the Constitution now and then; of course they did. We had willful judges then, and we will have willful judges until the end of time. But the difference is that prior to the last fifty years or so, prior to the advent of the "Living Constitution," judges did their distortions the good old-fashioned way, the honest way—they lied about it. They said the Constitution means such and such, when it never meant such and such.

It's a big difference that you now no longer have to lie about it, because we are in the era of the evolving Constitution. And the judge can simply say, "Oh yes, the Constitution didn't used to mean that, but it does now." We are in the age in which not only judges, not only lawyers, but even school children have come to learn the Constitution changes. I have grammar school students come into the Court now and then, and they recite very proudly what they have been taught: "The Constitution is a living document." You know, it morphs.

Well, let me first tell you how we got to the "Living Constitution." You don't have to be a lawyer to understand it. The road is not that complicated. Initially, the Court began giving terms in the text of the Constitution a meaning they didn't have when they were adopted. For example, the First Amendment, which forbids Congress to abridge the freedom of speech. What does the freedom of speech mean? Well, it clearly did not mean that Congress or government could not impose any restrictions upon speech. Libel laws, for example, were clearly constitutional. Nobody thought the First Amendment was *carte blanche* to libel someone. But in the famous case of *New York Times v. Sullivan*, the Supreme Court said, "But the First Amendment does prevent you from suing for libel if you are a public figure and if the libel was not malicious"—that is, the person, a member of the press or otherwise, thought that what the person said was true. Well, that had never been the law. I mean, it might be a good law. And some states could amend their libel law.

It's one thing for a state to amend its libel law and say, "We think that public figures shouldn't be able to sue." That's fine. But the courts have said that the First Amendment, which never meant this before, now means that if you are a public figure, that you can't sue for libel unless it's intentional, malicious. So that's one way to do it.

Another example is the Constitution guarantees the right to be represented by counsel. That never meant the state had to pay for your counsel. But you can reinterpret it to mean that.

That was step one. Step two, I mean, that will only get you so far. There is no text in the Constitution that you could reinterpret to create a right to abortion, for example. So you need something else. The something else is called the doctrine of "Substantive Due Process." Only lawyers can walk around talking about substantive process, inasmuch as it's a contradiction in terms. If you referred to substantive process or procedural substance at a cocktail party, people would look at you funny. But, lawyers talk this way all the time.

What substantive due process is is quite simple—the Constitution has a Due Process Clause, which says that no person shall be deprived of life, liberty, or property without due process of law. Now, what does this guarantee? Does it guarantee life, liberty, or property? No, indeed! All three can be taken away. You can be fined, you can be incarcerated, you can even be executed, but not without due process of law. It's a procedural guarantee. But the Court said, and this goes way back, in the 1920s at least—in fact the first case to do it was *Dred Scott*. But it became more popular in the 1920s. The Court said there are some liberties that are so important, that no process will suffice to take them away. Hence, substantive due process.

Now, what liberties are they? The Court will tell you. Be patient. When the doctrine of substantive due process was initially announced, it was limited in this way: the Court said it embraces only those liberties that are fundamental to a democratic society and rooted in the traditions of the American people.

Then we come to step three. Step three: that limitation is eliminated. Within the last twenty years, we have found to be covered by due process the right to abortion, which was so little rooted in the traditions of the American people that it was criminal for 200 years; the right to homosexual sodomy, which was so little rooted in the traditions of the American people that it was criminal for 200 years. So it is literally true, and I don't think this is an exaggeration, that the Court has essentially liberated itself from the text of the Constitution, from the text and even from the traditions of the American people. It is up to the Court to say what is covered by substantive due process.

What are the arguments usually made in favor of the Living Constitution? As the name of it suggests, it is a very attractive philosophy, and it's hard to talk people out of it—the notion that the Constitution grows. The major argument is the Constitution is a living organism; it has to grow with the society that it governs or it will become brittle and snap.

This is the equivalent of, an anthropomorphism equivalent to, what you hear from your stockbroker, when he tells you that the stock market is resting for an assault on the 11,000 level. The stock market panting at some base camp. The stock market is not a mountain climber and the Constitution is not a living organism, for Pete's sake; it's a legal document, and like all legal documents, it says some things, and it doesn't say other things. And if you think that the aficionados of the Living Constitution want to bring you flexibility, think again.

My Constitution is a very flexible Constitution. You think the death penalty is a good idea—persuade your fellow citizens and adopt it. You think it's a bad idea—persuade them the other way and eliminate it. You want a right to abortion—create it the way most rights are created in a democratic society: persuade your fellow citizens it's a good idea and enact it. You want the opposite—persuade them the other way. That's flexibility. But to read either result into the Constitution is not to produce flexibility, it is to produce what a constitution is designed to produce—rigidity. Abortion, for example, is offstage, it is off the democratic stage; it is no use debating it; it is unconstitutional. I mean prohibiting it is unconstitutional; I mean it's no use debating it anymore—now and forever, coast to coast, I guess until we amend the Constitution, which is a difficult thing. So, for whatever reason you might like the Living Constitution, don't like it because it provides flexibility.

That's not the name of the game. Some people also seem to like it because they think it's a good liberal thing—that somehow this is a conservative/liberal battle, and conservatives like the old-fashioned originalist Constitution and liberals ought to like the Living Constitution. That's not true either. The dividing line between those who believe in the Living Constitution and those who don't is not the dividing line between conservatives and liberals.

Conservatives are willing to grow the Constitution to cover their favorite causes just as liberals are, and the best example of that is two cases we announced some years ago on the same day, the same morning. One case was *Romer v. Evans*, in which the people of Colorado had enacted an amendment to the state constitution by plebiscite, which said that neither the state nor any subdivision of the state would add to the protected statuses against which private individuals cannot discriminate. The usual ones are race, religion, age, sex, disability and so forth. Would not add sexual preference—somebody thought that was a terrible idea, and, since it was a terrible idea, it must be unconstitutional. Brought a lawsuit, it came to the Supreme Court. And the Supreme Court said, "Yes, it is unconstitutional." On the basis of—I don't know. The Sexual Preference Clause of the Bill of Rights, presumably. And the liberals loved it, and the conservatives gnashed their teeth.

The very next case we announced is a case called *BMW v. Gore*. Not the Gore you think; this is another Gore. Mr. Gore had bought a BMW, which is a car supposedly advertised at least as having a superb finish, baked seven times in ovens deep in the Alps, by dwarfs. And his BMW apparently had gotten scratched on the way over. They did not send it back to the Alps, they took a can of spray paint and fixed it. And he found out about this and was furious, and he brought a lawsuit. He got his compensatory damages, a couple of hundred dollars—the difference between a car with a better paint job and a worse paint job—plus $2 million against BMW for punitive damages for being a bad actor, which is absurd of course, so it must be unconstitutional. BMW appealed to my Court, and my Court said, "Yes, it's unconstitutional." In violation of, I assume, the Excessive Damages Clause of the Bill of Rights. And if excessive punitive damages are unconstitutional, why aren't excessive compensatory damages unconstitutional? So you have a federal question whenever you get a judgment in a civil case. Well, that one the conservatives liked, because conservatives don't like punitive damages, and the liberals gnashed their teeth.

I dissented in both cases because I say, "A pox on both their houses." It has nothing to do with what your policy preferences are; it has to do with what you think the Constitution is.

Some people are in favor of the Living Constitution because they think it always leads to greater freedom—there's just nothing to lose, the evolving Constitution will always provide greater and greater freedom, more and more rights. Why would you think that? It's a two-way street. And indeed, under the aegis of the Living Constitution, some freedoms have been taken away.

Recently, last term, we reversed a 15-year-old decision of the Court, which had held that the Confrontation Clause—which couldn't be clearer, it says, "In all criminal prosecutions, the accused shall enjoy the right . . . to be confronted with the witness against him." But a Living Constitution Court held that all that was necessary to comply with the Confrontation Clause was that the hearsay evidence which is introduced—hearsay evidence means you can't cross-examine the person who said it because he's not in the court—the hearsay evidence has to bear indicia of reliability. I'm happy to say that we reversed it last term with the votes of the two originalists on the Court. And the opinion said that the only indicium of reliability that the Confrontation Clause acknowledges is confrontation. You bring the witness in to testify and to be cross-examined. That's just one example; there are others, of eliminating liberties.

So, I think another example is the right to jury trial. In a series of cases, the Court had seemingly acknowledged that you didn't have to have trial by jury of the facts that increase your sentence. You can make the increased sentence a "sentencing factor"—you get thirty years for burglary, but if the burglary is committed with a gun, as a sentencing factor the judge can give you another ten years. And the judge will decide whether you used a gun. And he will decide it, not beyond a reasonable doubt, but whether it's more likely than not. Well, we held recently, I'm happy to say, that this violates the right to a trial by jury. The Living Constitution would not have produced that result. The Living Constitution, like the legislatures that enacted these laws, would have allowed sentencing factors to be determined by the judge because all the Living Constitution assures you is that what will happen is what the majority wants to happen. And that's not the purpose of constitutional guarantees.

Well, I've talked about some of the false virtues of the Living Constitution; let me tell you what I consider its principle vices are. Surely the greatest—you should always begin with principle—its greatest vice is its illegitimacy. The only reason federal courts sit in judgment of the constitutionality of federal legislation is not because they are explicitly authorized to do so in the Constitution. Some modern constitutions give the constitutional court explicit authority to review German legislation or French legislation for its constitutionality; our Constitution doesn't say anything like that. But John Marshall says in *Marbury v. Madison*: Look, this is lawyers' work. What you have here is an apparent conflict between the Constitution and the statute. And, all the time, lawyers and judges have to reconcile these conflicts—they try to read the two to comport with each other. If they can't, it's judges' work to decide which ones prevail. When there are two statutes, the more recent one prevails. It implicitly repeals the older one. But when the Constitution is at issue, the Constitution prevails because it is a "superstatute." I mean, that's what Marshall says: It's judges' work.

If you believe, however, that the Constitution is not a legal text, like the texts involved when judges reconcile or decide which of two statutes prevail; if you think the Constitution is some exhortation to give effect to the most fundamental values of the society as those values change from year to year; if you think that it is meant to reflect, as some of the Supreme Court cases say, particularly those involving the Eighth Amendment, if you think it is simply meant to reflect the evolving standards of decency that mark the progress of a maturing society—if that is what you think it is, then why in the world would you have it interpreted by nine lawyers? What do I know about the evolving standards of decency of American society? I'm afraid to ask.

If that is what you think the Constitution is, then *Marbury v. Madison* is wrong. It shouldn't be up to the judges, it should be up to the legislature. We should have a system like the English—whatever the legislature thinks is constitutional is constitutional. They know the evolving standards of American society, I don't. So in principle, it's incompatible with the legal regime that America has established.

Secondly, and this is the killer argument—I mean, it's the best debaters' argument—they say in politics you can't beat somebody with nobody. It's the same thing with principles of legal interpretation. If you don't believe in originalism, then you need some other principle of interpretation. Being a non-originalist is not enough. You see, I have my rules that confine me. I know what I'm looking for. When I find it—the original meaning of the Constitution—I am handcuffed. If I believe that the First Amendment meant when it was adopted that you are entitled to burn the American flag, I have to come out that way even though I don't like to come out that way. When I find that the original meaning of the jury trial guarantee is that any additional time you spend in prison which depends upon a fact must depend upon a fact found by a jury—once I find that's what the jury trial guarantee means, I am handcuffed. Though I'm a law-and-order type, I cannot do all the mean conservative things I would like to do to this society. You got me.

Now, if you're not going to control your judges that way, what other criterion are you going to place before them? What is the criterion that governs the Living Constitutional judge? What can you possibly use, besides original meaning? Think about that. Natural law? We all agree on that, don't we? The philosophy of John Rawls? That's easy. There really is nothing else. You either tell your judges, "Look, this is a law, like all laws; give it the meaning it had when it was adopted." Or, you tell your judges, "Govern us. You tell us whether people under eighteen, who committed their crimes when they were under eighteen, should be executed. You tell us whether there ought to be an unlimited right to abortion or a partial right to abortion. You make these decisions for us." I have put this question—you know I speak at law schools with some frequency just to make trouble—and I put this question to the faculty all the time, or incite the students to ask their Living Constitutional professors: "Okay professor, you are not an originalist, what is your criterion?" There is none other.

And finally, this is what I will conclude with although it is not on a happy note. The worst thing about the Living Constitution is that it will destroy the Constitution. You heard in the introduction that I was confirmed, close to nineteen years ago now, by a vote of ninety-eight to nothing. The two missing were Barry Goldwater and Jake Games, so make it one hundred. I was known at that time to be, in my political and social views, fairly conservative. But still, I was known to be a good lawyer, an honest man—somebody who could read a text and give it its fair meaning—had judicial impartiality and so forth. And so I was unanimously confirmed. Today, barely twenty years later, it is difficult to get someone confirmed to the Court of Appeals. What has happened? The American people have figured out what is going on. If we are selecting lawyers, if we are selecting people to read a text and give it the fair meaning it had when it was adopted, yes, the most important thing to do is to get a good lawyer. If on the other hand, we're picking people to draw out of their own conscience and experience a new constitution with all sorts of new values to govern our society, then we should not look principally for good lawyers. We should look principally for people who agree with us, the majority, as to whether there ought to be this right, that right and the other right. We want to pick people that would write the new constitution that we would want.

And that is why you hear in the discourse on this subject, people talking about moderate—we want moderate judges. What is a moderate interpretation of the text? Halfway between what it really means and what you'd like it to mean? There is no such thing as a moderate interpretation of the text. Would you ask a lawyer, "Draw me a moderate contract?" The only way the word has any meaning is if you are looking for someone to write a law, to write a constitution, rather than to interpret one. The moderate judge is the one who will devise the new constitution that most people would approve of. So, for example, we had a suicide case some terms ago, and the Court refused to hold that there is a constitutional right to assisted suicide. We said, "We're not yet ready to say that. Stay tuned, in a few years, the time may come, but we're not yet ready." And that was a moderate decision, because I think most people would not want—if we had gone, looked into that and created a national right to assisted suicide—that would have been an immoderate and extremist decision.

I think the very terminology suggests where we have arrived—at the point of selecting people to write a constitution, rather than people to give us the fair meaning of one that has been democratically adopted. And when that happens, when the Senate interrogates nominees to the Supreme Court, or to the lower courts—you know, "Judge so-and-so, do you think there is a right to this in the Constitution? You don't? Well, my constituents think there ought to be, and I'm not going to appoint to the court someone who is not going to find that"—when we are in that mode, you realize, we have rendered the Constitution useless, because the Constitution will mean what the majority wants it to mean. The senators are representing the majority, and they will be selecting justices who will devise a constitution that the majority wants. And that, of course, deprives the Constitution of its principle utility. The Bill of Rights is devised to protect you and me against, who do you think? The majority. My most important function on the Supreme Court is to tell the majority to take a walk. And the notion that the justices ought to be selected because of the positions that they will take, that are favored by the majority, is a recipe for destruction of what we have had for 200 years.

To come back to the beginning, this is new—fifty years old or so—the Living Constitution stuff. We have not yet seen what the end of the road is. I think we are beginning to see. And what it is should really be troublesome to Americans who care about a Constitution that can provide protections against majoritarian rule. Thank you.

Stephen Breyer
Our Democratic Constitution

I shall focus upon several contemporary problems that call for governmental action and potential judicial reaction. In each instance I shall argue that, when judges interpret the Constitution, they should place greater emphasis upon the "ancient liberty," i.e., the people's right to "an active and constant participation in collective power." I believe that increased emphasis upon this active liberty will lead to better constitutional law, a law that will promote governmental solutions consistent with individual dignity and community need.

At the same time, my discussion will illustrate an approach to constitutional interpretation that places considerable weight upon consequences—consequences valued in terms of basic constitutional purposes. It disavows a contrary constitutional approach, a more "legalistic" approach that places too much weight upon language, history, tradition, and precedent alone while understating the importance of consequences. If the discussion helps to convince you that the more "consequential" approach has virtue, so much the better.

Three basic views underlie my discussion. First, the Constitution, considered as a whole, creates a framework for a certain kind of government. Its general objectives can be described abstractly as including (1) democratic self-government, (2) dispersion of power (avoiding concentration of too much power in too few hands), (3) individual dignity (through protection of individual liberties), (4) equality before the law (through equal protection of the law), and (5) the rule of law itself.

The Constitution embodies these general objectives in particular provisions. In respect to self-government, for example, Article IV guarantees a "republican Form of Government;" Article I insists that Congress meet at least once a year, that elections take place every two (or six) years, that a census take place every decade; the Fifteenth, Nineteenth, Twenty-fourth, and Twenty-sixth Amendments secure a virtually universal adult suffrage. But a general constitutional objective such as self-government plays a constitutional role beyond the interpretation of an individual provision that refers to it directly. That is because constitutional courts must consider the relation of one phrase to another. They must consider the document as a whole. And consequently the document's handful of general purposes will inform judicial interpretation of many individual provisions that do not refer directly to the general objective in question. My examples seek to show how that is so. And, as I have said, they will suggest a need for judges to pay greater attention to one of those general objectives, namely participatory democratic self-government.

Second, the Court, while always respecting language, tradition, and precedent, nonetheless has emphasized different general constitutional objectives at different periods in its history. Thus one can characterize the early nineteenth century as a period during which the Court helped to establish the authority of the federal government, including the federal judiciary. During the late nineteenth and early twentieth centuries, the Court underemphasized the Constitution's efforts to secure participation by black citizens in representative government— efforts related to the participatory "active" liberty of the ancients. At the same time, it overemphasized protection of property rights, such as an individual's freedom to contract without government interference, to the point where President Franklin Roosevelt commented that the Court's Lochner-era decisions had created a legal "no-man's land" that neither state nor federal regulatory authority had the power to enter.

The New Deal Court and the Warren Court in part reemphasized "active liberty." The former did so by dismantling various Lochner-era distinctions, thereby expanding the scope of democratic self-government. The latter did so by interpreting the Civil War Amendments in light of their purposes and to mean what they say, thereby helping African-Americans become members of the nation's community of self-governing citizens—a community that the Court expanded further in its "one person, one vote" decisions.

More recently, in my view, the Court has again underemphasized the importance of the citizen's active liberty. I will argue for a contemporary reemphasis that better combines "the liberty of the ancients" with that "freedom of governmental restraint" that Constant called "modern."

Third, the real-world consequences of a particular interpretive decision, valued in terms of basic constitutional purposes, play an important role in constitutional decision-making. To that extent, my approach differs from that of judges who would place nearly exclusive interpretive weight upon language, history, tradition and precedent. In truth, the difference is one of degree. Virtually all judges, when interpreting a constitution or a statute, refer at one time or another to language, to history, to tradition, to precedent, to purpose, and to consequences. Even those who take a more literal approach to constitutional interpretation sometimes find consequences and general purposes relevant. But the more "literalist" judge tends to ask those who cannot find an interpretive answer in language, history, tradition, and precedent alone to rethink the problem several times, before making consequences determinative. The more literal judges may hope to find in language, history, tradition, and precedent objective interpretive standards; they may seek to avoid an interpretive subjectivity that could confuse a judge's personal idea of what is good for that which the Constitution demands; and they may believe that these more "original" sources will more readily yield rules that can guide other institutions, including lower courts. These objectives are desirable, but I do not think the literal approach will achieve them, and, in any event, the constitutional price is too high. I hope that my examples will help to show you why that is so, as well as to persuade some of you why it is important to place greater weight upon constitutionally valued consequences, my consequential focus in this lecture being the effect of a court's decisions upon active liberty.

To recall the fate of Socrates is to understand that the "liberty of the ancients" is not a sufficient condition for human liberty. Nor can (or should) we replicate today the ideal represented by the Athenian agora or the New England town meeting. Nonetheless, today's citizen does participate in democratic self-governing processes. And the "active" liberty to which I refer consists of the Constitution's efforts to secure the citizen's right to do so.

To focus upon that active liberty, to understand it as one of the Constitution's handful of general objectives, will lead judges to consider the constitutionality of statutes with a certain modesty. That modesty embodies an understanding of the judges' own expertise compared, for example, with that of a legislature. It reflects the concern that a judiciary too ready to "correct" legislative error may deprive "the people" of "the political experience and the moral education that come from . . . correcting their own errors." It encompasses that doubt, caution, prudence, and concern—that state of not being "too sure" of oneself—that Learned Hand described as the "spirit of liberty." In a word, it argues for traditional "judicial restraint."

But active liberty argues for more than that. I shall suggest that increased recognition of the Constitution's general democratic participatory objectives can help courts deal more effectively with a range of specific constitutional issues. To show this I shall use examples drawn from the areas of free speech, federalism, privacy, equal protection and statutory interpretation. In each instance, I shall refer to an important modern problem of government that calls for a democratic response. I shall then describe related constitutional implications. I want to draw a picture of some of the different ways that increased judicial focus upon the Constitution's participatory objectives can have a positive effect.

* * *

I begin with free speech and campaign finance reform. The campaign finance problem arises out of the recent explosion in campaign costs along with a vast disparity among potential givers. * * * The upshot is a concern by some that the matter is out of hand—that too few individuals contribute too much money and that, even though money is not the only way to obtain influence, those who give large amounts of money do obtain, or appear to obtain, too much influence. The end result is a marked inequality of participation. That is one important reason why legislatures have sought to regulate the size of campaign contributions.

The basic constitutional question, as you all know, is not the desirability of reform legislation but whether, how, or the extent to which, the First Amendment permits the legislature to impose limitations or ceilings on the amounts individuals or organizations or parties can contribute to a campaign or the kinds of contributions they can make. * * *

One cannot (or, at least, I cannot) find an easy answer to the constitutional questions in language, history, or tradition. The First Amendment's language says that Congress shall not abridge "the freedom of speech." But it does not define "the freedom of speech" in any detail. The nation's Founders did not speak directly about campaign contributions. Madison, who decried faction, thought that members of Congress would fairly represent all their constituents, in part because the "electors" would not be the "rich" any "more than the poor." But this kind of statement, while modestly helpful to the campaign reform cause, is hardly determinative.

Neither can I find answers in purely conceptual arguments. Some argue, for example, that "money is speech"; others say "money is not speech." But neither contention helps much. Money is not speech, it is money. But the expenditure of money enables speech; and that expenditure is often necessary to communicate a message, particularly in a political context. A law that forbids the expenditure of money to convey a message could effectively suppress that communication.

Nor does it resolve the matter simply to point out that campaign contribution limits inhibit the political "speech opportunities" of those who wish to contribute more. Indeed, that is so. But the question is whether, in context, such a limitation abridges "the freedom of speech." And to announce that this kind of harm could never prove justified in a political context is simply to state an ultimate constitutional conclusion; it is not to explain the underlying reasons.

To refer to the Constitution's general participatory self-government objective, its protection of "active liberty" is far more helpful. That is because that constitutional goal indicates that the First Amendment's constitutional role is not simply one of protecting the individual's "negative" freedom from governmental restraint. The Amendment in context also forms a necessary part of a constitutional system designed to sustain that democratic self-government. The Amendment helps to sustain the democratic process both by encouraging the exchange of ideas needed to make sound electoral decisions and by encouraging an exchange of views among ordinary citizens necessary to encourage their informed participation in the electoral process. It thereby helps to maintain a form of government open to participation (in Constant's words "by all citizens without exception").

The relevance of this conceptual view lies in the fact that the campaign finance laws also seek to further the latter objective. They hope to democratize the influence that money can bring to bear upon the electoral process, thereby building public confidence in that process, broadening the base of a candidate's meaningful financial support, and encouraging greater public participation. They consequently seek to maintain the integrity of the political process—a process that itself translates political speech into governmental action. Seen in this way, campaign finance laws, despite the limits they impose, help to further the kind of open public political discussion that the First Amendment also seeks to encourage, not simply as an end, but also as a means to achieve a workable democracy.

For this reason, I have argued that a court should approach most campaign finance questions with the understanding that important First Amendment-related interests lie on both sides of the constitutional equation and that a First Amendment presumption hostile to government regulation, such as "strict scrutiny" is consequently out of place. Rather, the Court considering the matter without benefit of presumptions, must look realistically at the legislation's impact, both its negative impact on the ability of some to engage in as much communication as they wish and the positive impact upon the public's confidence, and consequent ability to communicate through (and participate in) the electoral process.

The basic question the Court should ask is one of proportionality. Do the statutes strike a reasonable balance between their electoral speech-restricting and speech-enhancing consequences? Or do you instead impose restrictions on that speech that are disproportionate when measured against their corresponding electoral and speech-related benefits, taking into account the kind, the importance, and the extent of those benefits, as well as the need for the restrictions in order to secure them?

The judicial modesty discussed earlier suggests that, in answering these questions, courts should defer to the legislatures' own answers insofar as those answers reflect empirical matters about which the legislature is comparatively expert, for example, the extent of the campaign finance problem, a matter that directly concerns the realities of political life. But courts cannot defer when evaluating the risk that reform legislation will defeat the very objective of participatory self-government itself, for example, where laws would set limits so low that, by elevating the reputation-related or media-related advantages of incumbency to the point where they would insulate incumbents from effective challenge.

I am not saying that focus upon active liberty will automatically answer the constitutional question in particular campaign finance cases. I argue only that such focus will help courts find a proper route for arriving at an answer. The positive constitutional goal implies a systemic role for the First Amendment; and that role, in turn, suggests a legal framework, i.e., a more particular set of questions for the Court to ask. Modesty suggests where, and how, courts should defer to legislatures in doing so. The suggested inquiry is complex. But courts both here and abroad have engaged in similarly complex inquiries where the constitutionality of electoral laws is at issue. That complexity is demanded by a Constitution that provides for judicial review of the constitutionality of electoral rules while granting Congress the effective power to secure a fair electoral system.

I next turn to a different kind of example. It focuses upon current threats to the protection of privacy, defined as "the power to control what others can come to know about you." It seeks to illustrate what active liberty is like in modern America, when we seek to arrive democratically at solutions to important technologically based problems. And it suggests a need for judicial caution and humility when certain privacy matters, such as the balance between free speech and privacy, are at issue.

First, I must describe the "privacy" problem. That problem is unusually complex. It has clearly become even more so since the terrorist attacks. For one thing, those who agree that privacy is important disagree about why. Some emphasize the need to be left alone, not bothered by others, or that privacy is important because it prevents people from being judged out of context. Some emphasize the way in which relationships of love and friendship depend upon trust, which implies a sharing of information not available to all. Others find connections between privacy and individualism, in that privacy encourages non-conformity. Still others find connections between privacy and equality, in that limitations upon the availability of individualized information lead private businesses to treat all customers alike. For some, or all, of these reasons, legal rules protecting privacy help to assure an individual's dignity.

For another thing, the law protects privacy only because of the way in which technology interacts with different laws. Some laws, such as trespass, wiretapping, eavesdropping, and search-and-seizure laws, protect particular places or sites, such as homes or telephones, from searches and monitoring. Other laws protect not places, but kinds of information, for example laws that forbid the publication of certain personal information even by a person who obtained that information legally. Taken together these laws protect privacy to different degrees depending upon place, individual status, kind of intrusion, and type of information.

Further, technological advances have changed the extent to which present laws can protect privacy. Video cameras now can monitor shopping malls, schools, parks, office buildings, city streets, and other places that present law left unprotected. Scanners and interceptors can overhear virtually any electronic conversation. Thermal imaging devices can detect activities taking place within the home. Computers can record and collate information obtained in any of these ways, or others. This technology means an ability to observe, collate and permanently record a vast amount of information about individuals that the law previously may have made available for collection but which, in practice, could not easily have been recorded and collected. The nature of the current or future privacy threat depends upon how this technological/legal fact will affect differently situated individuals.

These circumstances mean that efforts to revise privacy law to take account of the new technology will involve, in different areas of human activity, the balancing of values in light of prediction about the technological future. If, for example, businesses obtain detailed consumer purchasing information, they may create individualized customer profiles. Those profiles may invade the customer's privacy. But they may also help firms provide publicly desired products at lower cost. If, for example, medical records are placed online, patient privacy may be compromised. But the ready availability of those records may lower insurance costs or help a patient carried unconscious into an operating room. If, for example, all information about an individual's genetic make-up is completely confidential, that individual's privacy is protected, but suppose a close relative, a nephew or cousin, needs the information to assess his own cancer risk?

Nor does a "consent" requirement automatically answer the dilemmas suggested, for consent forms may be signed without understanding and, in any event, a decision by one individual to release or to deny information can affect others as well.

Legal solutions to these problems will be shaped by what is technologically possible. Should video cameras be programmed to turn off? Recorded images to self-destruct? Computers instructed to delete certain kinds of information? Should cell phones be encrypted? Should web technology, making use of an individual's privacy preferences, automatically negotiate privacy rules with distant web sites as a condition of access?

The complex nature of these problems calls for resolution through a form of participatory democracy. Ideally, that participatory process does not involve legislators, administrators, or judges imposing law from above. Rather, it involves law revision that bubbles up from below. Serious complex changes in law are often made in the context of a national conversation involving, among others, scientists, engineers, businessmen and -women, the media, along with legislators, judges, and many ordinary citizens whose lives the new technology will affect. That conversation takes place through many meetings, symposia, and discussions, through journal articles and media reports, through legislative hearings and court cases. Lawyers participate fully in this discussion, translating specialized knowledge into ordinary English, defining issues, creating consensus. Typically, administrators and legislators then make decisions, with courts later resolving any constitutional issues that those decisions raise. This "conversation" is the participatory democratic process itself.

The presence of this kind of problem and this kind of democratic process helps to explain, because it suggests a need for, judicial caution or modesty. That is why, for example, the Court's decisions so far have hesitated to preempt that process. In one recent case the Court considered a cell phone conversation that an unknown private individual had intercepted with a scanner and delivered to a radio station. A statute forbid the broadcast of that conversation, even though the radio station itself had not planned or participated in the intercept. The Court had to determine the scope of the station's First Amendment right to broadcast given the privacy interests that the statute sought to protect. The Court held that the First Amendment trumped the statute, permitting the radio station to broadcast the information. But the holding was narrow. It focused upon the particular circumstances present, explicitly leaving open broadcaster liability in other, less innocent, circumstances.

The narrowness of the holding itself serves a constitutional purpose. The privacy "conversation" is ongoing. Congress could well rewrite the statute, tailoring it more finely to current technological facts, such as the widespread availability of scanners and the possibility of protecting conversations through encryption. A broader constitutional rule might itself limit legislative options in ways now unforeseeable. And doing so is particularly dangerous where statutory protection of an important personal liberty is at issue.

By way of contrast, the Court held unconstitutional police efforts to use, without a warrant, a thermal imaging device placed on a public sidewalk. The device permitted police to identify activities taking place within a private house. The case required the Court simply to ask whether the residents had a reasonable expectation that their activities within the house would not be disclosed to the public in this way—a well established Fourth Amendment principle. Hence the case asked the Court to pour new technological wine into old bottles; it did not suggest that doing so would significantly interfere with an ongoing democratic policy conversation.

The privacy example suggests more by way of caution. It warns against adopting an overly rigid method of interpreting the constitution—placing weight upon eighteenth-century details to the point where it becomes difficult for a twenty-first-century court to apply the document's underlying values. At a minimum it suggests that courts, in determining the breadth of a constitutional holding, should look to the effect of a holding on the ongoing policy process, distinguishing, as I have suggested, between the "eavesdropping" and the "thermal heat" types of cases. And it makes clear that judicial caution in such matters does not reflect the fact that judges are mitigating their legal concerns with practical considerations. Rather, the Constitution itself is a practical document—a document that authorizes the Court to proceed practically when it examines new laws in light of the Constitution's enduring, underlying values.

My fourth example concerns equal protection and voting rights, an area that has led to considerable constitutional controversy. Some believe that the Constitution prohibits virtually any legislative effort to use race as a basis for drawing electoral district boundaries—unless, for example, the effort seeks to undo earlier invidious race-based discrimination. Others believe that the Constitution does not so severely limit the instances in which a legislature can use race to create majority-minority districts. Without describing in detail the basic argument between the two positions, I wish to point out the relevance to that argument of the Constitution's democratic objective.

That objective suggests a simple, but potentially important, constitutional difference in the electoral area between invidious discrimination, penalizing members of a racial minority, and positive discrimination, assisting members of racial minorities. The Constitution's Fifteenth Amendment prohibits the former, not simply because it violates a basic Fourteenth Amendment principle, namely that the government must treat all citizens with equal respect, but also because it denies minority citizens the opportunity to participate in the self-governing democracy that the Constitution creates. By way of contrast, affirmative discrimination ordinarily seeks to enlarge minority participation in that self-governing democracy. To that extent it is consistent with, indeed furthers, the Constitution's basic democratic objective. That consistency, along with its more benign purposes, helps to mitigate whatever lack of equal respect any such discrimination might show to any disadvantaged member of a majority group.

I am not saying that the mitigation will automatically render any particular discriminatory scheme constitutional. But the presence of this mitigating difference supports the view that courts should not apply the strong presumptions of unconstitutionality that are appropriate where invidious discrimination is at issue. My basic purpose, again, is to suggest that reference to the Constitution's "democratic" objective can help us apply a different basic objective, here that of equal protection. And in the electoral context, the reference suggests increased legislative authority to deal with multiracial issues.

The instances I have discussed encompass different areas of law—speech, federalism, privacy, equal protection, and statutory interpretation. In each instance, the discussion has focused upon a contemporary social problem— campaign finance, workplace regulation, environmental regulation, information-based technological change, race-based electoral districting, and legislative politics. In each instance, the discussion illustrates how increased focus upon the Constitution's basic democratic objective might make a difference—in refining doctrinal rules, in evaluating consequences, in applying practical cautionary principles, in interacting with other constitutional objectives, and in explicating statutory silences. In each instance, the discussion suggests how that increased focus might mean better law. And "better" in this context means both (a) better able to satisfy the Constitution's purposes and (b) better able to cope with contemporary problems. The discussion, while not proving its point purely through logic or empirical demonstration, uses example to create a pattern. The pattern suggests a need for increased judicial emphasis upon the Constitution's democratic objective.

My discussion emphasizes values underlying specific constitutional phrases, sees the Constitution itself as a single document with certain basic related objectives, and assumes that the latter can inform a judge's understanding of the former. Might that discussion persuade those who prefer to believe that the keys to constitutional interpretation instead lie in specific language, history, tradition, and precedent and who fear that a contrary approach would permit judges too often to act too subjectively?

Perhaps so, for several reasons. First, the area of interpretive disagreement is more limited than many believe. Judges can, and should, decide most cases, including constitutional cases, through the use of language, history, tradition, and precedent. Judges will often agree as to how these factors determine a provision's basic purpose and the result in a particular case. And where they differ, their differences are often differences of modest degree. Only a handful of constitutional issues—though an important handful—are as open in respect to language, history, and basic purpose as those that I have described. And even in respect to those issues, judges must find answers within the limits set by the Constitution's language. Moreover, history, tradition, and precedent remain helpful, even if not determinative.

Second, those more literalist judges who emphasize language, history, tradition, and precedent cannot justify their practices by claiming that is what the framers wanted, for the framers did not say specifically what factors judges should emphasize when seeking to interpret the Constitution's open language. Nor is it plausible to believe that those who argued about the Bill of Rights, and made clear that it did not contain an exclusive detailed list, had agreed about what school of interpretive thought should prove dominant in the centuries to come. Indeed, the Constitution itself says that the "enumeration" in the Constitution of some rights "shall not be construed to deny or disparage others retained by the people." Professor Bailyn concludes that the Framers added this language to make clear that "rights, like law itself, should never be fixed, frozen, that new dangers and needs will emerge, and that to respond to these dangers and needs, rights must be newly specified to protect the individual's integrity and inherent dignity." Instead, justification for the literalist's practice itself tends to rest upon consequences. Literalist arguments often seek to show that such an approach will have favorable results, for example, controlling judicial subjectivity.

Third, judges who reject a literalist approach deny that their decisions are subjective and point to important safeguards of objectivity. A decision that emphasizes values, no less than any other, is open to criticism based upon (1) the decision's relation to the other legal principles (precedents, rules, standards, practices, institutional understandings) that it modifies and (2) the decision's consequences, i.e., the way in which the entire bloc of decision-affected legal principles subsequently affects the world. The relevant values, by limiting interpretive possibilities and guiding interpretation, themselves constrain subjectivity, indeed the democratic values that I have emphasized themselves suggest the importance of judicial restraint. An individual constitutional judge's need for consistency over time also constrains subjectivity. That is why Justice O'Connor has explained that need in terms of a constitutional judge's initial decisions creating "footprints" that later decisions almost inevitably will follow.

Fourth, the literalist does not escape subjectivity, for his tools, language, history, and tradition, can provide little objective guidance in the comparatively small set of cases about which I have spoken. In such cases, the Constitution's language is almost always nonspecific. History and tradition are open to competing claims and rival interpretations. Nor does an emphasis upon rules embodied in precedent necessarily produce clarity, particularly in borderline areas or where rules are stated abstractly. Indeed, an emphasis upon language, history, tradition, or prior rules in such cases may simply channel subjectivity into a choice about: Which history? Which tradition? Which rules? It will then produce a decision that is no less subjective but which is far less transparent than a decision that directly addresses consequences in constitutional terms.

Finally, my examples point to offsetting consequences—at least if "literalism" tends to produce the legal doctrines (related to the First Amendment, to federalism, to statutory interpretation, to equal protection) that I have criticized. Those doctrines lead to consequences at least as harmful, from a constitutional perspective, as any increased risk of subjectivity. In the ways that I have set out, they undermine the Constitution's efforts to create a framework for democratic government—a government that, while protecting basic individual liberties, permits individual citizens to govern themselves.

To reemphasize the constitutional importance of democratic self-government may carry with it a practical bonus. We are all aware of figures that show that the public knows ever less about, and is ever less interested in, the processes of government. Foundation reports criticize the lack of high school civics education.

Comedians claim that more students know the names of the Three Stooges than the three branches of government. Even law school graduates are ever less inclined to work for government—with the percentage of those entering government (or nongovernment public interest) work declining at one major law school from 12 percent to 3 percent over a generation. Indeed, polls show that, over that same period of time, the percentage of the public trusting the government declined at a similar rate.

This trend, however, is not irreversible. Indeed, trust in government has shown a remarkable rebound in response to last month's terrible tragedy [September 11]. Courts cannot maintain this upward momentum by themselves. But courts, as highly trusted government institutions, can help some, in part by explaining in terms the public can understand just what the Constitution is about. It is important that the public, trying to cope with the problems of nation, state, and local community, understand that the Constitution does not resolve, and was not intended to resolve, society's problems. Rather, the Constitution provides a framework for the creation of democratically determined solutions, which protect each individual's basic liberties and assures that individual equal respect by government, while securing a democratic form of government. We judges cannot insist that Americans participate in that government, but we can make clear that our Constitution depends upon it. Indeed, participation reinforces that "positive passion for the public good," that John Adams, like so many others, felt a necessary condition for "Republican Government" and any "real Liberty."

That is the democratic ideal. It is as relevant today as it was 200 or 2,000 years ago. Today it is embodied in our Constitution. Two thousand years ago, Thucydides, quoting Pericles, set forth a related ideal—relevant in his own time and, with some modifications, still appropriate to recall today. "We Athenians," said Pericles, "do not say that the man who fails to participate in politics is a man who minds his own business. We say that he is a man who has no business here."

DISCUSSION QUESTIONS

1. Critics of the originalist perspective often point to ambiguities in the language of the Constitution. Justice Breyer outlines several of these in his speech. What are some other examples of ambiguous language in the Constitution? (Look at the Bill of Rights as a start.) What alternative interpretations can you develop?

2. Critics of the Living Constitution, such as Justice Scalia, often argue that judges substitute their own reading of what they think the law should be for what the law is. Do you think it is possible for justices to avoid having their own views shape their decisions? How could they protect against this happening?

3. Should judges take public opinion or changing societal standards into account when ruling on the constitutionality of a statute or practice? If so, what evidence of public opinion or societal standards should matter? Surveys? Laws enacted in states? If not, what are the risks in doing so?

4. Consider Scalia's examples of when the Court has employed a Living Constitution approach. How would Breyer's approach of active liberty decide these cases? Which approach do you think leads to the better outcomes: Scalia's textualist approach or Breyer's active liberty?

9

Public Opinion and the Media: Is Partisan Media Exposure Bad for Democracy?

From the 1960s through the 1980s, when people thought of media and news, they thought of newspapers and the broadcast television networks (ABC, CBS, NBC). Cable news soon emerged to provide an alternative (CNN, Fox, MSNBC), but one that for the most part followed the same style in their major nightly newscasts as the big networks. Late in the 1980s, talk radio, which had been around for some time, boomed in popularity and hosts such as Rush Limbaugh became household names. Hosts gleefully tweaked the mainstream media and embraced a much more aggressive, hard-hitting style that was explicitly ideological and partisan. There was, in this new forum, no pretense to being objective but, talk-radio fans would argue, the mainstream media were also not objective—they just pretended to be. News-oriented talk shows on CNN, Fox, and MSNBC followed the same pattern, as did politically oriented humor such as that offered by Jon Stewart, Stephen Colbert, and John Oliver. The rise of the Internet in the 1990s was the most recent dramatic change in communications technology. Today, Twitter receives much of the attention for breaking stories, blogs are prominent in presenting wide-ranging opinion and analysis, and Facebook provides an easy way for individuals to voice their opinions on the news.

Is it a problem for democracy if the media outlets consumed by the public are explicitly partisan and ideological? One side of this debate says that selective exposure to partisan media is good for democracy: it enhances participation in politics, influences the flow of ideas in public discourse, and potentially portrays American politics with more accuracy than the conventional "balanced" press. From another perspective, one-sided media exposure is harmful: it encourages extreme political beliefs, polarizes the electorate, creates an "echo chamber" that diminishes the ability to learn from opposing views, and leads to stalemate and gridlock in Washington.

This chapter's debate provides three perspectives on the effects of partisan media exposure. Political scientist John Sides argues that most Americans who watch news actually do so from a variety of different sources and notes that partisan media outlets do not polarize voters so much as they instead attract the already-polarized. Sides also argues that partisan media can have the positive outcome of spurring political engagement. Journalist Jihii Jolly describes a "filter bubble" (on new media platforms, prior search and reading behavior influences what articles are presented to readers as future options) that makes it easy for individuals to expose themselves selectively to one particular point of view without even knowing it. Should we worry about filter bubbles? Quoting one analyst, Jolly suggests we should, noting that even individuals visiting the same site will have a different experience and "not have a baseline to compare what is real and what is not." Political scientist Matthew Levendusky argues that partisan media has its strongest effects on those who are already at the ideological extremes, pushing them further to the extremes. But overall, this is a small group of people. At the same time, Levendusky notes that many important questions remain unanswered about the possible effects of partisan media exposure.

John Sides

Can Partisan Media Contribute to Healthy Politics?

On Monday at 5 p.m. I'm participating in a South by Southwest panel entitled "How Partisan Media Contributes to Healthy Politics." I prefer to think of this as a question: Can partisan media contribute to healthy politics? For my contribution, I want to do two things. The first is report on the available social science to show that partisan media might not be as powerful as is sometimes suggested. I think that's an important piece of context for this discussion. The second is to raise some questions about whether and how partisanship—an often maligned notion—can play a valuable role in democracy.

The Audience for Partisan News Is Not as Big as You Might Think

What percentage of Americans watches cable news for 10 minutes or more per day? Only about 10–15 percent, if you simply add up the audiences for Fox News, CNN, and MSNBC. This is based on calculations by political scientist Markus Prior, drawing on detailed data about what people actually watch and not what they report in a survey. Survey reports of news consumption are often highly inaccurate. Consider this comparison of a 2008 Pew survey to data on viewership from the Nielsen Company:

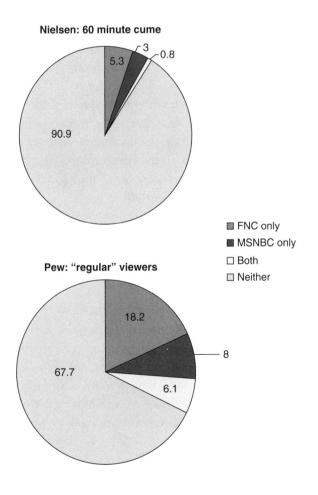

In the survey, almost a third of Americans believe they watch one of the three cable networks "regularly." It's not quite clear what "regularly" means, of course. This is one of the problems of using survey questions to measure media exposure. But if we assume that a regular viewer should watch at least an hour per week, then in reality only about 6–7 percent of Americas meet that description.

And even those numbers may be too high, because they double-count anyone who watches more than one of those channels. The seemingly inconceivable possibility that someone might watch both Fox and MSNBC leads to the next point.

Most People Are News Omnivores

Most people's "diet" of news isn't all that skewed by their partisans. There is actually a lot of overlap viewers of various cable news networks. Markus Prior reports that people who watch at least 1 minute of Fox News each week devote about 7.5 percent of their news consumption to Fox but 3.7 percent to other cable news channels. The same is true of CNN viewers. This is consistent with the research of Michael LaCour, who tracked media usage via devices that participants carried with them and that regularly recorded the ambient sounds around them. It is also consistent with the research of Matthew Gentzkow and Jesse Shapiro, who examined news consumption online and found that most consumers read ideologically diverse new outlets.

Unsurprisingly, if you isolate people who watch a lot of Fox News or a lot of MSNBC, their viewing habits reflect more skew. But this is a small group of people. The same is true of people who read political blogs: they are anything but omnivores, according to my research with Eric Lawrence and Henry Farrell, but they are also a small fraction of the public.

Prior has an excellent summary of these points:

> Automatic tracking of television viewing using two different technologies reveals that most people avoid cable news almost entirely. A large segment watches cable news infrequently and nonselectively, mixing exposure to different cable news channels. In the small slice of heavy cable news viewers, however, partisan selective exposure is not uncommon.

Partisan News May Not Polarize Partisans, but Attract Polarized Partisans

There is surprisingly little research that attempts to deal with a fundamental issue. Do people who watch partisan news become more polarized, or do people with polarized views simply like to watch partisan news? In one experiment political scientist Matthew Levendusky randomly assigned people to watch partisan news that either did or did not share their political outlook, or to a neutral news source. He found that partisan news that reinforced subjects' political outlook made their attitudes modestly more extreme. This effect was stronger among those who said that they preferred to consume news that shared their political outlook—suggesting that even if the people who watch partisan news are already pretty partisan, partisan news will make them more so.

However, other research by Kevin Arceneaux and Martin Johnson arrives at a different conclusion. They conducted a set of experiments and allowed people to choose whether they watched their side's partisan news, the other side's news, or entertainment programming that had no news content. They found that the news shows had no effects on attitudes as long as people were allowed to choose. This suggests that, in the real world, partisan news doesn't polarize. If anything, it may be that polarization creates an audience for partisan news.

A few experiments isn't much of an evidentiary base. Much more needs to be done. But it's worth noting that we don't really know that partisan news is polarizing us, and with more evidence, we may find that it isn't.

Learning to Love Partisanship

As you can tell from the title of the panel, it was deliberately framed as a provocation. It's sometimes (often? always?) hard to like partisan news and even partisanship itself. But here is the trade-off I want to emphasize. We want politics to involve calm, civil, rational deliberation about the common good. Partisanship doesn't necessarily facilitate that goal and can actively detract from it. But we also want politics to be full of active, eager, and engaged citizens. Partisanship does a very good job of facilitating engagement. It's one reason why voter turnout was so high in the late eighteenth century during the heyday of strong party organizations and a largely partisan press.

Indeed, if you look at partisans in the public, they look like ideal citizens in many respects. In a December 2011 YouGov poll, 65 percent of people who identified as "strong" Democrats or Republicans said they were "very much interested" in politics. Only 35 percent of those who identified as independents with no partisan leaning said that. Partisans are more likely not only to follow politics but to participate in it. Indeed, it is sort of odd to expect people to care deeply about something but then tell them they're not allowed to have strong opinions. It's like saying, "You should love baseball, but please don't actually root for a team."

I'm not suggesting that partisanship is an unalloyed good. Partisans can be misinformed if they are buying the spin their side is selling—spin that, by the way, they can usually hear in neutral news outlets doing "he said, she said" reporting, not simply in partisan news. Partisanship militates against other democratic goals, like tolerance for opposing points of view. Or compromise.

And, in any case, we've only got an hour in this panel, so we're hardly going to resolve this. I just think it's worth exploring these tensions in the folk theories we have about politics.

Jihii Jolly
How Algorithms Decide the News You See

Homepage traffic for news sites continues to decrease. This trend is the result of an "if the news is important, it will find me" mentality that developed with the rise of social media, when people began to read links that their friends and others in their networks recommended. Thus, readers are increasingly discovering news through social media, email, and reading apps.

Publishers are well aware of this, and have tweaked their infrastructure accordingly, building algorithms that change the site experience depending on where a reader enters from.

While publishers view optimizing sites for the reading and sharing preferences of specific online audiences as a good thing, because it gets users to content they are likely to care about quickly and efficiently, that kind of catering may not be good for readers.

"We can actually act on the psychological predisposition to just expose ourselves to things that we agree with," explains Nick Diakopoulos, research fellow at the Tow Center for Digital Journalism, where he recently published a report on algorithmic accountability reporting. "And what the algorithms do is they throw gasoline on the fire."

Visitors who enter BuzzFeed via Pinterest, for instance, see a larger "Pin It" button, no Twitter share button, and a "hot on Pinterest" module. Medium, launched less than two years ago by Twitter co-founder Evan Williams, recommends content to readers via an intelligent algorithm primarily based on how long users spend reading articles. Recommended content sidebars on any news site are calculated via algorithm, and Facebook has a recommended news content block that takes into account previous clicks and offers similar links.

Diakopoulos categorizes algorithms into several categories based on the types of decisions they make. *Prioritization*, for example, ranks content to bring attention to one thing at the expense of another. *Association* marks relationships between entities, such as articles or videos that share subject matter of features. *Filtering* involves the inclusion or exclusion of certain information based on a set of criteria.

"Algorithms make it much easier not just for you to find the content that you're interested in, but for the content to find you that the algorithm thinks you're interested in," Diakopoulos says. That is, they maximize for clicks by excluding other kinds of content, helping reinforce an existing worldview by diminishing a reader's chance of encountering content outside of what they already know and believe.

This type of exclusion on the internet has become known as the filter bubble, after a 2011 book by Eli Pariser. As [Columbia Journalism Review]'s Alexis Fitts explains in a recent feature about Pariser's viral site, Upworthy:

> In Pariser's conception, the filter bubble is the world created by the shift from "human gatekeepers," such as newspaper editors who curate importance by what makes the front page, to the algorithmic ones employed by Facebook and Google, which present the content they believe a user is most likely to click on. This new digital universe is "a cozy place," Pariser writes, "populated by our favorite people and things and ideas." But it's ultimately a dangerous one. These unique universes "alter the way we'd encounter ideas and information," preventing the kind of spontaneous encounters with ideas that promote creativity and, perhaps more importantly, encouraging us to throw our attention to matters of irrelevance.
>
> "It's easy to push 'Like' and increase the visibility of a friend's post about finishing a marathon or an instructional article about how to make onion soup," writes Pariser. "It's harder to push the 'Like' button on an article titled, 'Darfur sees bloodiest month in two years.'"

These types of algorithms create a news literacy issue because if readers don't know they are influencing content, they cannot make critical decisions about what they choose to read. In the print world, partisan media was transparent about its biases, and readers could therefore select which bias they preferred. Today, readers don't necessarily know how algorithms are biased and and how nuanced the filters they receive content through really are.

"Newspapers have always been able to have an editorial voice and to possibly even affect voting patterns based on that editorial voice," says Diakopoulos. "But what we're seeing [now] is the ability to scale across a population in a much more powerful way." Facebook recently did a study that found that simply showing more news in the newsfeed affects voting decisions.

Furthermore, the algorithms that social sites use to promote content don't evaluate the validity of the content, which can and has spread misinformation.

Beyond the filter bubble, algorithmic bias extends to search engine manipulation, which refers to the process undertaken by many companies, celebrities, and public figures to ensure that favorable content rises to the top of search engine results in particular regions. Though not intuitive to the average Web user, it's actually a form of soft censorship, explains Wenke Lee, Director of the Georgia Tech Information Security Center.

After reading Pariser's book, Lee and his research team set out to test the effect of personalized search results on Google and built a tool called Bobble a browser plug-in that runs simultaneous Google searches from different locations around the globe so users can see the difference between Google search returns for different people. They found that results differ based on several factors: Web content at any given time, the region from which a search is performed, recent search history, and how much search engine manipulation has occurred to favor a given result. Though Bobble has largely been confined to research purposes, it has been downloaded close to 10,000 times and has tremendous potential as a news literacy teaching tool.

"When we do this kind of work, there is always some pushback from people who say 'Why should people care? Why should people care about the filter bubble or biased news?'" says Lee. "But in the print media age, if somebody was to give me a manipulated version of *The New York Times*, I would be able to put my newspaper next to yours and find out that mine is different. But now? You and I can very likely see different front pages of newspapers online because they are customized for individuals, and that's pretty dangerous. Because that means I don't have a baseline to compare what is real and what is not."

For these reasons, the Center for News Literacy at Stony Brook University dedicates a portion of its curriculum to the filter bubble, covering issues of search engine manipulation and teaching how to search incognito on a Web browser—that is, without it storing your information.

Other efforts to mitigate media bias from algorithmic personalization include NewsCube, a Web service which automatically provides readers with multiple viewpoints on a given news item, and Balance, a research project at the University of Michigan that seeks to diversify the result sets provided by news aggregators (such as Google News).

Meanwhile, Diakopoulous is working on a framework for how to be transparent about algorithms, as well as processes for how they can be investigated, be it through reverse engineering by users (for which he offers methods in his report) or policy regulations on an institutional level.

"Transparency is important for the same reason why we want our newspaper editors to be transparent," he says. "If the purveyor of this very powerful media tool is honest with us about how they are using it, then at least we can be a little bit more trusting of them."

And it's also a way to give people the choice to be more media savvy—to exit the filter bubble, if they wish. "If I know your search engine works that way and I know someone else's search engine works a different way, then I can choose which one I would prefer to use."

Matthew Levendusky

Are Fox and MSNBC Polarizing America?

A generation ago, if ordinary Americans turned on the television at 6 P.M., they had basically one choice: to watch the evening news. They could have chosen to watch ABC, CBS, or NBC, but it wouldn't really have mattered, because they all basically gave the same news in a similar format. Today, if they did that, they would have hundreds of options, including not just the news, but also sports, movies, re-runs, and so forth. Even within news, they have a variety of choices. Not only would they have the major network news programs, but they would have many choices on cable, most notably the partisan outlets of Fox News and MSNBC (not to mention even more choices online). This choice of explicitly partisan outlets means that individuals can choose to hear messages that reinforce their beliefs, while avoiding those from alternative points of view, which some claim leads to polarization. Does this high-choice media environment, especially with its partisan outlets, polarize the public?

The evidence suggests that the media may contribute to polarization, but in a more circumscribed way than many commentators suggest. Take first the question, of choice, and in particular, whether people seek out media choices that reinforce their existing beliefs. The answer is (perhaps not surprisingly) yes: Republicans are more likely to tune in to Fox News and liberals are more likely to watch MSNBC. Researchers have also found that these effects are stronger for those who are more partisan and politically involved.

But there is perhaps an even more important type of selection at work. While the political can tune into Fox and MSNBC, those who dislike politics also have more options than ever for avoiding it. In lieu of the nightly news—or a televised presidential address—they can watch *Sports Center*, *Entertainment Tonight*, or a rerun of *The Big Bang Theory*. When confronted with a political option, they simply change the channel to something else that they find more agreeable. Even the most popular cable news programs get 2 to 3 million viewers on a typical evening in a country of 300 million Americans. In earlier decades, some of these individuals would have been incidentally exposed to political news and information (by, say, watching the television news at 6 o'clock, when there were no other options). Now that they can avoid news altogether, they know less about politics and are less likely to participate. So the growth of media choice strengthens the extremes while hollowing out the center, making the electorate more divided.

But what about the effects of partisan media on those who do watch these programs? While this research tradition is still relatively young, scholars have found a number of effects: on vote choice, participation, and attitudes toward bipartisanship and compromise, among others. The research looking at effects on attitudes finds that while there are effects, they are concentrated primarily among those who are already extreme. This suggests that these programs contribute to polarization not by shifting the center of the ideological distribution, but rather by lengthening the tails (i.e., moving the polarized even further away from the center).

It is vital to put these effects into context. As noted above, these programs attract a small audience, but those who watch these shows are more partisan, politically interested, and politically involved; these are the individuals who are more likely to make their voices heard in the halls of power. So to the extent that these shows matter, it is by influencing this relatively narrow audience. These programs have few direct effects on most Americans.

While scholars have learned a great deal about how media might shape polarization, there are still many questions to be answered. First, we know essentially nothing about the indirect effects of these shows: Do those who watch these shows transmit some of the effects to non-watchers through discussion in social networks? Does the Rachel Maddow fan in the cubicle next to you shape your opinions by telling you what she discussed on her show last night? Second, what is the effect of these shows on the broader media agenda, and on elites? Do the frames and issues that originate on Fox or MSNBC influence the broader media agenda? If so, that's an important finding, as it shows how these networks help to shape what a wider swath of Americans see.

In general, we understand little about how news outlets influence one another, especially in a 24-hour news cycle. Some recent work suggests that these outlets (particularly Fox) have shaped the behavior of members of Congress. The work discussed here has focused on the effects of cable TV news (with similar effects found previously for political talk radio). But there is an even broader range of material on the Internet, and few works have yet explored these effects. How the Internet—and especially social media sites like Twitter and Facebook—contributes to polarization will be an important topic in the years to come.

DISCUSSION QUESTIONS

1. Which part or parts of the news media—newspapers, television, websites, blogs, radio, Facebook, Twitter—do you rely on most? Which would you say you trust the most? What makes these sources the most trustworthy?

2. Considering the evidence presented in these three articles, how pervasive is exposure to news coverage that is implicitly or explicitly partisan or ideological? On balance, is this exposure good or bad for American democracy? What are the strongest areas of concern? What might be the chief benefits?

3. How do you know partisan bias when you see it? Define three criteria you would use to determine whether a media outlet is catering to readers' or viewers' partisan bias.

10

Elections and Voting: Voter ID Laws— Reducing Fraud or Suppressing Votes?

Recent national elections have raised many concerns about the voting system and the standards for administering elections in the United States. Charges of impropriety in voting procedures and vote counting, as well as complaints that certain voting technologies were systematically likely to produce more voter error or not accurately record voter choices, were legion. Massive voter mobilization campaigns on both the political left and right registered millions of new voters. Huge sums were poured into campaign advertising, further stoking the interest of these newly registered voters and the public in general. In such a charged political environment, concerns about the integrity of the voting process have taken on a particular urgency. One issue on which battle lines are frequently drawn is voter identification, especially the requirement that voters show a photo ID. Heading into the 2016 election, 32 states required voters to show some form of identification, with eight of those states requiring photo ID and eight requesting that voters provide a photo ID. During 2016 federal courts struck down in whole or in part voter ID laws in several states, concluding that the laws had a disparate impact that deterred minority and low-income voters.

The readings in this debate explore the issue of voter identification laws from three perspectives. John Fund points to examples where individuals posed undercover to commit voter fraud and were successful in their efforts. The gist of Fund's argument is that the claim that fraud is rare, often advanced by opponents of voter ID laws, ignores the ease by which fraud can actually occur and the difficulty in detecting it. To Fund, opposition to voter ID is rooted in the willingness of Democratic party officials to tolerate or benefit from individuals voting fraudulently. Peter Beinart does not take a position on the prevalence of voter fraud, but instead argues that voter ID laws are a modern-day equivalent of a poll tax. Before being declared unconstitutional, poll taxes were fees charged in some states for the ability to register to vote. He sees voter ID laws as imposing similar financial burdens on low-income voters and suggests that the main intent of the laws is to suppress minority and low-income voter turnout to the benefit of Republican party candidates. One possible implication of Beinart's argument is that even if fraud were frequent, voter ID might not be a desirable remedy due to its drawbacks. Finally, Lorraine Minnite argues that when there is fraud, it is likely party operatives, election officials, or politicians who commit it, not individual voters. Why, then, do states adopt voter ID laws? Minnite sees these laws as racially motivated and a stark continuation of attempts to thwart racial equality and inclusion by adopting voter regulations that disproportionately deter minority voters.

John Fund

Voter Fraud: We've Got Proof It's Easy

Liberals who oppose efforts to prevent voter fraud claim that there is no fraud—or at least not any that involves voting in person at the polls.

But New York City's watchdog Department of Investigations has just provided the latest evidence of how easy it is to commit voter fraud that is almost undetectable. DOI undercover agents showed up at 63 polling places last fall and pretended to be voters who should have been turned away by election officials; the agents assumed the names of individuals who had died or moved out of town, or who were sitting in jail. In 61 instances, or 97 percent of the time, the testers were allowed to vote. Those who did vote cast only a write-in vote for a "John Test" so as to not affect the outcome of any contest. DOI published its findings two weeks ago in a searing 70-page report accusing the city's Board of Elections of incompetence, waste, nepotism, and lax procedures.

The Board of Elections, which has a $750-million annual budget and a work force of 350 people, reacted in classic bureaucratic fashion, which prompted one city paper to deride it as "a 21st-century survivor of Boss Tweed–style politics."

The Board approved a resolution referring the DOI's investigators for prosecution. It also asked the state's attorney general to determine whether DOI had violated the civil rights of voters who had moved or are felons, and it sent a letter of complaint to Mayor Bill de Blasio. Normally, I wouldn't think de Blasio would give the BOE the time of day, but New York's new mayor has long been a close ally of former leaders of ACORN, the now-disgraced "community organizing" group that saw its employees convicted of voter-registration fraud all over the country during and after the 2008 election.

Greg Soumas, president of New York's BOE, offered a justification for calling in the prosecutors: "If something was done in an untoward fashion, it was only done by DOI. We [are] unaware of any color of authority on the part of [DOI] to vote in the identity of any person other than themselves—and our reading of the election law is that such an act constitutes a felony." The Board is bipartisan, and all but two of its members voted with Soumas. The sole exceptions were Democrat Jose Araujo, who abstained because the DOI report implicated him in hiring his wife and sister-in-law for Board jobs, and Republican Simon Shamoun.

Good-government groups are gobsmacked at Soumas's refusal to smell the stench of corruption in his patronage-riddled empire. "They should focus not on assigning blame to others, but on taking responsibility for solving the problems themselves," Dick Dadey of the watchdog group Citizens Union told the *Daily News*. "It's a case of the Board of Elections passing the buck." DOI officials respond that the use of undercover agents is routine in anti-corruption probes and that people should carefully read the 70-page report they've filed before criticizing it. They are surprised how little media attention their report has received.

You'd think more media outlets would have been interested, because the sloppiness revealed in the DOI report is mind-boggling. Young undercover agents were able to vote using the names of people three times their age, people who in fact were dead. In one example, a 24-year-old female agent gave the name of someone who had died in 2012 at age 87; the workers at the Manhattan polling site gave her a ballot, no questions asked. Even the two cases where poll workers turned away an investigator raise eyebrows. In the first case, a poll worker on Staten Island walked outside with the undercover investigator who had just been refused a ballot; the "voter" was advised to go to the polling place near where he used to live and "play dumb" in order to vote. In the second case, the investigator was stopped from voting only because the felon whose name he was using was the son of the election official at the polling place.

Shooting the messenger has been a typical reaction in other states when people have demonstrated just how easy it is to commit voter fraud. Guerrilla videographer James O'Keefe had three of his assistants visit precincts during New Hampshire's January 2012 presidential primary. They asked poll workers whether their books listed the names of several voters, all deceased individuals still listed on voter-registration rolls. Poll workers handed out ten ballots, never once asking for a photo ID. O'Keefe's team immediately gave back the ballots, unmarked, to precinct workers. Debbie Lane, a ballot inspector at one of the Manchester polling sites, later said: "I wasn't sure what I was allowed to do. . . . I can't tell someone not to vote, I suppose." The only precinct in which O'Keefe or his crew did *not* obtain a ballot was one in which the local precinct officer had personally known the dead "voter."

New Hampshire's Democratic governor, John Lynch, sputtered when asked about O'Keefe's video, and he condemned the effort to test the election system even though no actual votes were cast. "They should be prosecuted to the fullest extent of the law, if in fact they're found guilty of some criminal act," he roared. But cooler heads eventually prevailed, and the GOP state legislature later approved a voter-ID bill, with enough votes to override the governor's veto. Despite an exhaustive and intrusive investigation, no charges were ever filed against any of O'Keefe's associates.

Later in 2012, in Washington, D.C., one of O'Keefe's assistants was able to obtain Attorney General Eric Holder's ballot even though Holder is 62 years old and bears no resemblance to the 22-year-old white man who obtained it merely by asking if Eric Holder was on the rolls. But the Department of Justice, which is currently suing Texas to block that state's photo-ID law, dismissed the Holder ballot incident as "manufactured." The irony was lost on the DOJ that Holder, a staunch opponent of voter-ID laws, could have himself been disenfranchised by a white man because Washington, D.C., has no voter-ID law. Polls consistently show that more than 70 percent of Americans—including clear majorities of African Americans and Hispanics—support such laws.

Liberals who oppose ballot-security measures claim that there are few prosecutions for voter fraud, which they take to mean that fraud doesn't happen. But as the New York DOI report demonstrates, it is comically easy, given the sloppy-voter registration records often kept in America, to commit voter fraud in person. (A 2012 study by the Pew Research Center found that nationwide, at least 1.8 million deceased voters are still registered to vote.) And unless someone confesses, in-person voter fraud is very difficult to detect—or stop. New York's

Gothamist news service reported last September that four poll workers in Brooklyn reported they believed people were trying to vote in the name of other registered voters. Police officers observed the problems but did nothing because voter fraud isn't under the police department's purview.

What the DOI investigators were able to do was eerily similar to actual fraud that has occurred in New York before. In 1984, Brooklyn's Democratic district attorney, Elizabeth Holtzman, released a state grand-jury report on a successful 14-year conspiracy that cast thousands of fraudulent votes in local, state, and congressional elections. Just like the DOI undercover operatives, the conspirators cast votes at precincts in the names of dead, moved, and bogus voters. The grand jury recommended voter ID, a basic election-integrity measure that New York has steadfastly refused to implement.

In states where non-photo ID is required, it's also all too easy to manufacture records that allow people to vote. In 2012, the son of Congressman Jim Moran, the Democrat who represents Virginia's Washington suburbs, had to resign as field director for his father's campaign after it became clear that he had encouraged voter fraud. Patrick Moran was caught advising an O'Keefe videographer on how to commit in-person voter fraud. The scheme involved using a personal computer to forge utility bills that would satisfy Virginia's voter-ID law and then relying on the assistance of Democratic lawyers stationed at the polls to make sure the fraudulent votes were counted. Last year, Virginia tightened its voter-ID law and ruled that showing a utility bill was no longer sufficient to obtain a ballot.

Given that someone who is dead, is in jail, or has moved isn't likely to complain if someone votes in his name, how do we know that voter fraud at the polls isn't a problem? An ounce of prevention—in the form of voter ID and better training of poll workers—should be among the minimum precautions taken to prevent an electoral miscarriage or meltdown in a close race.

After all, even a small number of votes can have sweeping consequences. Al Franken's 312-vote victory in 2008 over Minnesota senator Norm Coleman gave Democrats a filibuster-proof Senate majority of 60 votes, which allowed them to pass Obamacare. Months after the Obamacare vote, a conservative group called Minnesota Majority finished comparing criminal records with voting rolls and identified 1,099 felons—all ineligible to vote—who had voted in the Franken–Coleman race. Fox News's random interviews with ten of those felons found that nine had voted for Franken, backing up national academic studies that show felons tend to vote strongly for Democrats.

Minnesota Majority took its findings to prosecutors across the state, but very few showed any interest in pursuing the issue. Some did, though, and 177 people have been convicted as of mid-2012—not just "accused" but actually *convicted*—of voting fraudulently in the Senate race. Probably the only reason the number of convictions isn't higher is that the standard for convicting someone of voter fraud in Minnesota is that the person must have been both ineligible and must have "knowingly" voted unlawfully. Anyone accused of fraud is apt to get off by claiming he didn't know he'd done anything wrong.

Given that we now know for certain how easy it is to commit undetectable voter fraud and how serious the consequences can be, it's truly bizarre to have officials at the New York City Board of Elections and elsewhere savage those who shine a light on the fact that their modus operandi invites fraud. One might even think that they're covering up their incompetence or that they don't want to pay attention to what crimes could be occurring behind the curtains at their polling places. Or both.

Peter Beinart

Should the Poor Be Allowed to Vote?

If Hong Kong's pro-democracy protesters succeed in booting C.Y. Leung from power, the city's unelected chief executive should consider coming to the United States. He might fit in well in the Republican Party.

In an interview Monday with *The New York Times* and other foreign newspapers, Leung explained that Beijing cannot permit the direct election of Hong Kong's leaders because doing so would empower "the people in Hong Kong who earn less than $1,800 a month." Leung instead defended the current plan to have a committee of roughly 1,200 eminent citizens vet potential contenders because doing so, in the *Times'* words, "would insulate candidates from popular pressure to create a welfare state, and would allow the city government to follow more business-friendly policies."

If that sounds vaguely familiar, it should. Leung's views about the proper relationship between democracy and economic policy represent a more extreme version of the views supported by many in today's GOP.

Start with Mitt Romney. In 2012, at a fundraiser with ultra-wealthy donors, the Republican nominee famously denigrated the "47 percent" of Americans who "believe that government has a responsibility to care for them, who believe that they are entitled to health care, to food, to housing"—to a welfare state. Because these self-appointed "victims" were voting in order to get things from government, Romney argued, their motives were inferior to the potential Romney voters who "take personal responsibility and care for their lives."

In distinguishing between Americans whose economic independence permits them to make reasoned political choices and those who because of their poverty cannot, Romney was channeling a hoary American tradition. In 1776, John Adams argued that men (let alone women) "who are wholly destitute of Property" were "too dependent upon other Men to have a Will of their own." In 1800, only three states allowed property-less white men to vote. For most of the twentieth century, southern states imposed "poll taxes" that effectively barred not only African Americans from voting but some poor whites as well.

Romney didn't suggest that the 47 percent be denied the right to vote, of course. But other Republicans have flirted with the idea. In 2010, Tea Party Nation President Judson Phillips observed that "The Founding Fathers . . . put certain restrictions on who gets the right to vote . . . one of those was you had to be a property owner. And that makes a lot of sense, because if you're a property owner you actually have a vested stake in the community." In 2011, Iowa Representative Steve King made a similar observation, noting approvingly, "There was a time in American history when you had to be a male property owner in order to vote. The reason for that was, because [the Founding Fathers] wanted the people who voted—that set the public policy, that decided on the taxes and the spending—to have some skin in the game. Now we have data out there that shows that 47 percent of American households don't pay taxes . . . But many of them are voting. And when they vote, they vote for more government benefits." In 2012, Florida House candidate Ted Yoho remarked, "I've had some radical ideas about voting and it's probably not a good time to tell them, but you used to have to be a property owner to vote." Yoho went on to win the election.

Philips, King, and Yoho are outliers. Most prominent Republicans would never propose that poor people be denied the franchise. But they support policies that do just that. When GOP legislatures make it harder to vote—either by restricting early voting, limiting the hours that polls remain open, requiring voter identification or disenfranchising ex-felons—the press usually focuses on the disproportionate impact on racial minorities and Democrats. But the most profound impact may be on the poor.

Voter-identification laws, in particular, act as a new form of poll tax. After Texas passed its voter-ID law, a study found that Texans who earned less than $20,000 per year were more than 10 times more likely to lack the necessary identification than Texans who earned more than $150,000. On the surface, this discrepancy might seem possible to remedy, since courts have generally demanded that the states that require voter identification provide some form of ID for free. But there's a catch. Acquiring that free ID requires showing another form of identification—and those cost money. In the states with voter-ID laws, notes a report by the Brennan Center for Justice at NYU Law School, "Birth certificates can cost between $8 and $25. Marriage licenses, required for married women whose birth certificates include a maiden name, can cost between $8 and $20. By comparison, the notorious poll tax—outlawed during the civil rights era—cost $10.64 in current dollars."

To make matters worse, roughly half a million people without access to a car live more than 10 miles from the nearest office that regularly issues IDs. And the states that require IDs, which just happen to be mostly in the south, also just happen to have some of the worst public transportation in the country.

Not surprisingly, a 2007 study by researchers at Washington University and Cal Tech found that, "registered voters with low levels of educational attainment or lower levels of income are less likely to vote the more restrictive the voter identification regime." Barring former felons from voting has an even more dramatic impact on the poor, since almost half of state prison inmates earned less than $10,000 in the year before their incarceration.

Obviously, the United States is not Hong Kong. But there's a reason some of the city's demonstrators have adopted the label "Occupy." Like the Americans who assembled in Zuccotti Park in 2011, they are fighting a system in which political exclusion and economic exclusion reinforce each other. Hong Kong's chief oligarch is named C.Y. Leung. But here in the United States, we have ours too.

Lorraine C. Minnite
The Myth of Voter Fraud

When there has been election fraud in American elections, it has usually been committed by politicians, party operatives, and election officials who have something at stake in electoral outcomes. Voters rarely commit fraud because for them, it is a motiveless crime, the individual benefits to the fraudulent voter are immaterial, while the costs are prohibitive.

The most important illustration of outright corruption of elections is the century-long success of white supremacists in the American South stripping African Americans of their right to vote. Elites and party bosses in the urban North followed the Southern example, using some of the same tricks to manipulate electoral outcomes and to disfranchise immigrants and the poor.

From this perspective, the impact of election fraud on American elections has been massive. It was only with the rise of the Black Freedom Movement and passage of the Voting Rights Act in 1965 that the tricks and political chicanery were halted. In fact, according to political historian J. Morgan Kousser, the Voting Rights Act is the most important fraud-prevention legislation ever passed.

In response to these victories, a reactionary movement arose to push back against progress in civil rights and to counter the thrust toward a more equal society. Over the last 40 years, that movement has made important gains, especially in the courts, where a conservative Supreme Court, in a 2013 case called *Shelby County v. Holder*, gutted one of the most effective features of the Voting Rights Act—the "preclearance" formula which forced states and localities with the most egregious histories of vote denial to obtain permission from the Justice Department before putting new election rules in place.

Prior to the contested 2000 presidential election, only 14 states either requested or required that voters show some form of identification at the polls. Since then, the number of states requiring ID to vote has doubled and the forms of acceptable identification have narrowed. In what is likely no coincidence, the rate at which states have adopted tougher photo identification requirements accelerated with the election of the nation's first black president and the demise of legally mandated federal oversight in the *Shelby* case.

In rapid succession, partisan lawmakers in state after state have pushed through the new rules, claiming tougher identity checks are necessary to staunch or prevent voter fraud. And yet, in no state adopting a photo ID requirement has any lawmaker or anyone else, for that matter, presented a credible showing of a problem with voters corrupting the electoral process. In other words, if the claimed reason of preventing voter fraud is taken at face value, there is no rational basis for the policy intervention. So what is actually going on?

I think the phony claims and renewed political chicanery are a reflection of the fact that a century and a half after the Civil War, and 50 years after the signing of the Voting Rights Act, a deeper struggle for democracy, equality, and inclusion continues. Beneath the skirmish over arcane voting rules is a fraught tension between our ideals and our fears, between what we profess to believe about the "sanctity" of the ballot, and racialized and class-based notions of worthiness embedded in the question of who is to be a citizen in the United States.

The myth of voter fraud persists because it is a racialized weapon in a power struggle over the soul of American democracy. To see this, we must set our current politics in a historical context. Long-standing fears about unworthy citizens polluting and distorting electoral outcomes are the underside of the usual celebratory story we like to tell ourselves of a progressive struggle for voting rights. In fact, the struggle has not unfolded in a linear fashion. Each successive advance has generated counter-movements rooted in alternative and reactionary histories aimed at "taking back" at least a part of what has been lost. In our own time, from the moment blacks began exercising their newly (re-)won right to vote, that right was undermined in ways that constrained its power to deliver social justice. The question of who is to be a citizen in our racially divided and injured society remains unresolved.

DISCUSSION QUESTIONS

1. Would you approve of a proposal that all voters be required to show photo identification at polling places? Do you think it would decrease turnout? If so, is this a reasonable cost to pay to ensure that people cannot vote using another person's name or cannot vote without proving that they live in the voting district? Or should turnout be prioritized and the risk that some people will vote inappropriately be accepted as a reasonable risk?

2. What are the advantages and drawbacks of using the kinds of evidence pointed to by Fund when crafting voter ID laws or public policy in general? How do you, or can you, distinguish between something that an undercover operation shows could happen and something that in fact happens regularly?

3. As a general matter, do you believe there is a trade-off between maximizing turnout and minimizing voter fraud? Or are these goals compatible? Why?

4. If photo IDs were provided free of charge and mailed to all potential voters, would that adequately address the concerns raised by Beinart and Minnite?

11

Political Parties: Should the United States Encourage Multi-Party Politics?

The American political system is dominated by the Republican and Democratic parties. Other political parties run candidates and occasionally win, but the electoral record of "third" or "minor" parties is generally quite poor. Political scientists point to a number of behavioral and structural reasons for this pattern.

As for behavior, most Americans sense that the two-party system is what is "normal" in American politics, and any other choices can seem risky. Voters are often reluctant to "waste" their vote for a candidate they believe has no chance to win, especially if they also believe that casting such a vote would increase the chances that a candidate they strongly dislike would win. Liberal Democrats faced this dilemma in 2000 when deciding whether to vote for Ralph Nader, the Green Party candidate for president, or Al Gore, the Democrat. When Gore lost by 537 votes in Florida, sealing the victory for Republican candidate George W. Bush, many of the more than 97,000 Floridians who voted for Ralph Nader no doubt wondered if they had made a mistake. In 2016, Libertarian Party candidate Gary Johnson and Green Party candidate Jill Stein created similar dilemmas for some Republicans and Democrats. The percentage of votes won by Johnson exceeded the margin of votes between Donald Trump and Hillary Clinton in nine of the ten closest states. Stein and other minor party candidates won additional votes in these states.

And as for structure, third parties face the need to raise substantial financial resources; the time and expense of getting on the ballot in all the states, which often involves lawsuits; and the relative lack of attention from news media. In addition, most electoral districts in the United States—for elections to the U.S. House or a state legislature, for example—elect a single person to an office, so that means the candidate with the highest number of votes will win. Because of this arrangement, potential smaller parties have an incentive to join forces with one of the larger parties, and skilled candidates are more likely to want to run on the ticket of one of those larger parties. It is certainly not impossible for more than two parties to have a solid, durable presence in such a system—the British system has a similar system of district-based elections and has two major parties and a competitive third party—but it is difficult. The most successful third party in American history, the Republican party, was not a "third" party for long, as it quickly replaced the collapsing Whig Party.

Despite these electoral struggles, political scientists and other supporters of multi-party politics point out other contributions that minor parties can make. Minor party candidates can raise issues that neither major party candidate is likely to raise. They can provide an alternative to voters who believe the major parties have become too extreme or have become too alike. Voters may sometimes support a third-party candidate before moving their support from one major party to another, giving these voters a means by which to shift their voting habits.

Should the United States encourage multi-party politics? Larry Diamond says yes. Americans are dissatisfied with their politics and their politicians. Diamond argues that the electoral system is rigid and slow to adapt, and this rigidity has consequences for addressing health, education, and other concerns. Although a majority of Americans voice support in public opinion surveys for having the option to vote for a minor party candidate—presumably, survey respondents mean voting for a candidate with a possibility of winning, since there are usually numerous minor party options on the ballot in most states for presidential elections—structural constraints make it hard for minor party candidates to be visible to voters. Diamond advocates for one specific change: making it easier for third-party candidates to participate in the presidential debates conducted by the Commission on Presidential Debates during the general election campaign. Ezra Klein takes a more pessimistic view toward third parties. While third parties might well introduce new issues into public discussion, Klein fears that in practice a third-party president would find himself or herself with two major parties unwilling to promote the president's agenda and determined to defeat it. And a Congress with third-party members would be unlikely to grant those newcomers any institutional power because to do so would mean reducing the influence of members of the major parties. In Klein's view, third parties are unlikely to reduce the frustrations that voters express about American politics.

Larry Diamond
Ending the Presidential-Debate Duopoly

The Democratic and Republican parties—which cannot seem to agree on anything else these days—have conspired to construct and defend a duopoly that closes competition to all other political alternatives. As a result, every current state governor and every one of the 535 members of Congress (save Maine Senator Angus King and Vermont Senator Bernie Sanders) was elected on one of the two party tickets. Governance in Washington is increasingly deadlocked between two parties that are being dragged to the extremes, while new alternatives that might fashion creative policy options and broader governing coalitions are stifled from competing. The political parties have become rigid and resistant to change, and have lost their capacity to find necessary and imaginative solutions to major problems.

Is it any wonder, then, that the polls show unprecedented disaffection among the American public? Sixty-two percent of Americans do not think the federal government has the consent of the governed, and 86 percent feel the political system is broken and does not serve the interests of the American people.

In *The Economist*'s 2013 democracy index, the United States is looking mediocre by international standards. It ranks only 19th in the quality of democracy. Americans should care about the quality and openness of their democracy for its own sake.

But there are also strong connections between the adaptability and competitiveness of its political institutions and the outcomes they produce. Globally, the United States ranks 14th in education, 19th in quality of infrastructure, 26th in child well-being, 26th in life expectancy, 33rd in Internet download speeds, and 44th in healthcare efficiency, but first in one thing—the rate of incarceration.

Nowhere is openness, innovation, and competition more sorely needed than in presidential politics. If competition is good for the economy, why shouldn't it be good for the political system as well? If economic markets thrive when there are low barriers to entry, why shouldn't the political marketplace—democracy—benefit from the same principle?

Two-thirds of Americans say they wish they had the option to vote for an independent candidate for president. But any alternative to the 162-year-old duopoly of Democrats and Republicans is blocked by the system the two parties have created. Leave aside the huge hurdles of organization and funding that independents must scale to collect enough signatures to qualify for the ballot across the states. Even more formidable is the obstacle imposed by a crucial but little known and unaccountable gatekeeper, the Commission on Presidential Debates (CPD). Members of this unelected and unaccountable commission have established a rule that makes it impossible for an independent, nonpartisan, or third-party ticket to gain access to the general-election debates. In the contemporary era, these debates have become such a dominant focus of political attention that no candidate (and particularly not a third one) can become president without participating.

Even if a third-party candidate does not manage to use the debate as a springboard to the Oval Office, his or her presence on the stage might reshape the conversation. With a third-party candidate in the race, both Democrats and Republicans would have a strong incentive to speak to the issues propelling that candidacy.

The CPD requires candidates for president to average over 15 percent in five polls (which they reserve the right to select, and which are open to manipulation) taken in September, just days before the debates. Since 1960 not one American who had not participated in a major-party primary has ever polled over 15 percent less than two weeks before the debates. (Ross Perot was polling in the single digits when he was permitted into the debates under an old rule.) For a candidate who has not run the gauntlet of the two major-party primaries, new research demonstrates that getting to that level of support in the polls by mid-September might require an expenditure of nearly $270 million. No independent campaign has ever spent, or ever will spend, that kind of money without knowing that its presidential and vice-presidential candidates can stand on the stage of the debates in the fall with a fall with a fair chance to compete.

In January, 49 prominent Republicans, Democrats, and independents—including current and former governors, members of Congress, cabinet members, academics, military leaders, and me—wrote to the CPD, asking it to change the rule and open up the debates to an independent voice. (Atlantic Media chairman David Bradley is also a signatory to the letter.) The letter proposed a different (or at least supplementary) means for earning a third spot on the debate stage: If one or more alternative candidates or parties qualified for the presidential ballot in states with enough electoral votes to win the election, then whichever one gathered the most signatures as part of the ballot-access process would be invited to participate in the debates. It urged that this decision be made by April 30 of the election year, to allow enough time for the candidate to mount a serious national campaign—and to be tested and scrutinized by the media. And it invited the CPD to propose other means by which an alternative ticket could reasonably qualify to enter the debates.

When a Petition for Rulemaking was filed with the FEC and posted for public comment in December, all but one of the 1,252 public comments endorsed the request for a new rule, Only the CPD claimed there was no need for a change. Despite this overwhelming backing, the CPD has stonewalled. In fact, the 17-member board has refused even to meet with the four dozen signers of the Change the Rule letter.

For more than two centuries, the United States has been a beacon of hope for democracy worldwide. For the last century, the United States has been the world's most successful and powerful democracy. But both of these elements of global leadership are now rapidly eroding. Making the election for America's highest office more open and competitive might renew the vigor and promise of its democracy.

Ezra Klein

A Third Party Won't Fix What's Broken in American Politics

The question I get more than any other about American politics is: The Democratic Party and the Republican Party both suck. Don't we need a third party to fix this?

Well, to paraphrase Bill Clinton, it depends what the meaning of "this" is.

If you think the problem with American politics is that there are ideas that are popular among voters but suppressed by the two major parties, then a third party could potentially help a lot.

But if you think the problem with American politics is that Congress is grid-locked, the president seems powerless to do anything about it, and Americans are increasingly frustrated, then a third party might well make things worse.

The Case for a Third Party

Political scientist Ronald Rapaport wrote the book on third parties. Literally. It's called *Three's a Crowd*, because of course it is. And the key thing he found about third parties is that "they need some sort of unique agenda. There has to be a reason why you're going to support a third party."

Third parties are a political weapon: they force the system to confront issues it might otherwise prefer to ignore. Take Ross Perot, the most successful leader of a third party in recent American history. "People like to think of Perot as being centrist. But he was not," says Rapaport. "He was extreme on the issues he cared about. And with Perot, it was economic nationalism and balancing the budget."

It's worth stopping on that point a moment. In Washington, the yearning for a third party is often by elites—and for elites. It's for the third party of Unity08, or No Labels, or Mike Bloomberg, or Simpson-Bowles. It's a third party of technocrats: fiscally moderate, socially permissive. A third party of sober moderates. A third party *of things people in Washington already care about.*

That third party won't work. The space for a third political party—if it exists—isn't in Washington's zone of elite agreement. It's in the zones of popular agreement that elites have little patience for. America's unaffiliated voters aren't moderates. They are, by Washington's standards, extremists—they're just extreme in a way that blithely crosses left and right lines, then doubles back on itself again. They support single-payer health care and tax cuts. Or they're against gay marriage but for a living wage. Or they're for open borders and cuts to social spending. Or they want a smaller military and sharp restrictions on abortions.

Perot's enthusiasts were a good example, Rapaport says. "His supporters, on issues like choice, were very pro-choice. On affirmative action, they were very against affirmative action."

Third parties like Perot's can force issues to the fore. But, typically, they get co-opted. Bill Clinton was much more intent on reducing the deficit because Perot showed the issue's power. Newt Gingrich's Contract With America echoed Perot's United We Stand. By 1996 there wasn't much left for Perot and his party to do.

Rapoport quotes historian Eric Hofstadter's famous line on American third parties: They're like bees. Once they've stung, they die.

The Problem with a Third-Party President

America's two-party duopoly has been going on a long time. What's new is the world where even the duopoly's favored ideas are stymied. Today, the chances of infrastructure investment or immigration reform aren't much better than the chances of single-payer health care. What's changed isn't that Washington is closed to new ideas. It's that it's closed to any ideas.

Could a third party break that deadlock? Probably not. In fact, it might well make it worse.

Imagine a third party that actually elects a new president. Right now, the basic problem in American politics is that one of the two major political parties has an interest in destroying the president. As incoming Senate Majority Leader Mitch McConnell said in 2010, "the single most important thing we want to achieve is for President Obama to be a one-term president."

The statement is often used to paint McConnell as uniquely Machiavellian, but in truth, it's banal: the single most important thing any minority political party wants to achieve is becoming the majority party. That's not because they're evil; it's because they believe being in the majority is the best way for them to do good. But the way for them to get there is to destroy the incumbent. Hence, the gridlock we see today.

A third-party president would change this in one big way: now *both* major political parties would have a direct incentive to destroy the president.

"The reason congressional parties work with the president from their party is that they share policy goals *and* because they share electoral goals," says Sarah Binder, a congressional scholar at the Brookings Institution. "You put a Michael Bloomberg at the top and maybe they still share policy goals but they don't share electoral goals. So you sever that electoral incentive."

In fact, the perverse reality of a third party is that the major party that agrees with it the most is also the most threatened by its existence. Think of Ralph Nader acting as a spoiler for Al Gore. So the fact of sharing policy goals often means they're directly opposed on electoral goals. No one in Congress is going to want to help an executive whose success is a threat to their chance of ever being in the majority again.

The Problem with a Third Party in Congress

Arguably, a third party could attack congressional gridlock at its source: by winning seats in Congress and then doing . . . something . . . to fix the chamber. But that something is hard to imagine.

I asked Binder for the rosiest possible scenario for a congressional third party. But she couldn't come up with much. "I can't even quite wrap my head around the politics, the electoral politics, the institutional politics, that would ever lead a third party to be in a position to make a difference in Congress," she said. "Everything in Congress is structured by the parties. If you want committee assignments, it's the parties that control committee assignments. Unless you can displace a major party I don't see how you get the toehold that gives you institutional power."

Rapoport didn't have much more of an answer. Third parties, he said, "are bad at process." They tend to be structured around a charismatic founder or a particular issue but, if they get far enough to actually wield power, they're ground to death by the byzantine institutions of American politics.

You can see that in Congress now, in fact. There are a number of third-party candidates serving in the Senate. Maine's Angus King, Vermont's Bernie Sanders, and Alaska's Lisa Murkowski were all elected as third-party candidates (Murkowski ran as a Republican write-in after losing the Republican primary). But in order to wield any power they've allied themselves with one of the two major parties. Sanders and King caucus with the Democratic Party and vote like typical Democrats—indeed, Sanders is thinking about running for president as a Democrat. Murkowski caucuses with the Republican Party and votes like a Republican. Even when Congress has three parties, it really only has two.

If a third party did win seats in Congress and accepted less institutional power for more party coherence, it's hard to say what problems it would solve. Congress is riven by disagreement and an inability to compromise. A third party would simply add another set of disagreements and another group who could potentially block action to the mix.

Which is all to say that the perverse incentives and byzantine structures that are causing so many problems for our two-party system would end up causing just as many problems, if not more, for a multi-party system. A third party might change the ideas Washington takes seriously. But it's hard to see it fixing the fact that Washington can't do much with the ideas it already does take seriously.

DISCUSSION QUESTIONS

1. Imagine that it is a presidential election year and you are living in a closely contested "battleground" state. Each of the major parties believes its candidate can win your state, and each will need your state in order to win a majority of the Electoral College votes and the election. Public opinion surveys indicate the election to be essentially tied between the two major party candidates. A third party candidate that you have strongly supported throughout the election year is also running. Supporters of one of the major party candidates urge you to forget about voting for the third party candidate because she cannot win. Even worse, because you are not voting for their candidate, you are in effect helping the other major party win, and you dislike that candidate most of all. Do you vote for the third party candidate, the major party candidate, or not vote at all? Why?

2. While voters have more options with multi-party elections, the likelihood increases that the winning candidate will not receive a majority of the vote. And as Klein argues, successful third-party candidates will face many roadblocks once they are in office. Considering these trade-offs, would American democracy be better off or worse off with more than two major parties?

3. The national presidential debates are the most-viewed events of the general election campaign and the most extended exposure most voters will have to the candidates. Given this information, do you support Diamond's proposal? Why or why not?

12

Groups and Interests: Donor Disclosure—Is Anonymous Campaign Funding a Problem?

The First Amendment of the U.S. Constitution says that "Congress shall make no law . . . abridging the freedom of speech." The Supreme Court must define the boundaries of what that broad prohibition means. Does it apply to pornography? To commercial speech? To speech that advocates the overthrow of the government or incites violence? Political advertising and campaign spending similarly generate a difficult set of questions. In its rulings, the Court has equated the use of money in campaigns with speech. In other words, money facilitates the making and spreading of messages. Supporting a candidate with a contribution is making a statement, and is thus speech, and the money itself helps the candidate speak through advertisements and other means. Spending independently to promote a candidate or message and not giving the money directly to a candidate is similarly a kind of speech—spending the money allows you to distribute the message. The Court has recognized a government interest in promoting fair elections that are free from corruption, so it has determined that some regulation of campaign finance is warranted. But the question is where to draw the line between activity that is permissible and that which is prohibited.

In its January 2010 decision in *Citizens United v. Federal Election Commission* (FEC), the Supreme Court decided that the First Amendment protects the right of non-profit and for-profit corporations and labor unions to spend directly to run ads calling for the election or defeat of a candidate in political campaigns, rather than having to set up political action committees (PACs). Political action committees must raise donations that they then either contribute directly to candidates and parties or spend independently to send a campaign message. The Court decision said that corporations and unions could bypass PACs and spend directly from their treasuries to speak on matters of interest to their organizations, including who they believe would be preferable candidates to elect. The amounts they could spend to support these messages, so long as they were not giving the money directly to a candidate or party, were not limited. The premise in the Court's decision was that the risk of the corrupting influence of money is most powerful when the money is going directly to a candidate or party's campaign coffers, not when an organization is spending money to transmit a message independently. *Citizens United* and subsequent lower court rulings and Federal Election Commission decisions also paved the way for so-called Super PACs, which can collect unlimited donations so long as they spend the money independently—for example, on TV ads—and did not contribute it to a candidate or party. For the most part, donors, including to Super PACs, must be named and submitted in federal campaign finance reports.

In the years since these decisions, debate has flared over campaign donations and spending that do not require disclosure of those spending or contributing the funds. Proponents of disclosure such as the Campaign Legal Center in this chapter note that although most funding must be disclosed, the amount that is undisclosed, often referred to as "dark money," is also significant. Their chief arguments are that voters have a right to know who is speaking through these funds and that non-disclosure increases the risk of corrupt activity and influence. Proponents of anonymous (un-disclosed) speech, such as Jon Riches of the Goldwater Institute in this chapter, who believe anonymous speech (including the provision of funds in campaigns) should be protected, say the issue is simple: we should care more about the message than who is delivering it. Supporters of this view note the prevalence of anonymous speech during the American Revolution. Better for democracy that the ideas be heard and voters can then decide. Moreover, it can sometimes be risky if one's support for particular causes is revealed. They point to Brendan Eich, the widely respected inventor of Javascript, who resigned under pressure as CEO of Mozilla in 2014 for a $1,000 donation he had made eight years earlier supporting California's Proposition 8, which prohibited same-sex marriage. Supporters of anonymous speech say that because government officials take actions and make decisions that affect the livelihood of organizations and individuals, these organizations and individuals must be able to spend funds in campaigns—maybe even to defeat these officials—without fear of reprisal. They worry that disclosure databases, rather than being of everyday use to voters, provide a tool for government officials and other powerful political figures to monitor their supporters and opponents.

Campaign Legal Center
Why Our Democracy Needs Disclosure

The disclosure of political spending has become a hot-button issue as many of those seeking to buy influence and sway election results with million-dollar checks would prefer to do it anonymously. The individuals and corporations writing the checks know they're doing it and so do the politicians that benefit. Only the public is left in the dark in this equation and that is a serious threat to our democracy. The amount of misinformation out there about disclosure is staggering, so the Legal Center has produced a primer on the topic to help separate the fact from the fiction.

Q: Why is disclosure of election-related fundraising and spending important?

A: Disclosure of money raised spent in elections has been the bedrock of our political system for many years, usually supported by all political parties. Voters deserve to know who is funding political communications in order to evaluate the full context of the message. Citizens need to know who has spent money to elect or defeat officials in order to hold those officeholders accountable and prevent corruption.

Justice Kennedy, in the only portion of last year's *Citizens United* opinion that had the support of eight of the nine Justices, noted the importance of disclosing the sources of campaign spending. He wrote that disclosure "provide[s] the electorate with information," makes sure "that voters are fully informed about the person or group who is speaking," and ensures people are "able to evaluate the arguments to which they are being subjected."

Justice Kennedy explained further: "The First Amendment protects political speech, and disclosure permits citizens and shareholders to react to the speech of corporate entities in a proper way. The transparency enables the electorate to make informed decisions and give proper weight to different speakers and messages." He also went on to say: "With the advent of the Internet, prompt disclosure of expenditures can provide shareholders and citizens with the information needed to hold corporations and elected officials accountable for their positions and supporters. Shareholders can determine whether their corporation's political speech advances the corporation's interest in making profits, and citizens can see whether elected officials are 'in the pocket' of so-called moneyed interests."

Justice Kennedy presumed that disclosure would serve as a check on potential misuse of independent expenditures, saying "[i]f elected officials succumb to improper influences from independent expenditures; if they surrender their best judgment; and if they put expediency before principle, then surely there is cause for concern."

Justice Scalia also made a forceful defense of election-related disclosure last year in a concurring opinion in *Doe v. Reed*. In that case, which upheld disclosure requirements for petition signers for ballot measures, Justice Scalia wrote: "Requiring people to stand up in public for their political acts fosters civic courage, without which democracy is doomed."

Q: What do you mean when you say disclosure?

A: Disclosure means shining a light on the money that is raised and spent to influence our elections. It should be clear who is paying for a TV advertisement or a piece of mail and where their money comes from. Already, candidates for federal office have to file reports detailing how much money they raised, where it came from, and what they spent it on. When they run an ad on TV or on the radio, the candidate has to personally state that they approved the message in the ad. Tens of millions of dollars were spent in 2010 on ads paid for by groups that reveal nothing about their donors. Far more of this undisclosed spending is anticipated in 2012.

Q: Why worry about disclosure? I thought most donations come from small donors.

A: Even in 2008, when more individuals donated to campaigns than ever before, only 12 percent of the money in congressional candidates' coffers came from small donations from individuals. That figure represents only a fraction of the total money spent on federal elections. The floodgates that the Supreme Court opened in *Citizens United* allow unlimited corporate and union money to drown out the voices of individual donors like never before. And without robust disclosure laws, the powerful interests behind that money remain in the shadows. Some groups have admitted receiving donations of tens of millions of dollars from one source—and many other large donations to elect or defeat candidates through these "outside" groups are completely hidden.

Q: Does disclosure really provide voters with useful information?

A: Full disclosure of the money in politics provides voters with information that is critical to holding representatives accountable through elections. In order to make that accountability meaningful, voters need to know if their elected officials will answer to them or to corporations, unions, and wealthy donors who pay for the advertisements that flood the airways. When special interest groups can spend large amounts of money while hidden in the shadows, it becomes easier for them to threaten political retribution to lawmakers who don't vote their way. Stronger disclosure laws will make clear the role that special interests play in our elections and will ensure that voters have all of the facts when they go to the polls.

It is also important for voters to know who is paying for the ads bombarding them, because voters will find some sources more "trustworthy" than others. Members of the NRA or the Brady Campaign to Prevent Gun Violence, or any citizen, will have different views about the reliability of an ad if they know that a pro- or anti-gun group paid for it. Ads about cigarette taxes may be seen as more or less reliable if you know they were paid for by tobacco companies or anti-smoking groups.

Q: I thought the *Citizens United* decision means corporations and labor unions can spend what they want on elections without disclosing where the money comes from.

A: No—in fact, *Citizens United* said the opposite. Eight Justices agreed that organizations attempting to influence our elections should be required to disclose their spending and contributors, and agreed that disclosure should include the funder of communications that discuss candidates in the midst of an election, and not merely those that expressly advocate for a candidate's election or defeat.

Q: So if Congress passed landmark campaign finance legislation ten years ago, and the Supreme Court has upheld disclosure requirements by an 8–1 margin, why don't we have effective disclosure now?

A: Simple—the Federal Election Commission (FEC) subverted the disclosure law that Congress wrote and that the Supreme Court upheld with a little-noticed "interpretation of law" that virtually gutted its effectiveness.

The McCain-Feingold campaign finance law passed by Congress and signed by President Bush in 2002 specified that disclosure is required of *all* persons who contributed $1,000 or more to groups running "electioneering communications"— the ads that flood the airwaves in the weeks before an election. But the FEC's interpretation required disclosure only of persons who contributed $1,000 or more expressly "for the purpose of furthering electioneering communications." The agency explained that disclosure is only required if the contribution is "*specifically designated* for [electioneering communications] by the donor." In other words, a donor can evade disclosure simply by contributing to the organization for general purposes and refraining from designating their money for political ads.

Q: Why is it a problem if only contributions designated for election activity have to be disclosed? Wouldn't that mean all contributions used to fund these new ads are reported?

A: Unfortunately, the FEC's enforcement of its own "interpretation of law," described above, has made it *even easier* for groups to keep the source of their campaign funds hidden in the shadows. Just a few months after the Supreme Court's overwhelming affirmance of disclosure requirements in *Citizens United*, the FEC ignored the recommendation of its general counsel and dismissed a complaint that a group called "Freedom's Watch" had violated the law when it spent more than $125,000 on a political ad without disclosing donors. In dismissing the complaint, the three Republican Commissioners narrowed the interpretation of the disclosure law even further—to require disclosure of contributions only if the donor specifies that their money should go to a *particular ad*. Since it is almost never the case that someone donates money to fund a specific ad—indeed, generally the ads are not created until after the money is raised—the FEC has neutered the disclosure law passed by Congress in 2002.

Q: What sort of secret spending is occurring?

A: Although candidates and some political organizations have to disclose information about their contributors and spending, many groups that work to influence elections do not. Corporations, unions, and non-profits can spend millions of dollars to support or oppose a candidate and the public will never know where that money is coming from. The newest and most troubling vehicles for this secret money are the new organizations with deliberately nondescript names like "Crossroads GPS" and "Priorities USA." They accept unlimited amounts of money from business corporations, labor unions, and the über-wealthy without ever disclosing their donors. The public has no way of knowing who really is spending money to influence their vote.

Q: Does disclosure violate the First Amendment?

A: Absolutely not. To the contrary, the Supreme Court has held that disclosure advances the public's First Amendment right to information. Disclosure empowers Americans to evaluate the people and organizations that are trying to influence their vote and to exercise that vote effectively.

Q: Some say that disclosure stifles free speech—is that true?

A: The Supreme Court has consistently upheld as constitutional candidate election-related disclosure laws, except where someone has shown specific evidence that disclosure of their name will result in *threats, harassment, or reprisals*. As recently as *Citizens United*, the Court held that the challenged federal disclosure requirement did not "impose a chill on speech or expression."

In the landmark 1976 case *Buckley v. Valeo*, the Supreme Court upheld blanket disclosure requirements and suggested that if contributors could give courts facts that show, for example, "specific evidence of past or present harassment," or a "pattern of threats or specific manifestations of public hostility," they might qualify for an exemption from disclosure requirements. But the Court has granted those exemptions when the facts of a case show that a speaker has been threatened with bodily harm. For example, in separate Supreme Court cases, the NAACP and the Socialist Workers Party were exempted from disclosure requirements after proving to the courts that their members would be subject to serious threats and bodily harm. The FEC has a similar procedure in place to exempt groups that can show that disclosure presents a personal risk.

Q: What about a right to anonymous speech?

A: There is no right to anonymous speech when an organization is trying to influence the outcome of a candidate's election. The Supreme Court has explicitly rejected "[t]he existence of a generalized right of anonymity in speech." After all, as Justice Stevens wrote for the Supreme Court in *City of Ladue v. Gilleo*, "the identity of the speaker is an important component of many attempts to persuade." In order for citizens to make informed choices when they go to the polls, they should know who has been trying to persuade them to vote one way or the other.

Q: Is campaign finance disclosure a partisan issue?

A: It should not be. Campaign finance reforms have historically passed with bipartisan support. Requiring disclosure of contributors to 527 organizations passed with overwhelming bipartisan support in 2000 when our elections were threatened with huge waves of secret spending. Congressional leaders like Speaker John Boehner, House Majority Leader Eric Cantor, and even Senate Majority Leader Mitch McConnell have in the past voiced their support for increased transparency and disclosure of political contributions. However, in the last Congress, the DISCLOSE Act became a partisan issue, with Republicans claiming they were kept out of the drafting and that the bill contained provisions that favored Democrats and unions. Democrats said they could not find Republican members willing to participate in drafting the bill.

Q: Why is support for disclosure so critical now?

A: We are at a unique moment in the relationship of money and politics. The FEC, created after the Watergate scandal and tasked with enforcing campaign finance laws, has become deadlocked and unable to perform its functions and ensure disclosure of money spent in federal elections. At the same time, the *Citizens United* decision has unleashed a torrent of unidentifiable but generously funded spending on our elections. The opponents of disclosure have been emboldened by victories on other campaign finance issues and are launching an assault on the decades-old disclosure laws that safeguard our elections. The basic principle that voters should have the information they need to make an informed choice in the voting booth is under attack by wealthy special interests.

Jon Riches

The Victims of 'Dark Money' Disclosure

The Dangers of Disclosure

Proponents of government-mandated disclosure have set forth several arguments for compelling private charitable organizations to disclose their donors. Those arguments range from the wrong but perhaps well-intentioned to the nefarious. In any event, the strongest arguments for government reporting are easily eclipsed by the dangers of disclosure. On the soft end of the spectrum are those government reporting advocates who claim they are not seeking to prevent speech, but only to inform the public of who is speaking. On the hard end of the spectrum are partisan political operatives who wish to use disclosure mandates to silence opposing views. As Arshad Hasan, executive director of the anti-privacy group ProgressNow put it, "The next step for us is to take down this network of institutions that are state-based in each and every one of our states." A similar sentiment was echoed by the sponsor of the DISCLOSE Act, the federal bill that would have mandated greater disclosure by nonprofit organizations, when he candidly proclaimed, "the deterrent effect on [political speech] should not be underestimated." Regardless of motive, the dangers of disclosure are far outweighed by any putative benefits.

Private association is a fundamental part of our nation's history and underpins a free society. Mandatory disclosure undermines core values that are essential for free speech and thus representative democracy. Specifically, mandatory disclosure: (1) prevents public discourse from focusing on the message, rather than the messenger; (2) allows for retaliation against speakers by those who disagree, particularly for minority opinions or when speaking truth to power; and (3) muddles regulations so that no one knows what speech is permitted and what is not, thus further chilling speech. Even assuming mandatory disclosure achieves its ostensible goals, an assumption that research does not appear to support, the costs of disclosure are simply too high.

Anonymous Speech Keeps Marketplace of Ideas Focused on the Message

Anonymous speech is an essential component of free speech, which is an essential component of representative democracy. One of the most important features of anonymous speech is that it focuses the dialogue on the message and issue, rather than the speaker. This is invaluable and irreplaceable in literary, social, and political dialogue. As the U.S. Supreme Court recognized in *Talley v. California*, "Anonymous pamphlets, leaflets, brochures and even books have played an important role in the progress of mankind."

Indeed, the ratification debate of our own Constitution was argued primarily under the pseudonym "Publius." The actual authors, Alexander Hamilton, James Madison, and John Jay, feared that their arguments would be eclipsed by *ad hominem* attacks had the papers not been published anonymously. At the time of ratification, Alexander Hamilton in particular was subject to personal attacks because of his foreign birth and perceived links to the British Crown. As one author noted, "Hamilton's anonymity meant to avoid prejudice and preclude obfuscation of his message, and these interests are still compelling justifications for speaking anonymously." Similarly, although a less controversial character, given the regional rivalries of the time, James Madison's Virginian roots would have made New Yorkers suspicious of his arguments had they been penned in his own name. Given these realities, an objective assessment of the U.S. Constitution would have been much less likely had it not been for anonymous political speech in the *Federalist Papers*. Put simply, the Constitution may never have been ratified had it not been for anonymous political speech.

The *Federalist Papers* are also instructive for another reason. In *Citizens United v. FCC*, writing for the majority, Justice Kennedy cited to James Madison's *Federalist* 10 in observing that factions will necessarily exist in our republic, "but the remedy of destroying the liberty of some factions is worse than the disease." Justice Kennedy went on to observe, "Factions should be checked by permitting them all to speak . . . and by entrusting the people to judge what is true and what is false." In our republic, citizens should be trusted to judge the value of the speech, irrespective of the speaker. Competing arguments ought to be weighed on their merits. Indeed, even under the most ideal circumstances, the value of government reporting mandates is negligible when the *content* of the speech, rather than its *source*, is the primary consideration in evaluating the strength of competing arguments, particularly in the political context. How many Americans are tired of *ad hominem* attacks on and by political actors, divorced from their positions on political issues? How worn is the country by character assassinations perpetrated by political campaigns? Is there not a yearning for dialogue that is above the caliber of gossip columns? Unfortunately, disclosure mandates drive political dialogue in the opposite direction. The result, as Madison and Justice Kennedy observed, is a "remedy" worse than the "disease" and an affront to the sensibilities of free people who should be entrusted to weigh the value of free speech.

The value of anonymous speech is not limited to purely political dialogue. Authors of literary works as well as editorials and news articles have long published anonymously or under assumed names. Lewis Carroll published anonymously to maintain his privacy. George Orwell wrote under a pen name because he was embarrassed of his early poverty. Both Charlotte and Emily Brontë published their classics under pseudonyms to avoid the significant gender biases of the time. Other authors may do so out of fear of economic or social retaliation. As the U.S. Supreme Court recognized in *McIntyre*, "Whatever the motivation may be, at least in the field of literary endeavor, the interest in having anonymous works enter the marketplace of ideas unquestionably outweighs any public interest in requiring disclosure as a condition of entry."

The same is true of the news media. Reporters routinely rely on anonymous sources to reveal major and significant newsworthy events. For example, the identity of Bob Woodward's and Carl Bernstein's primary source, Deep Throat, who provided information on the Nixon Administration's involvement in the Watergate scandal was not revealed until 2005—over 30 years after President

Nixon resigned. Indeed, reporters have faced incarceration for refusing to reveal their anonymous sources, even during national security investigations. These reporters reason, correctly, that anonymous speech often encourages truthful reporting, particularly from those who fear retaliation or retribution for speaking.

In addition to news reporting, every major newspaper in the country continues to publish anonymous editorials and commentary pieces. It can hardly be argued that media reports and truth in reporting are not tremendously important public values. But imagine a law that compelled the disclosure of news sources who choose to be anonymous or mandated that every newspaper editorial include a byline—and the names of every stockholder in the media corporation that owns the newspaper. The outrage would be swift and justified. The same should be true in the context of donor disclosure to nonprofit organizations—and for the same reasons. The real value of free speech is in the message, not the messenger, and the dangers of disclosure far outweigh any supposed benefits. One of the most significant such dangers is preventing retaliation against speakers who choose to be anonymous by those who disagree, particularly when speaking truth to power.

Anonymous Speech Prevents Retaliation, Especially When Speaking Truth to Power

Writing for the majority in *Talley v. California*, Justice Black wrote, "Persecuted groups and sects from time to time throughout history have been able to criticize oppressive practices and laws either anonymously or not at all." Political actors have routinely sought the identities of speakers with whom they disagree in order to harass, humiliate, and ultimately silence them.

During the Civil Rights era, for example, the Alabama attorney general sought to compel the National Association for the Advancement of Colored People ("NAACP") to turn over the names and addresses of all of its members to the state. This act of force and intimidation was fortunately rebuffed by the U.S. Supreme Court as a violation of the NAACP's and its members' First Amendment rights.

Even staunch advocates for free speech, such as John Adams, could not help using the power of government to silence critics, when, in 1798, he signed the Sedition Act. That statute made it a federal crime to "write, print, utter or publish . . . any false, scandalous and malicious writing or writings against the government of the United States." Of course, Adams punished such criminal acts only if their "scandalous" writings "pertained to him or his allies." Unfortunately, judicial review had yet to be established in 1798. Had it been, perhaps Mr. Adams would have received an admonishment from the Supreme Court, such as the one that echoed over two centuries later in *Citizens United*:

> When Government seeks to use its full power, including the criminal law, to command where a person may get his or her information or what distrusted source he or she may not hear, it uses censorship to control thought. This is unlawful. The First Amendment confirms the freedom to think for ourselves.

Unfortunately, efforts to compel disclosure in order to silence critics continue today. These include threats from government bureaucrats, like we saw when Dina Galassini tried to organize some friends and neighbors to oppose a local bond measure in Fountain Hills, Arizona. They include threats from other citizens, such as when Margie Christoffersen lost her job as a restaurant manager after her $100 donation to the campaign to ban gay marriage in California became public. And perhaps most ominously, these include threats from those wielding law enforcement authority, like the controversial Arizona sheriff, Joe Arpaio, who has jailed journalists critical of his office as well as political opponents. As the U.S. Supreme Court has long recognized, public disclosure of donations undoubtedly discourages political participation and exposes contributors to harassment and retaliation. Anonymous speech protected by the First Amendment has been the one barrier to prevent these abuses.

Regulatory Labyrinths Chill Free Speech

In order for opportunities for robust and free speech to be open to every speaker—not just the sophisticated or well-connected—the rules of the road must be simple and clear. Citizens and citizens groups must know what is permissible and what is impermissible, so they can steer their conduct accordingly. This is, in fact, a constitutional precept that negates vague and overbroad laws, particularly in the context of the First Amendment. Unfortunately, in the area of campaign finance law and mandatory donor disclosure, the rules of the road can be anything but simple and clear. Regulations are so often muddled that the average speaker does not know what is permissible and what is not. The unfortunate and inevitable result is less speech.

The U.S. Supreme Court in *Citizens United* recognized the importance of simplicity and clarity in the context of campaign finance speech restrictions:

> The First Amendment does not permit laws that force speakers to retain a campaign finance attorney, conduct demographic marketing research, or seek declaratory rulings before discussing the most salient political issues of our day. Prolix laws chill speech for the same reason that vague laws chill speech: People of common intelligence must necessarily guess at [the law's] meaning and differ as to its application.

A recent law review article provided one example of a small group of concerned citizens in a rural county who wanted to run a message about an environmental policy to illustrate how average Americans might get caught in the morass of campaign finance restrictions. The authors estimated that in order to form a political action committee to comply with federal election law, an average issue group would likely have to spend $9,000 in legal fees and ongoing compliance costs of $2,800. This expense alone makes political advocacy for most Americans cost-prohibitive.

Even more dangerous is the possibility that citizens who do choose to speak will get ensnared in the complexities of campaign finance restrictions. Dina Galassini had firsthand experience with this when Fountain Hills labeled her efforts to e-mail friends and organize a street protest a "political committee." The predictable result was that Ms. Galassini was scared her grassroots efforts were illegal, and she ceased her communications. As the U.S. Supreme Court observed, "As a practical matter . . . given the complexity of the regulations and the deference courts show to administrative determinations, a speaker who wants to avoid threats of criminal liability and the heavy costs of defending against FEC enforcement must ask a governmental agency for prior permission to speak." This acts as a prior-restraint on communication, the effect of which is to prevent speech—an outcome that is anathema to the First Amendment. Moreover, as the Court forecast in a FEC enforcement case, "Faced with the need to assume a more sophisticated organizational form, to adopt specific accounting procedures, to file periodic detailed reports . . . it would not be surprising if at least some groups decided that the contemplated political activity was simply not worth it."

In this sense, mandatory disclosure laws have the precise effect they were intended to have by many government reporting advocates—they silence opposing views. In his concurring opinion in *Citizens United*, Justice Thomas observed that the intimidation tactics by government reporting advocates have spurred a "cottage industry that uses forcibly disclosed donor information to preempt citizens' exercise of their First Amendment rights." Justice Thomas then cited a *New*

York Times article that described a new nonprofit group formed in the run-up to the 2008 elections that "plann[ed] to confront donors to conservative groups, hoping to create a chilling effect that will dry up contributions . . . [by exposing donors to] legal trouble, public exposure, and watchdog groups digging through their lives." This organization's leader described his donor disclosure efforts simply as "going for the jugular."

Cloaked as advocates of greater information and transparency, the enemies of free speech are at the gate. Defenders of the First Amendment must be ready to identify the dangers of donor disclosure and challenge efforts to compel government reporting wherever they occur. The courts should be one such battleground.

DISCUSSION QUESTIONS

1. Supporters of anonymous speech worry about reprisals from government officials or from others who might oppose the political views of a donor. How heavily do you weigh this concern in deciding whether or to what degree to require disclosure of campaign funding?

2. Imagine you hear a campaign advertisement that you fully agree with, but you then find that the major donors sponsoring the ad support many causes that you strongly oppose. Would you be more likely to dismiss the message or to reevaluate your view of the donor? Does your answer affect your views on the value of disclosure?

3. What kinds of disclosure in support of political causes or candidates would you support? All campaign-related funds? Or are there limits you would support? For example, currently donations to federal candidates under $200 do not have to be disclosed. Do you support this threshold? Should it be higher? Lower?

4. There are no disclosure requirements on social media posts, hours spent volunteering, and other ways in which individuals and groups can support a candidate and the issue positions the candidate supports. Campaign funding to support candidates and issues does have extensive, though not complete, disclosure requirements. Is campaign funding inherently different from other forms of political support, or should additional forms of campaign support have mandatory disclosure? Or should none of these activities require disclosure?

13

Government and the Economy: Is Income Inequality a Problem?

By any measure, income and wealth are distributed unequally in the United States. That may not come as a surprise, but the degree to which wealth and income are concentrated might be. According to recent Census figures, the top 1 percent of adults earned $1.3 million in 2014 compared to $428,000 in 1980 (in constant 2014 dollars), an increase of more than threefold. In contrast, the average income of the bottom 50 percent has stagnated at $16,000 per adult over this 34-year period. The concentration of wealth is even more pronounced than income inequality, with the richest 14,000 families in the United States (the top .01 percent) owning more than five times as much as the bottom 90 percent, or over 133 million families.

The fact of income inequality is indisputable. Whether that inequality has negative effects (and what to do about it) is a more complicated question. To many, high levels of income inequality signify gross failure of basic norms of fairness, and have harmful consequences for cohesion, civil life, and ultimately, even political stability. In this view, income inequality is both a cause and a consequence of political inequality, as the rich are better equipped to rig the system in their favor through favorable tax laws and regulations that further protect and concentrate wealth. Those who aren't wealthy wind up with the scraps: underfunded public schools, dangerous neighborhoods, crumbling infrastructure, inadequate services, and on and on. Others maintain that inequality is not a serious problem, and that even if it were, the alternative—draconian policies that forcefully redistribute wealth—is even worse. Moreover, since nobody can say what distribution of income would be fair, any attempt to achieve balance is arbitrary.

In the 2016 presidential campaign, income inequality was the centerpiece of Bernie Sanders's campaign in the primaries. Hillary Clinton emphasized the issue as well, but Donald Trump emerged as the favorite of white working class voters with his theme of "making America great again." The direction of Trump's economic policies are still unclear at the time of this writing, but income inequality remains a central concern.

Ray Williams makes the case that income inequality threatens democracy. He begins with an almost mind-numbing set of statistics on income and wealth inequality and argues that high-income inequality is associated with "more crime, less happiness, poorer mental and physical health, less racial harmony, and less civic and political participation." One of the more interesting studies cited by Williams found that Americans greatly underestimate the degree of wealth inequality in our nation and would prefer a more equal distribution, like Sweden's. George Will counters that "income inequality in a capitalist system is truly beautiful" because it is the engine of economic growth. Will argues that people like Mark Zuckerberg, Michael Dell, Bill Gates, Jeff Bezos, and Steve Jobs become wealthy because they have great ideas that produce innovative products. In turn, these ideas create thousands of jobs and create innovations that keep consumer prices down. The secret to creating economic growth is allowing the wealthy to keep their wealth to create jobs.

Barton Hinkle provides the angle that is likely to get the most sympathetic hearing from the Trump administration: we should tackle inequality by easing regulations that impede economic growth. This libertarian perspective of relying on the free market to create growth and wealth has moved into the mainstream in the past several decades. Airlines, trucking, telecommunications, and utilities industries were all deregulated in the past thirty years. However, according to Hinkle there are still some "low-hanging fruit" of inefficient regulations that are holding back growth and contributing to inequality. Copyrights and patents, immigration policies, especially for high-skilled workers, occupational licensing, and zoning all should be modified to encourage more entrepreneurship and job creation. Hinkle's suggestion on immigration policy may be resisted by the Trump administration, but small-government, pro-free market Republicans in Congress should be sympathetic to his agenda.

Ray Williams

Why Income Inequality Threatens Democracy

Rising economic inequality is threatening not only economic progress but also the democratic political system in the United States.

Emerging from the 2008–09 financial crisis, the global economy is strengthening. Yet around the world, prosperity evades most people. Increasingly the biggest benefits of economic prosperity are being accrued by a tiny elite. We live in a world where a small number of the richest people own half of the world's wealth.

In the United States, the increase in the income share of the top one percent is at its highest level since the eve of the Great Depression. In India, the number of billionaires has increased tenfold in the past decade. In Europe, poor people struggle with post-recovery austerity policies while moneyed investors benefit from bank bailouts. Africa has had a resource boom in the last decade but most people there still struggle daily for food, clean water, and health care.

Many economic and political experts have argued that extreme concentrations of wealth are not just morally questionable but that concentration in the hands of a few stunts long-term economic growth, too, making it more difficult to reduce poverty. What must now be admitted is that extreme income inequality also is undermining democracy.

Let's take a look at the evidence for increasing income inequality and its negative impact in the United States:

- The poorest half of the Earth's population owns 1 percent of the Earth's wealth. The richest 1 percent of the Earth's population owns 46 percent. The poorest half of the U.S. population owns 2.5 percent of the country's wealth. The top 1 percent owns 35 percent of it;
- The United States is the most economically stratified society in the western world. As *The Wall Street Journal* reported, a recent study found that the top .01 percent or 14,000 American families hold 22.2 percent of wealth, and the bottom 90 percent, or over 133 million families, just 4 percent of the nation's wealth;
- The U.S. Census Bureau and the World Wealth Report 2010 both report increases for the top 5 percent of households even during the recent recession. Based on Internal Revenue Service figures, the richest 1 percent has tripled their cut of America's income pie in one generation;

- In 81 percent of American counties, the median family income, about $52,000, is less than it was 15 years ago. This is despite the fact that the economy has grown 83 percent in the past quarter-century and corporate profits have doubled. American workers produce twice the amount of goods and services as 25 years ago, but get less of the pie;
- The amount of money that was given out in bonuses on Wall Street last year is twice the amount workers earned in the country combined;
- The wealthiest 85 people on the planet have more money that the poorest 3.5 billion people combined;
- The median wealth per adult number is only about $39,000, placing the United States about 27th among the world's nations, behind Australia, most of Europe, and even small countries like New Zealand, Ireland and Kuwait;
- The top 1 percent of America owns 50 percent of investment assets (stocks, bonds, mutual funds). The poorest half of America owns just .5 percent of the investments;
- The poorest Americans do come out ahead in one statistic: the bottom 90 percent of America owns 73 percent of the debt;
- Since 1990, CEO compensation has increased by 300 percent. Corporate profits have doubled. The average worker's salary has increased 4 percent. Adjusted for inflation, the minimum wage has actually decreased. CEOs in 1965 earned about 24 times the amount of the average worker. In 1980 they earned 42 times as much. Today, CEOs earn 325 times the average worker;
- In a study of 34 developed countries, the United States had the second highest level of income inequality, ahead of only Chile;
- Young people in the United States are getting poorer. The median wealth of people under 35 has dropped 68 percent since 1984. The median wealth of older Americans has increased 42 percent in the same period;
- Four hundred Americans have wealth equal to the GDP of Russia.
- In 1946, a child born into poverty had about a 50-percent chance of scaling the income ladder into the middle class. In 1980, the chances were 40 percent. A child born today has about a 33-percent chance.
- Twenty-five of the largest corporations in America in 2010 paid their CEOs more money than they paid in taxes that year.
- Some hedge fund mangers made $4 billion annually, enough to pay the salaries of every public school teacher in New York City, according to Paul Buchheit of DePaul University.

Robert Reich, former Secretary of Labor under President Bill Clinton, recently cited a *Forbes* story that reported "only twice before in American history has so much been held by so few, and the gap between them and the great majority been a chasm—in the late 1920s and in the era of the robber barons in the 1880s."

Dominic Barton, Managing Director of McKinsey and Co., argues "Few would disagree that unchecked increases in inequality will be costly for capitalism in the long run—due to the divisions that it creates within society and the strain that it puts on social safety nets."

The Pew Foundation study, reported in the *New York Times*, concluded, "The chance that children of the poor or middle class will climb up the income ladder, has not changed significantly over the last three decades." *The Economist's* special report, *Inequality in America*, concluded, "The fruits of productivity gains have been skewed towards the highest earners and towards companies whose profits have reached record levels as a share of GDP."

A joint effort by the Russell Sage Foundation, the Carnegie Corporation, and the Lyle Spencer Foundation has released several reports based on research on the issue of income inequality. They have concluded that over the past three decades, the United States has experienced a slow rise in economic inequality and as a result, the fruits of economic growth have gone largely to the wealthy; median incomes have stagnated; and the poor have increasingly been left behind.

In their book, *Winner-Take-All Politics: How Washington Made The Rich Richer—And Turned Its Back On The Middle Class*, Jacob Hacker and Paul Pearson argue that since the late 1970s, an intense campaign of anti-democracy policy changes have resulted in an intense concentration of wealth and income to very few individuals and corporations in the United States.

Many people believe it is only the recession that has had a negative impact on the economic welfare of people in the United States, but wealthy individuals and corporations have fared well during tough economic times.

According to Richard Wolff, professor of Economics at the University of Massachusetts, U.S. corporations, particularly the large ones, "have avoided taxes as effectively as they have controlled government expenditures to benefit them." Wolff points out that during the Depression and World War II, federal income tax receipts from individuals and corporations were fairly equal, but by 1980, individual income taxes were four times higher than corporate taxes. "Since World War II, corporations have shifted much of the federal tax burden for themselves to the public—and especially onto the middle class," Wolff says.

The most comprehensive recent study of corporate taxes by professors at Duke, MIT, and the University of California concluded, "We find a significant percent of firms that appear to be successfully avoiding large portions of the corporate income over a sustained period of time." For example, the *New York Times* reported that GE's total tax was 14.3 percent over the last 5 years, while in 2009 receiving a $140-billion bailout guarantee of its debt from the federal government.

What happens to societies where there are large and growing gaps in wealth? Significant social problems, and declining indicators of well-being and happiness, recent research seems to suggest.

British epidemiologists Richard Wilkinson and Kate Pickett, authors of *The Spirit Level: Why Greater Equality Makes Societies Stronger*, argue that almost every indicator of social health in wealthy societies is related to its level of economic equality. The authors, using data from the United States and other developed nations, contend that GDP and overall wealth are less significant than the gap between the rich and the poor, which is the worst in the United States among developed nations. "In more unequal societies, people are more out for themselves, their involvement in community life drops away." Wilkinson says. If you live in a state or country where level of income is more equal, "you will be less likely to have mental illness and other social problems," he argues.

A University of Leicester psychologist, Adrian White, has produced the first ever "world map of happiness," based on over 100 studies of more than 80,000 people and by analyzing data from the CIA, UNESCO, The New Economics Foundation, the World Health Organization, and European databases. The well-being index that was produced was based on the prediction variables of health, wealth, and education. According to this study, Denmark was ranked first, Switzerland second, Canada tenth and the United States twenty-third.

A study published in *Psychological Science* by Mike Morrison, Louis Tay, and Ed Diener, which is based on the Gallup World Poll of 128 countries and 130,000 people, found that the more satisfied people are with their country, the better they feel about themselves. Recent surveys in the United States show a significant percentage of Americans who are unhappy about their country. According to the World Values Survey of over 80 countries, the United States ranks only 16th, behind such countries such as Switzerland, the Netherlands, Sweden, and Canada, with Denmark ranked first.

Linda McQuaig and Neil Brooks, authors of *The Trouble with Billionaires* argue that increasing poverty due to economic inequality in the United States and Canada has detrimental effects on health and social conditions and undermines democracy. They cite the fact that while the United States has the most billionaires in the world; it ranks poorly in the Western world in terms of infant mortality, life expectancy, crime levels—particularly violent crime—and electoral participation.

Between 1983 and 1999, men's life expectancy decreased in more than 50 U.S. counties, according to a study by Majid Ezzati, associate professor of international health at the Harvard School of Public Health. For women, the news was even worse: life expectancy decreased in more than 900 counties—more than a quarter of the total. The United States no longer boasts anywhere near the world's longest life expectancy. It doesn't even make the top 40. In this and many other ways, the richest nation on earth is not the healthiest.

Ezzati's results are one example. There is also evidence that living in a society with wide disparities—in health, in wealth, in education—is worse for all the society's members, even the well off. Life-expectancy statistics hint at this. People at the top of the U.S. income spectrum "live a very long time," says Lisa Berkman, Director of Harvard University's Center Population and Development Studies, "but people at the top in some other countries live a lot longer."

A meta-analysis published by the *British Medical Journal* shows a link between income inequality and mortality and health. The researchers concluded that people living in regions with high-income inequality had an increased risk of premature death, independent of their individual socioeconomic status, age, or gender. While it is logical to assume the lowest-income citizens would be at greater health risk, the study concluded that income inequality is "detrimental to the more affluent members of society, since these citizens experience psychosocial stress from the inequality and loss of social cohesion."

Often popular media portrays the image of everyone favoring and wanting to be wealthy, but that may be deceiving.

Recent neuroscience search reveals that the brain rejects inequality and prefers equitable balance—physiological, emotional, social, and psychological. E. Tricomi and colleagues advanced this argument, published in the journal *Nature*. They contend the human brain dislikes inequality when it comes to money. And other behavioral and anthropological evidence shows that humans dislike social inequality and unfair distribution of outcomes. Researchers at the California Institute of Technology and Trinity College in Ireland have identified reward centers in the brain that are sensitive to inequality. This research shows a dislike of unfairness and inequality is more than just a social convention. On a physiological level, people may not be as selfish as once believed. Other studies have shown that many wealthy people want to restore equality and balance by charitable donations to assuage their guilt and decrease their own discomfort over having more than other people.

Research indicates that high inequality reverberates through societies on multiple levels, correlating with, if not causing, more crime, less happiness, poorer mental and physical health, less racial harmony, and less civic and political participation. Tax policy and social-welfare programs, then, take on importance far beyond determining how much income people hold onto.

In their report, "Building, A Better America—One Wealth Quintile At A Times," Dan Ariely of Duke University and Michael I. Norton of Harvard Business School showed that across ideological, economic, and gender groups, Americans thought the richest 20 percent of American society controlled about 59 percent of the country's wealth, while the real number is actually 84 percent. At the same time, the survey respondents believed that the top 20 percent should own only 32 percent of the wealth. In contrast, in Sweden, a country with significantly greater economic equality, 20 percent of the richest people there control only 36 percent of the wealth of the country. In the American survey, 92 percent of the respondents said they'd rather live in a country with Sweden's wealth distribution. They concluded that a majority of Americans they surveyed "dramatically underestimated the current level of inequality," and "respondents constructed ideal wealth distributions that were far more equitable even than their immensely low estimates of the actual distribution." They contend that all demographic groups including conservatives like Republicans and the wealthy "desired more equal distribution of wealth than the status quo."

In an article in the *New York Times* Eduardo Porter argues, "Comparisons across countries suggest a fairly strong, negative link between the level of inequality and the odds of advancement across the generations. And the United States appears at extreme ends along both of these dimensions—with some of the highest inequality and lowest mobility in the industrial world." He goes on to say,

> If the very rich can use the political system to slow or stop the ascent of the rest, the United States could become a hereditary plutocracy under the trappings of liberal democracy.
>
> One doesn't have to believe in equality to be concerned about these trends. Once inequality becomes very acute, it breeds resentment and political instability, eroding the legitimacy of democratic institutions. It can produce political polarization and gridlock, splitting the political system between

haves and have-nots, making it more difficult for governments to address imbalances and respond to brewing crises. That too can undermine economic growth, let alone democracy.

Frederick Soft, writing in the *American Journal of Political Science* provides an analysis of economic inequality and democratic political engagement, concluding "higher levels of income inequality powerfully depress political interest, the frequency of political discussion and participation in elections among all but the most affluent citizens, providing compelling evidence that greater economic inequality yields greater political inequality."

So while income inequality is a growing serious problem for the economic and social health of the U.S. population, it's fair to say it's also a threat to its democratic system.

George Will
How Income Inequality Benefits Everybody

Every day the Chinese go to work, Americans get a raise: Chinese workers, many earning each day about what Americans spend on a Starbucks latte, produce apparel, appliances, and other stuff cheaply, thereby enlarging Americans' disposable income. Americans similarly get a raise when they shop at the stores that made Sam Walton a billionaire.

The ranks of billionaires are constantly churned. Most of the people on the original Forbes 400 list of richest Americans in 1982 were off the list in 2013. Mark Zuckerberg, Facebook's chief executive, was not born until 1984. America needs more billionaires like him, Michael Dell, Bill Gates, Jeff Bezos, and Steve Jobs. With the iPod, iPhone and iPad, unique products when introduced, Jobs's Apple created monopolies. But instead of raising their prices, Apple has cut them because "profits attract imitators and innovators." Which is one reason why monopolies come and go. When John D. Rockefeller began selling kerosene in 1870, he had approximately 4 percent of the market. By 1890, he had 85 percent. Did he use this market dominance to gouge consumers? Kerosene prices fell from 30 cents a gallon in 1869 to 6 cents in 1897. And in the process of being branded a menacing monopoly, Rockefeller's Standard Oil made gasoline so cheap that Ford found a mass market for Model T's.

Monopoly profits are social blessings when they "signal to the ambitious the wealth they can earn by entering previously unknown markets." So "when the wealth gap widens, the lifestyle gap *shrinks*." Hence, "income inequality in a capitalist system is truly beautiful" because "it provides the incentive for creative people to gamble on new ideas, and it turns luxuries into common goods." Since 2000, the price of a 50-inch plasma TV has fallen from $20,000 to $550.

Henry Ford doubled his employees' basic wage in 1914, supposedly to enable them to buy Fords. Actually, he did it because in 1913 annual worker turnover was 370 percent. He *lowered* labor costs by reducing turnover and the expense of constantly training new hires.

All these thoughts are from John Tamny, a one-man antidote to economic obfuscation and mystification. Thomas Carlyle (1795–1881), who called economics "the dismal science," never read Tamny, a *Forbes* editor, editor of Real-ClearMarkets and now author of the cheerful, mind-opening book, *Popular Economics: What the Rolling Stones,* Downton Abbey, *and LeBron James Can Teach You About Economics.*

In the early 1970s, when the Rolling Stones were coining money and Britain's top tax rate was 83 percent, Keith Richards, guitarist and social philosopher, said: "That's the same as being told to leave the country." The Stones decamped to France, leaving Britain, Tamny notes, to collect 83 percent of nothing.

Americans execrate "outsourcing," which supposedly involves sending "American jobs" overseas. Well. Nike employs 40 times more manufacturing workers in Vietnam than in the United States, but it could not afford as many American workers as it has without the efficiencies of outsourcing. Tamny cites Enrico Moretti, an economist at the University of California at Berkeley, who says that when Americans buy an iPhone online, it is shipped from China and the only American who touches it is the UPS delivery person. Is it regrettable that Americans are not doing the assembly jobs for which Chinese are paid the "latte wage"?

Actually, Americans incessantly "outsource" here at home by, for example, having Iowans grow their corn and dentists take care of their teeth, jobs at which Iowans and dentists excel and the rest of us do not. LeBron James could be an adequate NFL tight end, but why subtract time from being a superb basketball player? The lesson, says Tamny, is that individuals—and nations—should do what they do better than others and let others do other things.

Millions of jobs, he says, would be created if we banned computers, ATMs, and tractors. The mechanization of agriculture destroyed millions of jobs performed with hoes and scythes. Was Cyrus McCormick—founder of what would later become the International Harvester Co.—a curse?

The best way to (in Barack Obama's 2008 words to Joe the Plumber) "spread the wealth around," is, Tamny argues, "to leave it in the hands of the wealthy." Personal consumption absorbs a small portion of their money and the remainder is not idle. It is invested by them, using the skill that earned it. Will it be more beneficially employed by the political class of a confiscatory government?

"Nothing," Tamny demonstrates, "is easier to understand than economics. It is everywhere you look." Readers of his book will subsequently look at things differently.

A. Barton Hinkle

How to Fix the Economy, and Income Inequality, the Libertarian Way

Conservatives want to get the economy roaring again. Republican presidential candidate Jeb Bush, for instance, wants to bring back 4-percent growth. Liberals want to reduce economic inequality. Hence the surging support for Bernie Sanders. The two goals often seem to work at cross purposes. But what if there were an idea that could do both? Brink Lindsey, a scholar at the Cato Institute, has written a paper that identifies not just one such idea, but four. Each of them addresses what he terms "regressive regulations": government rules that "redistribute income and wealth up the socioeconomic scale." Those rules have two other common features: They impede economic progress, and they have few disinterested defenders anywhere along the political spectrum. Nearly the only people who support them are the moneyed interests that benefit from them. They are, therefore, "low-hanging fruit guarded by dragons." Tackle them, and you can do a great deal of good.

Lindsey's ideas address:

1. Overly Restrictive Copyrights and Excessive Patents

Copyrights and patents are supposed to incentivize innovation by protecting property rights. Lindsey argues they have gone too far. A 1998 extension of copyright protection, for instance, was retroactive—even though "it is impossible to change incentives with respect to works that are already created. Retroactive extension thus amounted to a straight-up wealth transfer from consumers—and would-be adapters and remixers—to copyright holders."

Patents have exploded, from 61,620 in 1983 to more than 300,000 today—even though research and development outlays, as well as the rate of technological breakthroughs, have remained steady. Now you can patent such nebulous things as "methods of doing business."

The proliferation of patents has fed an army of "patent trolls," who buy patents on the cheap from distressed companies. As the Electronic Frontier Foundation explains, "the Patent Office has a habit of issuing patents for ideas that are neither new nor revolutionary, and these patents can be very broad. . . . (T)he troll will then send out threatening letters to those they argue infringe their patent(s)," demanding exorbitant licensing fees as the price of staying out of court—and in business.

Indeed, the majority of patent infringement suits today are "brought by firms that make no products . . . and whose chief activity is to prevent other companies" from making any. Result: the stifling of innovation, often by struggling entrepreneurs.

2. Too-Tight Immigration Policies, Especially for High-Skilled Workers

"The most straightforward way to increase economic output," Lindsey notes, "is simply to add more inputs used in production—namely, capital and labor." He recaps reams of research showing that immigrants "are disproportionately entrepreneurial and innovative."

One-fourth of Silicon Valley companies have at least one founder born abroad, for instance, even though immigrants make up less than 13 percent of the U.S. population. Others have reported that immigrants are now twice as likely to start a business as native-born Americans, and in 2011 created one out of every four new businesses in the United States.

Immigrants might be poorer than the typical American when they arrive here, but many don't stay that way, and those who climb the economic ladder bring many native-born Americans with them: immigrant-owned businesses have created 4 million jobs here. Unfortunately, only 7 percent of permanent resident visas go to "individuals who qualify on the basis of their work skills or other economic value," Lindsey writes.

3. Occupational Licensing

Nearly one-third of American occupations now require a permission slip from the government—up from 10 percent in 1970—including makeup artists, auctioneers, bartenders, florists, and ballroom dance instructors.

This causes harm in several ways. It acts as a drag on employment, which impedes economic growth. It raises prices for consumers, sometimes by as much as one-third, which hits the poor the hardest. It erects barriers to entry for the less educated: Thirty-two percent of Americans have a college degree, but 43 percent of people in licensed jobs are required to have one.

And for what? Not for health or safety. Lindsey points out that if health and safety were the principal drivers of licensing, then most states would license the same basket of occupations. That's not the case. Moreover, as Matthew Yglesias notes, in a Vox article on how the Obama administration is encouraging states to rethink excessive occupational licensing: "You can tell from the enormous state-to-state variation that rules are often going well beyond what's needed for safety." Alaska requires three days of training for manicurists; Alabama, 163.

Yglesias adds another point: "Licensing has in some cases become a cudgel with which to punish the already disadvantaged. Over a dozen states have rules that can make nonpayment of student loans into grounds for license revocation—turning state licensing boards into debt collectors. And rules barring people with felony convictions from obtaining licenses are widespread, which tends to exacerbate all the problems with racial and socioeconomic disparities in the criminal justice system."

4. Zoning

From 1950 to 1970, housing prices moved in tandem with construction costs. Then prices began to outstrip costs, and the trend "has been especially dramatic in America's big coastal cities."

Density might explain that—maybe some cities are just filling up—except that home prices do not correlate highly with density. However, prices do apparently correlate with "the progressive tightening of land-use restrictions." This "regulatory tax" can add as much as 50 percent to the cost of a dwelling.

Zoning, Lindsey says, exists "to protect homeowners' property values at the expense of housing for everybody else . . . and accomplishes its objectives by keeping poor people away from rich people." Not surprisingly, zoning "controls tend to be strictest in the cities with the highest per capita incomes."

As a result, and contrary to historical trends, people are moving away from big coastal cities—which are, by the way, "the country's most productive places," the ones that have "incubated the greatest productivity gains."

High prices caused by zoning are forcing people—non-rich people—to move to less productive regions, which hurts both their own economic prospects and the economy overall. (Lindsey cites a writer for *The Economist* who terms the phenomenon "moving to stagnation.")

It's customary in contemporary political discourse to pit economic liberty against economic equality: A laissez-faire economy supposedly brutalizes the weak, while a controlled economy slowly chokes to death on its own red tape. Lindsey has done the country a service by reminding everyone this dichotomy is too simplistic. Sometimes the best way to give the poor a hand up is simply to take government's boot off their neck.

DISCUSSION QUESTIONS

1. If Williams is right and people really do want a more equal distribution of income and wealth, why haven't policies been changed to reflect those desires?

2. If Will is right and income and wealth inequality is good for the economy, why have the incomes of the bottom half been stagnant for the past three decades, while the income of the top 1 percent has tripled? Is there some way to create more jobs while also allowing incomes at the bottom to grow?

3. Which of Hinkle's suggestions make the most sense to you? Which of the regulations may be important to protect other social goals?

14

Government and Society: Should the Affordable Care Act (Obamacare) Be Repealed?

The Affordable Care Act ("Obamacare") was the most significant domestic legislation enacted in the United States since the 1960s, and also one of the most controversial. Its supporters lauded its regulation of the health insurance industry, its cost controls, and its expansion of programs and subsidies that increased the number of people with health insurance. Its critics attacked the "individual mandate" requiring everyone to purchase health insurance, and its taxes on certain categories of medical equipment. Opposition to the law spurred the rise of the Tea Party and played a central role in the Republican Party's gains in the House and Senate in the 2010 midterm elections. Donald Trump made "repeal and replace" a central part of his successful presidential campaign.

The three pillars of the ACA are (a) prohibiting health insurers from denying coverage to individuals based on pre-existing conditions; (b) a requirement that all individuals have health insurance, either through employers, government programs like Medicare or Medicaid, or on the private insurance market; and (c) income-based subsidies to help with the affordability of coverage.

According to President Obama's article in the *Journal of the American Medical Association*, the law has succeeded: it has reduced the rate of uninsured Americans from 16 percent to 9 percent, allowing 20 million previously uninsured to obtain coverage. It has expanded access to basic preventive services. It has slowed the rate of growth of health care costs, reducing increases in the cost of private insurance and actually *lowering* costs in Medicare and Medicaid. And it has improved outcomes, lowering hospital readmission rates and the frequency of hospital-acquired infections. Because of the ACA, argues Obama, "Americans can now count on access to health coverage throughout their lives, and the federal government has an array of tools to bring the rise of health care costs under control."

Nonsense, responds Haislmaier and his co-authors, contesting nearly every claim about the ACA's success. Millions of people lost insurance they liked, and many people had their relationships with doctors disrupted as insurers narrowed provider networks. The costs of insurance grew, with premiums for many plans increasing by more than 10 percent a year, in part by imposing inflexible rules that prevent people from buying the kind of coverage they want, rather than what the federal government says they need. The ACA increased taxes, including those on middle class families, by $770 billion over 10 years. And the "widely despised" individual mandate takes away any element of individual choice. These authors propose an alternative reform that uses "market-based" reforms reliant on competition tax changes, and state-level regulation to improve efficiency and lower costs.

If there is one place in which the two readings agree, it is that health care reform will continue to be a controversial and contested policy.

Barack Obama

United States Health Care Reform: Progress to Date and Next Steps

Health care costs affect the economy, the federal budget and virtually every American family's financial well-being. Health insurance enables children to excel at school, adults to work more productively, and Americans of all ages to live longer, healthier lives. When I took office, health care costs had risen rapidly for decades, and tens of millions of Americans were uninsured. Regardless of the political difficulties, I concluded comprehensive reform was necessary.

The result of that effort, the Affordable Care Act (ACA), has made substantial progress in addressing these challenges. Americans can now count on access to health coverage throughout their lives, and the federal government has an array of tools to bring the rise of health care costs under control. However, the work toward a high-quality, affordable, accessible health care system is not over.

In this Special Communication, I assess the progress the ACA has made toward improving the U.S. health care system and discuss how policy makers can build on that progress in the years ahead. I close with reflections on what my administration's experience with the ACA can teach about the potential for positive change in health policy in particular and public policy generally.

Impetus for Health Reform

In my first days in office, I confronted an array of immediate challenges associated with the Great Recession. I also had to deal with one of the nation's most intractable and long-standing problems, a health care system that fell far short of its potential. In 2008, the United States devoted 16 percent of the economy to health care, an increase of almost one-quarter since 1998 (when 13 percent of the economy was spent on health care), yet much of that spending did not translate into better outcomes for patients. The health care system also fell short on quality of care, too often failing to keep patients safe, waiting to treat patients when they were sick rather than focusing on keeping them healthy, and delivering fragmented, poorly coordinated care.

Moreover, the U.S. system left more than 1 in 7 Americans without health insurance coverage in 2008. Despite successful efforts in the 1980s and 1990s to expand coverage for specific populations, like children, the United States had not seen a large, sustained reduction in the uninsured rate since Medicare and Medicaid began (Figure 1). The United States' high uninsured rate had negative consequences for uninsured Americans, who experienced greater financial insecurity, barriers to care, and odds of poor health and preventable death; for the health care system, which was burdened with billions of dollars in uncompensated care; and for the U.S. economy, which suffered, for example, because workers were concerned about joining the ranks of the uninsured if they sought additional education or started a business. Beyond these statistics were the countless, heartbreaking stories of Americans who struggled to access care because of a broken health insurance system. These included people like Natoma Canfield, who had overcome cancer once but had to discontinue her coverage due to rapidly escalating premiums and found herself facing a new cancer diagnosis uninsured.

In 2009, during my first month in office, I extended the Children's Health Insurance Program and soon thereafter signed the American Recovery and Reinvestment Act, which included temporary support to sustain Medicaid coverage as well as investments in health information technology, prevention, and health

Figure 1. Percentage of Individuals in the United States without Health Insurance, 1963–2015

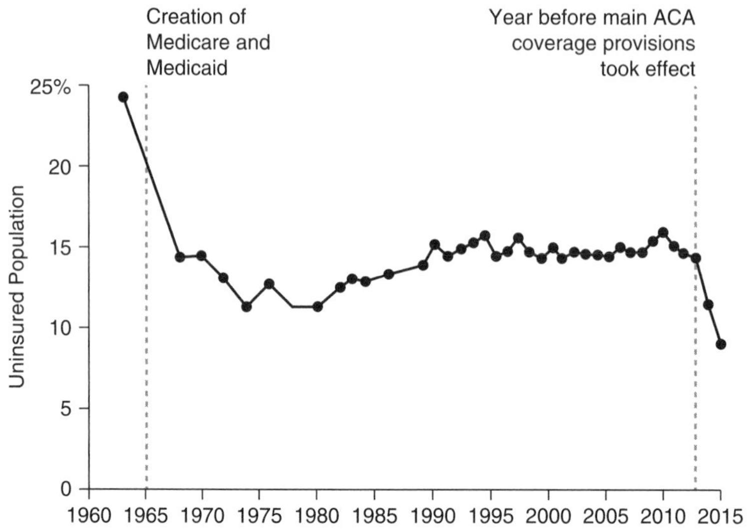

Creation of
Medicare and
Medicaid

Year before main ACA
coverage provisions
took effect

Uninsured Population

25%

20

15

10

5

0

1960 1965 1970 1975 1980 1985 1990 1995 2000 2005 2010 2015

SOURCE: Data are derived from the National Health Interview Survey and, for years prior to 1982, supplementary information from other survey sources and administrative records. For years 1989 and later, data are annual. For prior years, data are generally but not always biannual. ACA indicates Affordable Care Act.

research to improve the system in the long run. In the summer of 2009, I signed the Tobacco Control Act, which has contributed to a rapid decline in the rate of smoking among teens, from 19.5 percent in 2009 to 10.8 percent in 2015, with substantial declines among adults as well.

Beyond these initial actions, I decided to prioritize comprehensive health reform not only because of the gravity of these challenges but also because of the possibility for progress. Massachusetts had recently implemented bipartisan legislation to expand health insurance coverage to all its residents. Leaders in Congress had recognized that expanding coverage, reducing the level and growth of health care costs, and improving quality was an urgent national priority. At the same time, a broad array of health care organizations and professionals, business leaders, consumer groups, and others agreed that the time had come to press ahead with reform. Those elements contributed to my decision, along with my deeply held belief that health care is not a privilege for a few, but a right for all. After a long debate with well-documented twists and turns, I signed the ACA on March 23, 2010.

Progress Under the ACA

The years following the ACA's passage included intense implementation efforts, changes in direction because of actions in Congress and the courts, and new opportunities such as the bipartisan passage of the Medicare Access and CHIP Reauthorization Act (MACRA) in 2015. Rather than detail every development in the intervening years, I provide an overall assessment of how the health care system has changed between the ACA's passage and today.

The evidence underlying this assessment was obtained from several sources. To assess trends in insurance coverage, this analysis relies on publicly available government and private survey data, as well as previously published analyses of survey and administrative data. To assess trends in health care costs and quality, this analysis relies on publicly available government estimates and projections of health care spending; publicly available government and private survey data; data on hospital readmission rates provided by the Centers for Medicare & Medicaid Services; and previously published analyses of survey, administrative, and clinical data. The dates of the data used in this assessment range from 1963 to early 2016.

Expanding and Improving Coverage

The ACA has succeeded in sharply increasing insurance coverage. Since the ACA became law, the uninsured rate has declined by 43 percent, from 16.0 percent in 2010 to 9.1 percent in 2015, with most of that decline occurring after the law's main coverage provisions took effect in 2014 (Figure 1). The number of uninsured individuals in the United States has declined from 49 million in 2010 to 29 million in 2015. This is by far the largest decline in the uninsured rate since the creation of Medicare and Medicaid 5 decades ago. Recent analyses have concluded these gains are primarily because of the ACA, rather than other factors such as the ongoing economic recovery. Adjusting for economic and demographic changes and other underlying trends, the Department of Health and Human Services estimated that 20 million more people had health insurance in early 2016 because of the law.

Each of the law's major coverage provisions—comprehensive reforms in the health insurance market combined with financial assistance for low- and moderate-income individuals to purchase coverage, generous federal support for states that expand their Medicaid programs to cover more low-income adults, and improvements in existing insurance coverage—has contributed to these gains.

States that decided to expand their Medicaid programs saw larger reductions in their uninsured rates from 2013 to 2015, especially when those states had large uninsured populations to start with (Figure 2). However, even states that have not adopted Medicaid expansion have seen substantial reductions in their uninsured rates, indicating that the ACA's other reforms are increasing insurance coverage. The law's provision allowing young adults to stay on a parent's plan until age 26 years has also played a contributing role, covering an estimated 2.3 million people after it took effect in late 2010.

Early evidence indicates that expanded coverage is improving access to treatment, financial security, and health for the newly insured. Following the expansion through early 2015, nonelderly adults experienced substantial improvements in the share of individuals who have a personal physician (increase of 3.5 percentage points) and easy access to medicine (increase of 2.4 percentage points) and substantial decreases in the share who are unable to afford care (decrease of 5.5 percentage points) and reporting fair or poor health (decrease of 3.4 percent-

Figure 2. Decline in Adult Uninsured Rate from 2013 to 2015 vs. 2013 Uninsured Rate by State

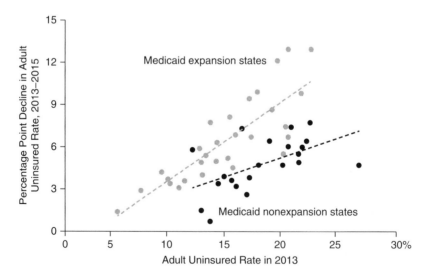

SOURCE: Data are derived from the Gallup-Healthways Well-Being Index and reflect uninsured rates for individuals 18 years or older. Dashed lines reflect the result of an ordinary least squares regression relating the change in the uninsured rate from 2013 to 2015 to the level of the uninsured rate in 2013, run separately for each group of states. The 29 states in which expanded coverage took effect before the end of 2015 were categorized as Medicaid expansion states, and the remaining 21 states were categorized as Medicaid nonexpansion states.

age points) relative to the pre-ACA trend. Similarly, research has found that Medicaid expansion improves the financial security of the newly insured (for example, by reducing the amount of debt sent to a collection agency by an estimated $600–$1000 per person gaining Medicaid coverage). Greater insurance coverage appears to have been achieved without negative effects on the labor market, despite widespread predictions that the law would be a "job killer." Private-sector employment has increased in every month since the ACA became law, and rigorous comparisons of Medicaid expansion and nonexpansion states show no negative effects on employment in expansion states.

The law has also greatly improved health insurance coverage for people who already had it. Coverage offered on the individual market or to small businesses must now include a core set of health care services, including maternity care and treatment for mental health and substance use disorders, services that were sometimes not covered at all previously. Most private insurance plans must now cover recommended preventive services without cost-sharing, an important step in light of evidence demonstrating that many preventive services were underused. This includes women's preventive services, which has guaranteed an estimated 55.6 million women coverage of services such as contraceptive coverage and screening and counseling for domestic and interpersonal violence. In addition, families now have far better protection against catastrophic costs related to health care. Lifetime limits on coverage are now illegal and annual limits typically are as well. Instead, most plans must cap enrollees' annual out-of-pocket spending, a provision that has helped substantially reduce the share of people with employer-provided coverage lacking real protection against catastrophic costs (Figure 3). The law is also phasing out the Medicare Part D coverage gap. Since 2010, more than 10 million Medicare beneficiaries have saved more than $20 billion as a result.

Reforming the Health Care Delivery System

Before the ACA, the health care system was dominated by "fee-for-service" payment systems, which often penalized health care organizations and health care professionals who find ways to deliver care more efficiently, while failing to reward those who improve the quality of care. The ACA has changed the health care payment system in several important ways. The law modified rates paid to many that provide Medicare services and Medicare Advantage plans to better align them with the actual costs of providing care. Research on how past changes in Medicare payment rates have affected private payment rates implies that these

Figure 3. Percentage of Workers with Employer-Based Single Coverage without an Annual Limit on Out-of-pocket Spending

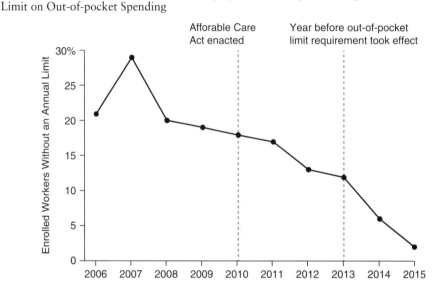

SOURCE: Data from the Kaiser Family Foundation/Health Research and Education Trust Employer Health Benefits Survey.

changes in Medicare payment policy are helping decrease prices in the private sector as well. The ACA also included numerous policies to detect and prevent health care fraud, including increased scrutiny prior to enrollment in Medicare and Medicaid for health care entities that pose a high risk of fraud, stronger penalties for crimes involving losses in excess of $1 million, and additional funding for antifraud efforts. The ACA has also widely deployed "value-based payment" systems in Medicare that tie fee-for-service payments to the quality and efficiency of the care delivered by health care organizations and health care professionals. In parallel with these efforts, my administration has worked to foster a more competitive market by increasing transparency around the prices charged and the quality of care delivered.

Most importantly over the long run, the ACA is moving the health care system toward "alternative payment models" that hold health care entities accountable for outcomes. These models include bundled payment models that make a single payment for all of the services provided during a clinical episode and population-based models like accountable care organizations (ACOs) that base payment on the results health care organizations and health care professionals achieve for all of their patients' care. The law created the Center for Medicare and Medicaid Innovation (CMMI) to test alternative payment models and bring them to scale if they are successful, as well as a permanent ACO program in Medicare. Today, an estimated 30 percent of traditional Medicare payments flow through alternative payment models that broaden the focus of payment beyond individual services or a particular entity, up from essentially none in 2010. These models are also spreading rapidly in the private sector, and their spread will likely be accelerated by the physician payment reforms in MACRA.

Trends in health care costs and quality under the ACA have been promising (Figure 4). From 2010 through 2014, mean annual growth in real per-enrollee Medicare spending has actually been *negative*, down from a mean of 4.7 percent per year from 2000 through 2005 and 2.4 percent per year from 2006 to 2010 (growth from 2005 to 2006 is omitted to avoid including the rapid growth associated with the creation of Medicare Part D). Similarly, mean real per-enrollee growth in private insurance spending has been 1.1 percent per year since 2010,

Figure 4. Rate of Change in Real per-Enrollee Spending by Payer

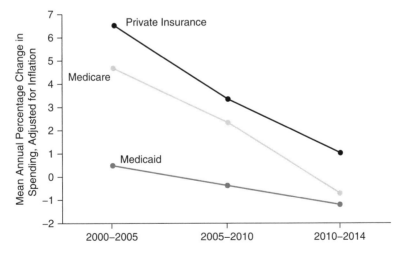

SOURCE: Data are derived from the National Health Expenditure Accounts. Inflation adjustments use the Gross Domestic Product Price Index reported in the National Income and Product Accounts. The mean growth rate for Medicare spending reported for 2005 through 2010 omits growth from 2005 to 2006 to exclude the effect of the creation of Medicare Part D.

compared with a mean of 6.5 percent from 2000 through 2005 and 3.4 percent from 2005 to 2010.

As a result, health care spending is likely to be far lower than expected. For example, relative to the projections the Congressional Budget Office (CBO) issued just before I took office, CBO now projects Medicare to spend 20 percent, or about $160 billion, less in 2019 alone. The implications for families' budgets of slower growth in premiums have been equally striking. Had premiums increased since 2010 at the same mean rate as the preceding decade, the mean family premium for employer-based coverage would have been almost $2,600 higher in 2015. Employees receive much of those savings through lower premium costs, and economists generally agree that those employees will receive the remainder as higher wages in the long run. Furthermore, while deductibles have increased in recent years, they have increased no faster than in the years preceding 2010. Multiple sources also indicate that the overall share of health care costs that enrollees in employer coverage pay out of pocket has been close to flat since 2010 (Figure 5),

Figure 5. Out-of-pocket Spending as a Percentage of Total Health Care Spending for Individuals Enrolled in Employer-Based Coverage

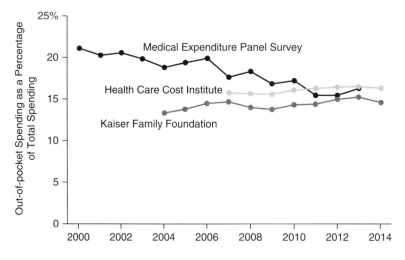

SOURCE: Data for the series labeled Medical Expenditure Panel Survey (MEPS) were derived from MEPS Household Component and reflect the ratio of out-of-pocket expenditures to total expenditures for nonelderly individuals reporting full-year employer coverage. Data for the series labeled Health Care Cost Institute (HCCI) were derived from the analysis of the HCCI claims database: to capture data revisions, the most recent value reported for each year was used. Data for the series labeled Kaiser Family Foundation were derived from the analyses of the Trueven Marketscan claims database reported by KFF in 2016.

most likely because the continued increase in deductibles has been canceled out by a decline in co-payments.

At the same time, the United States has seen important improvements in the quality of care. The rate of hospital-acquired conditions (such as adverse drug events, infections, and pressure ulcers) has declined by 17 percent, from 145 per 1000 discharges in 2010 to 121 per 1000 discharges in 2014. Using prior research on the relationship between hospital-acquired conditions and mortality, the Agency for Healthcare Research and Quality has estimated that this decline in the rate of hospital-acquired conditions has prevented a cumulative 87,000 deaths over 4 years. The rate at which Medicare patients are readmitted to the hospital within 30 days after discharge has also decreased sharply, from a mean of 19.1 percent during 2010 to a mean of 17.8 percent during 2015 (Figure 6; written communication; March 2016; Office of Enterprise Data and Analytics, Centers for Medicare & Medicaid Services). The Department of Health and Human Services has estimated that lower hospital readmission rates resulted in 565,000 fewer total readmissions from April 2010 through May 2015.

Figure 6. Medicare 30-Day, All-Condition Hospital Readmission Rate

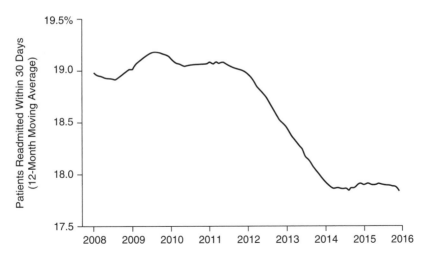

SOURCE: Data were provided by the Centers for Medicare & Medicaid Service (written communication; March 2016). The plotted series reflects a 12-month moving average of the hospital readmission rates reported for discharges occurring in each month.

While the Great Recession and other factors played a role in recent trends, the Council of Economic Advisers has found evidence that the reforms introduced by the ACA helped both slow health care cost growth and drive improvements in the quality of care. The contribution of the ACA's reforms is likely to increase in the years ahead as its tools are used more fully and as the models already deployed under the ACA continue to mature.

Building on Progress to Date

I am proud of the policy changes in the ACA and the progress that has been made toward a more affordable, high-quality, and accessible health care system. Despite this progress, too many Americans still strain to pay for their physician visits and prescriptions, cover their deductibles, or pay their monthly insurance bills; struggle to navigate a complex, sometimes bewildering system; and remain uninsured. More work to reform the health care system is necessary, with some suggestions offered below.

First, many of the reforms introduced in recent years are still some years from reaching their maximum effect. With respect to the law's coverage provisions, these early years' experience demonstrate that the Health Insurance Marketplace is a viable source of coverage for millions of Americans and will be for decades to come. However, both insurers and policy makers are still learning about the dynamics of an insurance market that includes all people regardless of any preexisting conditions, and further adjustments and recalibrations will likely be needed, as can be seen in some insurers' proposed Marketplace premiums for 2017. In addition, a critical piece of unfinished business is in Medicaid. As of July 1, 2016, 19 states have yet to expand their Medicaid programs. I hope that all 50 states take this option and expand coverage for their citizens in the coming years, as they did in the years following the creation of Medicaid and CHIP.

* * *

Second, while the ACA has greatly improved the affordability of health insurance coverage, surveys indicate that many of the remaining uninsured individuals want coverage but still report being unable to afford it. Some of these individuals may be unaware of the financial assistance available under current law, whereas others would benefit from congressional action to increase financial assistance to purchase coverage, which would also help middle-class families who have coverage but still struggle with premiums. The steady-state cost of the ACA's coverage provisions is currently projected to be 28 percent below CBO's original projections, due in significant part to lower-than-expected Marketplace premiums, so increased financial assistance could make coverage even more affordable while still keeping federal costs below initial estimates.

Third, more can and should be done to enhance competition in the Marketplaces. For most Americans in most places, the Marketplaces are working. The ACA supports competition and has encouraged the entry of hospital-based plans, Medicaid managed care plans, and other plans into new areas. As a result, the majority of the country has benefited from competition in the Marketplaces, with 88 percent of enrollees living in counties with at least 3 issuers in 2016, which helps keep costs in these areas low. However, the remaining 12 percent of enrollees live in areas with only 1 or 2 issuers. Some parts of the country have struggled with limited insurance market competition for many years, which is one reason that, in the original debate over health reform, Congress considered and I supported including a Medicare-like public plan. Public programs like Medicare often deliver care more cost-effectively by curtailing administrative overhead and securing better prices from providers. The public plan did not make it into the final legislation. Now, based on experience with the ACA, I think Congress should revisit a public plan to compete alongside private insurers in areas of the country where competition is limited. Adding a public plan in such areas would strengthen the Marketplace approach, giving consumers more affordable options while also creating savings for the federal government.

Fourth, although the ACA included policies to help address prescription drug costs, like more substantial Medicaid rebates and the creation of a pathway for approval of biosimilar drugs, those costs remain a concern for Americans, employers, and taxpayers alike—particularly in light of the 12 percent increase in prescription drug spending that occurred in 2014. In addition to administrative actions like testing new ways to pay for drugs, legislative action is needed. Congress should act on proposals like those included in my fiscal year 2017 budget to increase transparency around manufacturers' actual production and development costs, to increase the rebates manufacturers are required to pay for drugs prescribed to certain Medicare and Medicaid beneficiaries, and to give the federal government the authority to negotiate prices for certain high-priced drugs.

* * *

Lessons for Future Policy Makers

While historians will draw their own conclusions about the broader implications of the ACA, I have my own. These lessons learned are not just for posterity: I have put them into practice in both health care policy and other areas of public policy throughout my presidency.

The first lesson is that any change is difficult, but it is especially difficult in the face of hyperpartisanship. Republicans reversed course and rejected their own ideas once they appeared in the text of a bill that I supported. For example, they supported a fully funded risk-corridor program and a public plan fallback in the Medicare drug benefit in 2003 but opposed them in the ACA. They supported the individual mandate in Massachusetts in 2006 but opposed it in the ACA. They supported the employer mandate in California in 2007 but opposed it in the ACA—and then opposed the administration's decision to delay it. Moreover, through inadequate funding, opposition to routine technical corrections, excessive oversight, and relentless litigation, Republicans undermined ACA implementation efforts. We could have covered more ground more quickly with cooperation rather than obstruction. It is not obvious that this strategy has paid political dividends for Republicans, but it has clearly come at a cost for the country, most notably for the estimated 4 million Americans left uninsured because they live in GOP-led states that have yet to expand Medicaid.

The second lesson is that special interests pose a continued obstacle to change. We worked successfully with some health care organizations and groups, such as major hospital associations, to redirect excessive Medicare payments to federal subsidies for the uninsured. Yet others, like the pharmaceutical industry, oppose any change to drug pricing, no matter how justifiable and modest, because they believe it threatens their profits. We need to continue to tackle special interest dollars in politics. But we also need to reinforce the sense of mission in health care that brought us an affordable polio vaccine and widely available penicillin.

The third lesson is the importance of pragmatism in both legislation and implementation. Simpler approaches to addressing our health care problems exist at both ends of the political spectrum: the single-payer model vs government vouchers for all. Yet the nation typically reaches its greatest heights when we find common ground between the public and private good and adjust along the way. That was my approach with the ACA. We engaged with Congress to identify the combination of proven health reform ideas that could pass and have continued to adapt them since. This includes abandoning parts that do not work, like the voluntary long-term care program included in the law. It also means shutting down and restarting a process when it fails. When HealthCare.gov did not work on day one, we brought in reinforcements, were brutally honest in assessing problems, and worked relentlessly to get it operating. Both the process and the website were successful, and we created a playbook we are applying to technology projects across the government.

While the lessons enumerated above may seem daunting, the ACA experience nevertheless makes me optimistic about this country's capacity to make meaningful progress on even the biggest public policy challenges. Many moments serve as reminders that a broken status quo is not the nation's destiny. I often think of a letter I received from Brent Brown of Wisconsin. He did not vote for me and he opposed "ObamaCare," but Brent changed his mind when he became ill, needed care, and got it thanks to the law. Or take Governor John Kasich's explanation for expanding Medicaid: "For those that live in the shadows of life, those who are the least among us, I will not accept the fact that the most vulnerable in our state should be ignored. We can help them." Or look at the actions of countless health care providers who have made our health system more coordinated, quality-oriented, and patient-centered. I will repeat what I said 4 years ago when the Supreme Court upheld the ACA: I am as confident as ever that looking back 20 years from now, the nation will be better off because of having the courage to pass this law and persevere. As this progress with health care reform in the United States demonstrates, faith in responsibility, belief in opportunity, and ability to unite around common values are what makes this nation great.

Edmund F. Haislmaier, Robert E. Moffit, Nina Owcharenko, and Alyene Senger

A Fresh Start for Health Care Reform

Despite President Barack Obama's insistence that the national health care debate is over, and that he will not "re-litigate" the misnamed Patient Protection and Affordable Care Act (PPACA), the practical concerns, aggravated by implementation glitches and policy failures, guarantee that the debate over the PPACA is far from over.

In the next phase of the health care debate, supporters of the PPACA will undoubtedly attempt to fix or tweak the weaknesses and failures of the law. Such an approach would be based on preserving and expanding the government's role in health care. Indeed, some analysts have already proposed policies that would further strengthen the government's hand in managing and regulating the health care system.

Those who reject the notion of increasing government control in health care can pursue an alternative path—a path based on the principles of patient-centered, market-based health care reforms. That alternative path not only gives individuals greater choice, but also empowers them to make their own health care decisions.

Better Solutions

The need for health care reform has never been questioned by health care policy analysts on either side of the political spectrum. Furthermore, the broad goals of controlling costs, improving quality, and expanding access are widely shared. Yet, while both sides agree that reform is necessary, their policy solutions differ dramatically, most importantly on the question of who controls the key decisions in health care.

For the Obama Administration and defenders of the PPACA, the common conviction is that for major issues in health care, government officials should be the key decision makers. Those government decisions are imposed through detailed federal rules and regulations. The PPACA epitomizes this approach, and the course of its regulatory implementation—strewn with the broken promises of the President—provides an excellent guide to the consequences and inherent challenges of such an approach.

In contrast, those who believe in a patient-centered, market-based approach to reform trust individuals, not the government, to be the key decision makers in the financing of health care. To achieve this goal, Congress should embark on a reform agenda that is grounded in the following policy cornerstones: (1) reforming the tax treatment of health insurance so that individuals choose the health care coverage that best fits their needs (not the government's dictates); (2) restoring commonsense regulation of health insurance by devolving it back to the states; and modernizing (3) Medicare and (4) Medicaid by adopting policies that harness the powerful free-market forces of choice and competition.

The PPACA: Broken Promises

During the public campaign in support of President Obama's health plan, the President made numerous promises to the American people about the law's effect on everyday Americans. Four years into its implementation, it is growing ever more apparent that these promises have all but vanished.

Promise #1: "If you like your health care plan, you'll be able to keep your health care plan, period."

Reality: Millions of Americans have already lost, and more will likely lose, their coverage due to the PPACA. The PPACA has significantly disrupted the market for those who buy coverage on their own by imposing new coverage and benefit mandates, causing a reported 4.7 million health insurance cancelations in 32 states in 2013.

The same is true for those with employer-sponsored insurance. During the first half of 2014, Heritage Foundation analysis of the market enrollment data found that net enrollment in employer-group coverage declined by almost 4 million individuals, offsetting the gains in individual-purchased coverage by 61 percent.

Promise #2: "If you like your doctor, you will be able to keep your doctor, period."

Reality: Many Americans have not been able to keep their doctors as insurers try to offset the added costs of the PPACA by limiting the number of providers in their networks. In many of the PPACA's exchange plans, access to providers is limited; nationwide, 48 percent of all exchange plan provider networks are deemed to be "narrowed" and of those narrowed networks, nearly 40 percent are classified as "ultra-narrow." Likewise, due to significant payment reductions in the PPACA, some seniors with Medicare Advantage plans are being forced to find new doctors. UnitedHealth, the largest provider of these plans, has recently reduced its provider networks in at least 14 states.

In addition to these network access issues, there is the impact of the PPACA on the health care workforce, in particular its effects on workforce shortages and greater administrative burdens.

Promise #3: "In an Obama Administration we'll lower premiums by up to $2,500 for a typical family per year."

Reality: Premiums for those who purchase coverage in the individual market have significantly increased in a majority of states, and premiums in the group market also continue to rise. In 2014, PPACA coverage in the exchanges was more expensive than comparable 2013 coverage in the pre-PPACA individual market in 42 states. For Americans with employer-sponsored coverage, premium costs also continue to increase. Family premiums for employer-sponsored coverage have increased by an average of $3,459 since 2009.

Although 2015 premium rates have not been finalized, an initial analysis of 19 states with available data shows that 28 percent of Silver-level exchange plans will have premium increases greater than 10 percent, while only 14 percent of silver-level exchange plans will have rate decreases of more than 10 percent.

Promise #4: "Under my plan, no family making less than $250,000 a year will see any form of tax increase."

Reality: The PPACA contains 18 separate tax increases, fees, and penalties, many of which heavily impact the middle class. Altogether, the PPACA's taxes and penalties will collect more than $770 billion in new federal government revenues over 10 years. The individual mandate, the medical device tax, the federal health insurer tax, and new penalties and limits on health savings accounts and flexible spending accounts are just a few of the taxes that affect middle class Americans.

Promise #5: "I will protect Medicare."

Reality: The PPACA cuts Medicare to offset new health care spending. The PPACA makes unprecedented and unrealistic payment reductions to Medicare providers and Medicare Advantage plans in order to finance the law's new spending on subsidized coverage for the non-Medicare population. The cuts amount to over $700 billion from 2013 to 2022. If these draconian reductions take place as scheduled, they will significantly impact seniors' ability to access treatments and the quality of their care.

With such a lackluster record, it is not surprising that public opposition to the law remains strong and consistent. As a matter of fact, when all polls are averaged, the level of public opposition to the PPACA has always been higher than the level of public support.

Principles of Patient-Centered, Market-Based Health Care Reform

Traditionally, terms such as "patient-centered" or "market-based" have been used to contrast an alternative approach to greater government control in health care. However, the vocabulary of health care policy is often elastic, and different people sometimes use the same terms to express significantly different concepts. For example, the Obama Administration recently changed its description of the government-run health exchange to "marketplace."

The linguistic elasticity adds to the general confusion among the public and policymakers that seems to plague this already complex area of public policy. Consequentially, clarifying the rationale, objectives, and principles of patient-centered health care reform is important for properly understanding the concepts and implications of this approach. Specifically, truly patient-centered, market-based health reform means that:

- **Individuals are the key decision makers in the health care system.** That would be a major departure from most current arrangements under which governments or employers determine the type and scope of health care benefits and how those benefits are financed. In normal markets, consumers drive the system through their choices of products and services, reflecting their personal needs and preferences. In response, the providers of goods and services compete to meet consumer demands and preferences by supplying products that offer consumers better value in terms of price, quality, and features. The only way to achieve the same results in health care is by putting basic decision-making authority into the hands of consumers and patients.
- **Individuals buy and own their own health insurance coverage.** In a normal market, when individuals exchange money for a good or service, they acquire a property right in that good or service, but in today's system, individuals and families rarely have property rights in their health insurance coverage. The policy is owned and controlled by a third party—either the employer or government bureaucrats. In a reformed system, individuals would own their health insurance, just as they own virtually every other type of insurance or virtually any other product in other sectors of the economy.
- **Individuals are able to choose from a wide range of options.** Individuals, not employers or government officials, would choose their own health plan and level of coverage. Having a choice among health plans is particularly important

because, of necessity, it incorporates a whole set of other implicit choices— such as what the plan will pay for versus what the consumer will purchase directly from providers, how and from whom the patient will receive care, and any informational tools or services the plan provides to assist patients in deciding among competing providers and treatment options. The corollary is that suppliers of medical goods and services, including health plans, must have the necessary flexibility to offer consumers and patients innovative and better-value solutions. That means that government rules and regulations should be limited to those that are necessary to ensure safety and a level playing field. Laws and regulations that favor particular providers, suppliers, business models, or plan designs over others, or that create unreasonable barriers to market entry by new competitors, are inherently anti-consumer.

The challenge for policymakers is to undertake the reforms needed to transform the present system into one that rewards the search for and creation of better value. As other economic sectors show, health care need not be a zero-sum game in which costs can be controlled only by limiting benefits and benefits can be expanded only by increasing costs. Rather, a value-maximizing system would simultaneously demand and reward continuous benefit improvements accompanied by continuous cost reductions.

Such a value-maximizing result can be achieved in health care only if the system is restructured to make the consumer the key decision maker. When individual consumers decide how the money is spent, either directly for medical care or indirectly through their health insurance choices, the incentives will be aligned throughout the system to generate better value—in other words, to produce more for less.

A Fresh Start to Health Care Reform: The Right Policy

As it stands, the PPACA is burdened by practical infirmities that render it unworkable and unfair. Its policy prescriptions are unaffordable. This combination of bad policy and inherently flawed management has had, and will have, consequences that render the law persistently unpopular.

Congress should start fresh. It should repeal the PPACA and focus on the fundamentals: reform of the tax treatment of health care; devolving health insurance regulation back to the states; and reform of the major health care entitlement programs of Medicare and Medicaid.

Time to Reform the Tax Treatment of Health Care

The current tax treatment of health insurance is largely a relic of World War II wage and price controls. While those laws regulated cash wages, they exempted "insurance and pension benefits" of a "reasonable amount" from the definition of "wages" and "salaries," to which the controls were applied. Faced with labor shortages (as working-age men joined the armed forces) employers used that loophole to effectively skirt the wage controls by offering increased compensation in the form of employer-paid health insurance.

This distinction between cash wages and certain non-cash employee benefits also raised the issue of how the value of such benefits should be treated for tax purposes. When Congress enacted a major revision of the federal tax code in 1954 it explicitly excluded from the calculation of gross income any employer payments for a worker's medical care or health insurance. Moreover, this exclusion applies to both federal income and payroll (Social Security and Medicare) taxes. Thus, the tax exclusion for employer-sponsored health insurance meant that working families could fund their medical care with income that was completely tax-free.

Furthermore, unlike the case with most other tax breaks, Congress did not set a limit on the amount of income that could be diverted into paying for employer-sponsored health benefits on a pre-tax basis. Thus, having more of their compensation paid in the form of tax-free health benefits, and less in the form of taxable wages, became particularly attractive to workers in periods of higher inflation and higher marginal tax rates, such as during the 1970s.

The aggregate value of this federal tax preference in 2014 is about $250 billion per year, with reductions in federal personal income tax accounting for about $175 billion of that figure and reductions in payroll taxes accounting for the other $75 billion.

The principal effect of this policy was the widespread adoption of employer-sponsored health benefits as the dominant form of health coverage for American workers and their families. The share of the non-elderly population covered by employer-sponsored health insurance peaked at an estimated 71.4 percent in 1980. Even though the share has gradually declined since then, in 2012, an estimated 58.5 percent of the non-elderly population was still covered under such plans.

Yet that decline reveals some of the major drawbacks of this tax policy. Back in the 1950s and 1960s, it was fairly common for a worker to spend his entire career with the same employer. Yet the American workforce has become far more mobile since then. For instance, a Department of Labor survey of workers born between 1957 and 1964, found that they had an average of 11 jobs between the ages of 18 and 46. Obviously, a tax policy that links health insurance to the place of work means that each time a worker changes employers, he must change his health plan.

This tax policy also produces what economists call "horizontal inequity," meaning that if two individuals have the same income, but one has employer-sponsored health benefits while the other buys his own health insurance, the first individual receives a larger tax break than the second. At the same time, this tax policy also creates "vertical inequity." If two individuals work for the same employer and participate in the same health plan with the same cost, but have different incomes, the tax benefit each receives will vary based on their different marginal tax rates. That is so because the value of the tax exclusion for employer-sponsored coverage is equal to an individual's combined marginal tax rates for both income and payroll taxes, with the consequence that the size of the tax relief provided by the tax exclusion varies according to the different marginal tax rates imposed at different income levels.

Yet, the biggest problem with the tax exclusion from the health policy perspective is that while it offers workers substantial tax relief, it does so only if the workers let their employers decide how that portion of their compensation is spent. That translates to less choice and competition in health insurance, reduced consumer awareness of the true costs and value of medical care, and incentives to tailor health plans more toward meeting the interests of employers than to the preferences of the workers and their families.

The PPACA and the Tax Treatment of Health Care

Not only does the PPACA fail to correct these flaws in long-standing health care tax policy, it layers new complexity and distortions onto the existing system. It provides new, and substantial, subsidies for buying health insurance, but only to those individuals who have incomes between 100 percent and 400 percent of the federal poverty level (FPL) and purchase their coverage through government-run exchanges. Furthermore, it denies those new subsidies to individuals with access to employer-sponsored coverage, while at the same time imposing fines on employers with 50 or more full-time workers if they do not offer coverage.

Indeed, the only helpful change to health care tax policy that the PPACA makes is to limit the amount of employer-provided coverage that may be excluded from taxation. However, Congress did even that in a convoluted fashion. Rather than simply setting a limit—as Congress previously did with the tax exclusion for contributions to retirement plans—the PPACA imposes a punitive excise tax on any employer health plan whose value exceeds specified amounts.

A Better Approach

The proper goals for a true reform of the tax treatment of health insurance should be to make the system simpler and fairer for individuals, while also ensuring that it is neutral both with respect to how an individual obtains coverage (whether directly or through an employer or an association) as well as with respect to an individual's choice of plan design (such as a health-maintenance organization (HMO), a preferred-provider organization (PPO), a high-deductible plan, or another arrangement).

Various proposals for health care tax reform have been offered over the years. Most would repeal the tax exclusion and replace it with a new, universal tax deduction or tax credit for health expenses.

Replacing the current tax treatment of health benefits with a new design for health care tax relief that is both revenue and budget neutral (based on pre-PPACA levels) is the first step in transforming the American health system into one that is more patient-centered, market-based, and value-focused. No amount of government regulation or micromanagement of the system—such as tinkering with provider reimbursement rates or payment arrangements—can produce better value. That desired result will only be achieved by giving consumers more control over how to spend their health care dollars, thus forcing health insurers and medical providers to respond to consumer demand by offering better quality and prices for their products and services.

Even so, there is the practical concern that simply replacing the tax exclusion with a new design for health care tax relief would be an abrupt and major change in tax policy—resulting in further dislocation, at least initially, to the existing health care financing arrangements of millions of Americans. One way to avoid that problem is by including a transitional mechanism in the design, as follows:

First, instead of eliminating the tax exclusion, convert the existing limitation on high-cost employer health plans into a straightforward cap on the value of the exclusion.

Second, replace all the other narrower health care tax breaks (such as the tax deduction for coverage purchased by the self-employed, the Trade Adjustment

Assistance health care tax credit for dislocated workers, and the itemized deduction for medical expenses) with an alternative health care tax relief option available to all taxpayers, regardless of income or source of coverage.

Third, permit individuals with access to employer-sponsored coverage to choose whether the tax exclusion, or the new tax relief option, should be applied to the value of their employer-sponsored benefits. Each worker would simply instruct his employer, on his W-4 form, which type of health care tax relief to apply in calculating his tax withholding.

Fourth, index the cap on the amount of the exclusion to decrease as needed in future years, so as to maintain at a baseline level the aggregate amount of tax relief provided by both the new option and the exclusion. For years in which the combined aggregate amount of tax relief provided by the alternative tax relief option and the exclusion exceeded the baseline level, the Treasury Department would be required to apply the indexing adjustment to lower the exclusion cap for the following year to make up the difference.

Under this approach there would be no abrupt dislocation of existing coverage arrangements. Those with employer-sponsored coverage could stay in their plans. The only difference would be that each worker could choose the form of the tax treatment to be applied. In general, most lower-wage workers would likely benefit more under the new tax option than the exclusion, while most higher-wage workers would likely find that they are better off continuing to claim the tax exclusion.

This arrangement would not only avoid the PPACA's problem of creating incentives for employers to discontinue coverage, but might actually result in more lower-wage workers enrolling in employer-sponsored coverage. That is because employer coverage would become more affordable to those workers if they opted to apply the new tax relief option, instead of the tax exclusion, to that coverage.

Over time, the indexing of the cap on the exclusion would eventually bring the value of the tax exclusion into parity with the value of the new tax relief option. However, that would occur gradually—not abruptly—and as a byproduct of individual workers exercising their personal preferences.

Commonsense Insurance-Market Reforms

Beyond reforming health care tax policy, the next step in creating a more patient-centered, market-based health system is to reform the regulation of health insurance to make coverage more competitive and value-focused. It is necessary not only for consumers to have incentives to seek better value, but also for insurers to have sufficient scope to innovate in offering better value products.

America's private health insurance market consists of two basic subgroups: the employer-group market, and the individual insurance market. Plans purchased from commercial insurers—whether individual or employer-group policies—are primarily regulated by state insurance laws.

There are, however, instances where federal regulations apply. The Employee Retirement and Income Security Act (ERISA), for example, establishes federal protections for the arrangements that an employer makes for providing benefits to his workers. The state, however, still regulates the commercial products that the employer might choose to purchase.

In 1996, Congress enacted the Health Insurance Portability and Accountability Act (HIPAA). That act, among other policy changes, set in place basic market rules for employer-group coverage and individual-market coverage. For employer plans, HIPAA included policies on a number of issues relating to guarantee issue, guarantee renewability, limitations on pre-exclusions, and prohibition on discrimination based on health status. For individual plans, HIPAA was limited to guarantee renewability and rules in the case of workers who lost their group coverage.

The PPACA and Insurance Regulation

While there were certainly some problems with insurance market regulation prior to the PPACA, those relatively modest problems could easily have been remedied with a few thoughtful and limited reforms. Instead, Congress enacted in the PPACA a raft of new regulations on insurers and health plans that standardize coverage, restrict innovation in plan design, and increase premiums for many Americans. Consequently, many of the new requirements imposed on insurers by the PPACA—such as the new federal benefit mandates that standardize coverage and the rating rules that artificially increase premiums for younger adults—are counterproductive and lead to the need for the widely despised individual mandate to offset their destabilizing effects.

A Better Approach

State governments have performed the basic function of regulating insurance reasonably well for over a century, and there is no need for the federal government to supplant these efforts as it is now doing under the PPACA. Therefore,

Congress should immediately devolve the regulation of health insurance back to the states.

From there, states should initiate a policy agenda that aims to stabilize the market while expanding choice and competition by reducing burdensome and costly rating rules and benefit mandates. State lawmakers should also pursue policies to achieve greater harmonization among the states. For instance, reciprocity agreements between states would permit residents in one state to buy coverage that is issued and regulated in another state. In 2011, Maine included such a reciprocity provision in its broader health insurance reform law. Enacting such policies would expand the choices available to consumers, increase competition among insurers, and help clear the way for potential federal interstate purchase legislation. Finally, states should advance medical liability reforms to help improve access and bring down the cost of practicing medicine.

To address the outstanding concern over protections for those individuals with pre-existing conditions, Congress could solve this issue in a relatively simple fashion without resorting to the kind of sweeping and complex regulation enacted in the PPACA.

Dating back to the 1996 HIPAA law, Congress enacted a set of modest and reasonable rules for employer-group coverage that specified that individuals switching from one group plan to another (or from group coverage to an individual plan) could not be denied new coverage, be subjected to pre-existing-condition exclusions, or be charged higher premiums because of their health status. Thus, in the group market, pre-existing-condition exclusions could only be applied to those without prior coverage, or to those who wait until they need medical care to enroll in their employer's plan. Furthermore, there were limits even in those cases. Such individuals could still obtain the group coverage, and any pre-existing medical condition could not be excluded from that coverage for more than 12 months.

Under these employer group rules, individuals who received and kept coverage are rewarded, and individuals who wait until they are sick to enroll in coverage are penalized, but the penalties were neither unreasonable nor severe. That was also why those rules worked without needing to mandate that individuals purchase coverage, as required by the PPACA.

The problem, however, is that the same kind of rules did not apply to the individual market. Thus, an individual could have purchased non-group health insurance for many years, and still be denied coverage or face pre-existing-condition exclusions when he needed or wanted to pick a different plan. Not only was that unfair to those individuals who had bought insurance while they were healthy, it also did little to encourage other healthy individuals to purchase coverage before they needed it.

Thus, the obvious, modest, and sensible reform would be to apply a set of rules to the individual-health-insurance market similar to the ones that already govern the employer-group-coverage market.

* * *

Opportunity for a Fresh Start

The debate over reforming America's health care system is far from over. The ongoing implementation and technical problems plaguing the PPACA, combined with consistent opposition to the law as a whole, will necessitate another debate over healthcare reform. That will offer opportunities for Congress to advance a much better alternative. The alternative is one that does not reinforce greater government control as does the PPACA, but rather provides a fresh approach based on patient-centered, market-based principles. Such an approach would address the ongoing challenges associated with the tax treatment of health insurance, the over-regulation of insurance markets, and the pressing need for serious reforms to health care entitlements.

DISCUSSION QUESTIONS

1. Critics of the "market-based" reform theory argue that health care cannot be understood as a market. People are not sensitive to costs, and are rarely in a position to shop around to find bargains (if you go to the ER with symptoms of a heart attack or appendicitis, you probably won't have much interest in comparison pricing or choosing which treatment to have based on cost). If market forces do not exist, can a market-based reform ever work?

2. One common way of conceptualizing health care reform is to think of the system in terms of three things: advanced care, universal access, and affordability. You can choose two. Which ones are most important?

3. What are the challenges involved in repealing and replacing the Affordable Care Act, something that both congressional Republicans and President Trump

support? The first attempt to do so failed in 2017 because it proved difficult to satisfy both conservative Republicans who favored complete repeal and moderate Republicans who wanted to keep Medicare funding and maintain coverage levels. What are the challenges in coming up with a replacement?

4. Should health care be a "right," in the sense that individuals ought to be guaranteed access to health services by government? What would the consequences of such a right be? Does not recognizing health care as a right mean that some individuals might be unable to get access to health care, even that they might die as a result?

15

Foreign Policy and World Politics: How Dangerous Is ISIS?

The Islamic State has emerged as the most significant terror group of the past decade, easily supplanting the Taliban and Al Qaeda. It has sponsored terrorism all over the world, and claimed responsibility for or inspired attacks in San Bernardino, CA (December 2015, 14 dead), Orlando, FL (June 2016, 49 dead), and Ft. Hood, Texas (November 2009, 13 dead).

ISIS, in the words of Matthew Olsen, former Director of the National Counterterrorism Center, constitutes "the most urgent threat to our security in the world today." He argues that ISIS has become more sophisticated even as it loses territory, and that its ability to communicate to and inspire followers anywhere in the world makes it a significant risk to global stability. He advocates a combined response of military action, increased surveillance and intelligence action, and communication efforts that combat the radicalization of people inside the United States.

Pillar takes a broader view, arguing that proposed action against ISIS must be understood in the larger context of the history of the American military abroad. Until World War II, Americans had a record of unbroken military success, combined with infrequent wars. In recent decades, military intervention has become more common and less successful, and "an entire generation of Americans has come of age with its country perpetually at war." This has led to the impulse that military action is the first option in dealing with any threat, even when it was an initial military response that caused the threat, and when the continued application of force (through, for example, drone strikes) is a continuing cause of radicalization.

The main reason ISIS exists is the Iraq War and the chaos and power vacuum in the region that resulted. The urge to fight the group with military force merely repeats the initial error, and plays into ISIS's hands. Even "toppling the ISIS command structure" would not eliminate the threat; it would take hundreds of thousands of U.S. troops, and would result in another lengthy and unsuccessful war.

The questions both authors address—even as they come to very different conclusions—are how to understand the threats to the United States, and, once those threats are identified, how to fight them.

Matthew G. Olsen

The Spread of ISIS and Transnational Terrorism

Thank you Chairman Corker, Ranking Member Cardin, and distinguished members of the Committee. I am honored to have this opportunity to appear before you to discuss the spread of the Islamic State in Iraq and Syria and the threat from transnational terrorism.

We meet this morning in the wake of the horrific attacks in Brussels last month and the recent attacks in Paris and in San Bernardino late last year. These massacres serve both as a sobering reminder of the complexity of the threats we face from terrorist groups of global reach and as a call for action in the ongoing struggle against terrorism. Indeed, these attacks give this hearing added significance, as you convene to examine the threat to the United States and our interests around the world and the steps we should take to counter terrorist groups both at home and abroad.

By any measure, ISIS presents the most urgent threat to our security in the world today. The group has exploited the conflict in Syria and sectarian tensions in Iraq to entrench itself in both countries, now spanning the geographic center of the Middle East. Using both terrorist and insurgent tactics, the group has seized and is governing territory, while at the same time securing the allegiance of allied terrorist groups across the Middle East and North Africa. ISIS's sanctuary enables it to recruit, train, and execute external attacks, as we have now seen in Europe, and to incite assailants around the world. It has recruited thousands of militants to join its fight in the region and uses its propaganda campaign to radicalize countless others in the West. And at the same time, we continue to face an enduring threat from Al Qaeda and its affiliates, who maintain the intent and capacity to carry out attacks in the West.

In my remarks today, I will focus first on the nature of the terrorist threat from transnational terrorist groups, focusing on ISIS and Al Qaeda. I then will address some of the key elements of the strategy to degrade and defeat these groups, as well as the challenges we face ahead.

The Spread of ISIS

Let me begin with the spread of ISIS from its roots in Iraq. ISIS traces its origin to the veteran Sunni terrorist, Abu Mus'ab al-Zarqawi, who founded the group in 2004 and pledged his allegiance to bin Laden. Al Qaeda in Iraq, as it was then known, targeted U.S. forces and civilians to pressure the United States and other countries to leave Iraq and gained a reputation for brutality and tyranny.

In 2007, the group's continued targeting and repression of Sunni civilians in Iraq caused a widespread backlash—often referred to as the Sunni Awakening—against the group. This coincided with a surge in U.S. and coalition forces and Iraq counterterrorism operations that ultimately denied ISIS safe haven and led to a sharp decrease in its attack tempo. Then in 2011, the group began to reconstitute itself amid growing Sunni discontent and the civil war in Syria. In 2012, ISIS conducted an average of 5–10 suicide attacks in Iraq per month, an attack tempo that grew to 30–40 attacks per month in 2013.

While gaining strength in Iraq, ISIS exploited the conflict and chaos in Syria to expand its operations across the border. The group established the al-Nusrah Front as a cover for its activities in Syria, and in April 2013, the group publicly declared its presence in Syria under the ISIS name. Al-Nusrah leaders immediately rejected ISIS's announcement and publicly pledged allegiance to Al Qaeda. And by February 2014, Al Qaeda declared that ISIS was no longer a branch of the group.

At the same time, ISIS accelerated its efforts to remove Iraqi and Syrian government control of key portions of their respective territories, seizing control of Raqqa, Syria, and Fallujah, Iraq, in January 2014. The group marched from its safe haven in Syria, across the border into northern Iraq, slaughtering thousands of Iraqi Muslims, Sunni and Shia alike, on its way to seizing Mosul in June 2014.

Through these battlefield victories, the group gained weapons, equipment, and territory, as well as an extensive war chest. In the summer of 2014, ISIS declared the establishment of an Islamic caliphate under the name the "Islamic State" and called for all Muslims to pledge support to the group and its leader, Abu Bakr al-Baghdadi.

Three overarching factors account for the rise and rapid success of ISIS over the past three years.

First, ISIS has exploited the civil war in Syria and the lack of security in northern Iraq to establish a safe haven. At the same time, Assad's brutal suppression of the Syrian people acted as a magnet for extremists and foreign fighters. In western Iraq, the withdrawal of security forces during the initial military engagements with ISIS left swaths of territory ungoverned. ISIS has used these areas to establish sanctuaries in Syria and Iraq from where the group could amass and coordinate fighters and resources with little interference. With virtually no security forces along the Iraq-Syria border, ISIS was able to move personnel and supplies with ease within its held territories.

Second, ISIS has proven to be an effective fighting force. Its battlefield strategy employs a mix of terrorist operations, hit-and-run tactics, and paramilitary assaults to enable the group's rapid gains. These battlefield advances, in turn, sparked other Sunni insurgents into action, and they have helped the group hold and administer territory. Disaffected Sunnis have had few alternatives in Iraq or Syria. The leadership in both countries has pushed them to the sidelines in the political process for years, failing to address their grievances. ISIS has been recruiting these young Sunnis to fight. Since September 2014, the U.S.-led military coalition has halted ISIS's momentum and reversed the group's territorial gains, but ISIS has sought to adapt its tactics in the face of coalition air strikes.

Third, ISIS views itself as the new leader of the global jihad. The group has developed an unprecedented ability to communicate with its followers worldwide. It operates the most sophisticated propaganda machine of any terrorist group. ISIS disseminates timely, high-quality media content on multiple platforms, including on social media, designed to secure a widespread following for the group. ISIS uses a range of media to tout its military capabilities, executions of captured soldiers, and battlefield victories.

ISIS's media campaign also is aimed at drawing foreign fighters to the group, including many from Western countries. The media campaign also allows ISIS to recruit new fighters to conduct independent or inspired attacks in the West. ISIS's propaganda outlets include multiple websites, active Twitter feeds, YouTube channels, and online chat rooms. ISIS uses these platforms to radicalize and mobilize potential operatives in the United States and elsewhere. The group's supporters have sustained this momentum on social media by encouraging attacks in the United States and against U.S. interests in retaliation for our airstrikes. As a result, ISIS threatens to outpace Al Qaeda as the dominant voice of influence in the global extremist movement.

The Threat from ISIS Today

Today, ISIS reportedly has between 20,000 and 25,000 fighters in Iraq and Syria, an overall decrease from the number of fighters in 2014. ISIS controls much of the Tigris-Euphrates basin. Significantly, however, ISIS's frontlines in parts of northern and central Iraq and northern Syria have been pushed back, according to the Defense Department, and ISIS probably can no longer operate openly in approximately 25 to 30 percent of populated areas in Iraq and Syria that it dominated in August 2014.

ISIS also has branched out, taking advantage of the chaos and lack of security in countries like Yemen to Libya to expand to new territory and enlist new followers. ISIS can now claim formal alliances with eight affiliated groups across an arc of instability and unrest stretching from the Middle East across North Africa.

Libya is the most prominent example of the expansion of ISIS. There, ISIS's forces include as many as 6,500 fighters, who have captured the town of Sirte and 150 miles of coastline over the past year. This provides ISIS with a relatively safe base from which to attract new recruits and execute attacks elsewhere, including on Libya's oil facilities. In addition, ISIS has proven its ability to conduct operations in western Libya, including a suicide bombing at a police training, which killed at least 60 people earlier this year.

From this position, ISIS poses a multi-faceted threat to Europe and to the United States. The strategic goal of ISIS remains to establish an Islamic caliphate through armed conflict with governments it considers apostate—including European nations and the United States. In early 2014, ISIS's leader Abu Bakr al-Baghdadi warned that the United States will soon "be in direct conflict" with the group. In September 2014, the group's spokesperson Abu Muhammad al-Adnani released a speech instructing supporters to kill disbelievers in Western countries "in any manner or way," without traveling to Syria or waiting for direction.

ISIS has established an external operations organization under Adnani's leadership. This unit reportedly is a distinct body inside ISIS responsible for identifying recruits, supplying training and cash, and arranging for the delivery of weapons. The unit's main focus has been Europe, but it also has directed deadly attacks outside Europe, including in Turkey, Egypt, Tunisia, and Lebanon.

A recent *New York Times* report attributes 1,200 deaths to ISIS outside Iraq and Syria, and about half of the dead have been local civilians in Arab countries, many killed in attacks on mosques and government offices. In the past two years ISIS reportedly has directed or inspired more than 80 external attacks in as many as 20 nations. And ISIS has carried out or inspired at least 29 deadly assaults targeting Westerners around the world, killing more than 650 people.

Most concerning, the recent attacks in Brussels and Paris demonstrate that ISIS now has both the intent and capability to direct and execute sophisticated attacks in Western Europe. These attacks reflect an alarming trend. Over the past year, ISIS has increased the complexity, severity, and pace of its external attacks. The Brussels and Paris attacks were not simply inspired by ISIS, but rather they were ISIS-planned and directed. And they were conducted as part of a coordinated effort to maximize casualties by striking some of the most vulnerable targets in the West: a train station and airport in Brussels, and a nightclub, cafe, and sporting arena in Paris. Further, recent reports that ISIS has used chemical weapons in Syria, and that it conducted surveillance of Belgium nuclear facilities, raise the specter that the group is intent on using weapons of mass destruction.

In the United States, the threat from ISIS is on a smaller scale but persistent. We have experienced attacks that ISIS has inspired—including the attacks in San Bernardino and in Garland, Texas—and there has been an overall uptick over the past year in the number of moderate-to-small scale plots. Lone actors or insular groups—often self-directed or inspired by overseas groups, like ISIS—pose the most serious threat to carry out attacks here. Homegrown violent extremists will likely continue gravitating to simpler plots that do not require advanced skills, outside training, or communication with others. The online environment serves a critical role in radicalizing and mobilizing homegrown extremists towards violence. Highlighting the challenge this presents, the FBI Director said last year that the FBI has homegrown violent extremist cases, totaling about 900, in every state. Most of these cases are connected to ISIS.

Several factors are driving this trend toward the increasing pace and scale of terrorist-related violence. First, the sheer number of Europeans and other

Westerners who have gone to Syria to fight in the conflict and to join ISIS is supplying a steady flow of operatives to the group. Reports indicate that more than 6,000 Europeans—including many French, German, British, and Belgian nationals—have travelled to Syria to join the fight. This is part of the total of approximately 40,000 foreign fighters in the region. Among the Europeans who have left for Syria, several hundred fighters have returned to their home countries, typically battle-hardened, trained, and further radicalized. The number of Americans who have travelled to Syria or Iraq, or have tried to, exceeds 250.

As such, we should not underestimate the potential of an ISIS-directed attack in the United States. While the principal threat from ISIS in the United States is from homegrown, ISIS-inspired actors, the fact that so many Americans have travelled to Syria and Iraq to fight, along with thousands more from visa waiver countries in Europe, raises the real concern that these individuals could be deployed here to conduct attacks similar to the attacks in Paris and Brussels.

Second, ISIS has developed more advanced tactics in planning and executing these attacks. In both Brussels and Paris, the operatives staged coordinated attacks at multiple sites, effectively hampering police responses. The militants exploited weaknesses in Europe's border controls in order to move relatively freely from Syria to France and Belgium. The group has also moved away from previous efforts to attack symbolically significant targets—such as the 2014 attack on a Jewish museum in Brussels—and appears to have adopted the guidance of a senior ISIS operative in the group's online magazine, who directed followers "to stop looking for specific targets" and to "hit everyone and everything." Further, the explosives used in Paris and likely in Brussels indicate the terrorists have achieved a level of proficiency in bomb making. The use of TATP in Paris and the discovery of the material in raids in Brussels suggest that the operatives have received sophisticated explosives training, possibly in Syria.

Third, existing networks of extremists in Europe are providing the infrastructure to support the execution of attacks there. The investigations of the Paris and Belgium attacks have revealed embedded radical networks that supply foreign fighters to ISIS in Syria and operatives and logistical support for the terrorist attacks in those cities. While such entrenched and isolated networks are not present in the United States, ISIS continues to target Americans for recruitment, including through the use of focused social media, in order to identify and mobilize operatives here.

Looking more broadly, the rise of ISIS should be viewed as a manifestation of the transformation of the global jihadist movement over the past several years.

We have seen this movement diversify and expand in the aftermath of the upheaval and political chaos in the Arab world since 2010. Instability and unrest in large parts of the Middle East and North Africa have led to a lack of security, border control, and effective governance. In the last few years, four states—Iraq, Syria, Libya, and Yemen—have effectively collapsed. ISIS and other terrorist groups exploit these conditions to expand their reach and establish safe havens. As a result, the threat now comes from a decentralized array of organizations and networks, with ISIS being the group that presents the most urgent threat today.

Specifically, Al Qaeda core continues to support attacking the West and is vying with ISIS to be the recognized leader of the global jihad. There is no doubt that sustained U.S. counterterrorism pressure has led to the steady elimination of Al Qaeda's senior leaders and limited the group's ability to operate, train, and recruit operatives. At the same time, the core leadership of Al Qaeda continues to wield substantial influence over affiliated and allied groups, such as Yemen-based Al Qaeda in the Arabian Peninsula. On three occasions over the past several years, AQAP has sought to bring down an airliner bound for the United States. And there is reason to believe it still harbors the intent and substantial capability to carry out such a plot.

In Syria, veteran Al Qaeda fighters have traveled from Pakistan to take advantage of the permissive operating environment and access to foreign fighters. They are focused on plotting against the West. Al-Shabaab also maintains a safe haven in Somalia and threatens U.S. interests in the region, asserting the aim of creating a caliphate across east Africa. The group has reportedly increased its recruitment in Kenya and aims to destabilize parts of Kenya. Finally, AQIM (and its splinter groups) and Boko Haram—now an official branch of ISIS—continue to maintain their base of operations in North and West Africa and have demonstrated sustained capabilities to carry out deadly attacks against civilian targets.

The Strategy to Defeat ISIS

Against this backdrop, I will briefly address the current strategy to confront and ultimately defeat ISIS. As formidable as ISIS has become, the group is vulnerable. Indeed, the U.S.-led military campaign has killed thousands of ISIS fighters and rolled back ISIS's territorial gains in parts of Iraq and Syria. ISIS has not had any major strategic military victories in Iraq or Syria for almost a year. As ISIS loses its hold on territory, its claim that it has established the "caliphate" will be eroded, and the group will lose its central appeal.

On the military front, a coalition of twelve nations has conducted more than 8,700 airstrikes in Syria and Iraq, according to the Defense Department. These strikes have taken out a range of targets, including ISIS vehicles, weaponry, training camps, oil infrastructure, and artillery positions. In addition, several nations have joined the United States in deploying military personnel to assist the Iraqi government, training more than 17,000 Iraqi security forces.

The military effort also has included the successful targeting of ISIS leaders. United States special operations forces have gone into Syria to support the fight against ISIS, bringing a unique set of capabilities, such as intelligence gathering, enabling local forces, and targeting high-value ISIS operatives and leaders.

From a counterterrorism perspective, the United States is pursuing multiple lines of effort. First, the United States is focusing on stemming the flow of foreign fighters to Syria, and disrupting ISIS's financial networks. The government reports that at least 50 countries plus the United Nations now contribute foreign terrorist fighter profiles to INTERPOL, and the United States has bilateral arrangements with 40 international partners for sharing terrorist travel information. In 2015, the U.S. government sanctioned more than 30 ISIS-linked senior leaders, financiers, foreign terrorist facilitators, and organizations, helping isolate ISIS from the international financial system. In addition, since 2014, the FBI has arrested approximately 65 individuals in ISIS-related criminal matters.

Second, to counter ISIS propaganda, the United States is strengthening its efforts to prevent ISIS from radicalizing and mobilizing recruits. The White House recently announced the creation of an interagency countering violent extremism (CVE) task force under the leadership of the Department of Homeland Security and the Department of Justice, with additional staffing from the FBI and National Counterterrorism Center. The CVE task force is charged with integrating whole-of-government programs and activities and establishing new CVE efforts. As part of this initiative, the DHS Office for Community Partnerships is developing innovative ways to support communities that seek to discourage violent extremism and to undercut terrorist narratives.

Third, and more broadly, the United States continues to lead the international diplomatic effort to resolve the underlying conflicts in the region. This includes working toward a negotiated political transition that removes Bashar al-Asad from power and ultimately leads to an inclusive government that is responsive to the needs of all Syrians. This effort also includes supporting the Iraqi government's progress toward effective and inclusive governance, stabilization efforts, and reconciliation.

To augment this strategy, there are a number of initiatives that merit consideration.

One is a surge in our intelligence capabilities. Such a surge should include enhancing our technical surveillance capabilities, providing additional resources for the development of sources to penetrate ISIS, and fostering closer relationships with intelligence services in the region. This focus on intelligence collection would help address the fact that our law enforcement and intelligence agencies have found it increasingly difficult to collect specific intelligence on terrorist intentions and plots. This intelligence gap is due in part to the widespread availability and adoption of encrypted communication technology. Indeed, ISIS has released a how-to manual to its followers on the use of encryption to avoid detection. The gap also is the result of the illegal disclosures of our intelligence collection methods and techniques. These disclosures have provided terrorists with a roadmap on how to evade our surveillance. Therefore, rebuilding our intelligence capabilities should be an imperative.

Next, the United States should continue to work in concert with European partners and support Europe's effort to break down barriers to information sharing among agencies and among nations and to strengthen border controls. Today, European nations do not always alert each other when they encounter a terrorism suspect at a border. Europe should incorporate the lessons we learned after 9/11 and adopt structural changes that enable sharing of information between law enforcement and intelligence agencies and that support watchlisting of suspected terrorists.

Finally, the United States should redouble its efforts to counter ISIS on the ideological front. This begins with a recognition that the United States, along with nations in Europe, must build and maintain trust and strong relationships with Muslim communities who are on the front lines of the fight against radicalization. This also means we must reject unambiguously the hateful rhetoric that erodes that trust. The U.S. strategy should focus on empowering Muslim American communities to confront extremist ideology, working to galvanize and amplify networks of people, both in the government and private sector, to confront ISIS's ideology of oppression and violence. While the government has made strides in this direction, the pace and scale of the effort has not matched the threat.

Conclusion

In the wake of the terrorist attacks in Europe and here in the United States, our continued focus on ISIS and transnational terrorist threats is absolutely warranted. We should not underestimate the capacity of ISIS and other groups to adapt and evade our defenses and to carry out acts of violence, both here at home and around the world.

But no terrorist group is invincible. The enduring lessons of 9/11 are that we can overcome and defeat the threat of terrorism through strength, unity, and adherence to our founding values, and that American leadership is indispensible to this fight.

Paul R. Pillar

Welcome to Generation War*

Since World War II—the largest military effort ever by the United States, and one ending with clear victory—the use of U.S. military force overseas has exhibited two patterns. One is the increasing frequency and duration of the application of force. This trend has become especially noticeable since the turn of the twenty-first century, with the United States fighting its two longest major military campaigns, in Afghanistan and Iraq. Simultaneously, Washington has conducted combat operations in Libya, Syria, and elsewhere, all under the indeterminate rubric of "war on terror." An entire generation of Americans has come of age with its country perpetually at war.

This state of permanent warfare is hard to explain in terms of national self-image. Americans have traditionally seen themselves as peace-loving folks who strike back only when someone else picks a fight. In the words of John Quincy Adams, they tend not to seek out "monsters to destroy." The United States has not been a latter-day Sparta, defining its virtue in terms of martial spirit.

The second pattern makes the first even more difficult to comprehend: the overall results of all this fighting overseas have been poor. Uncle Sam has regularly

---

* Paul R. Pillar. "Welcome to Generation War," *The National Interest*, July/August 2016. Reprinted by permission of The National Interest.

cried "uncle." The Korean War ended in a draw. The only major U.S. war since then to register a win was Operation Desert Storm, the expulsion of Iraqi forces from Kuwait in 1991. The other large U.S. military campaigns of the last sixty years fall on the opposite side of the ledger. They include the Vietnam and Iraq fiascos, as well as a war in Afghanistan that has gone on for fourteen years and shows no sign of ending. More modestly sized uses of air power have brought only mixed results: some success in the Balkans in the 1990s, but extremist-infested chaos in Libya after the intervention in 2011. Smaller U.S. operations on the ground also have had mixed outcomes, ranging from achievement of some modest objectives in the Caribbean to significant U.S. casualties in, and an embarrassing withdrawal from, Lebanon in the early 1980s.

The United States has been employing military force overseas more than what prudent pursuit of its interests would call for. Yet it keeps coming back for more. An impulse for more foreign military expeditions, despite its poor record, is reflected not only in the two-decade trend toward permanent warfare but also in current pressure in American public debate to do still more militarily in the Middle East. This impulse is not just a matter of policymakers misunderstanding foreign conflicts. More fundamental elements of American thinking are at work and are affecting today's debates about military force in Syria, Iraq, and Afghanistan.

One possible way to explain the trend toward permanent U.S. engagement in warfare concerns long-term changes in the international system and the position of the United States in it. There is some validity to this approach. The United States evolved into a superpower with the increased opportunities and responsibilities that come with it. But the ability to project military power across the globe does not imply that it is prudent to do so, particularly given the United States' string of poor results. Political scientist Barry Posen explains that although the unmatched ability to project military power gives the United States command of the global commons (e.g., sea lanes and international air space), it does not give Washington the ability to control events wherever it wants. The expansion of U.S. military capabilities has prompted excessive applications of force, much as a person who owns a nifty hammer tends to perceive nails everywhere.

Theories elevating terrorism to a new and systemic threat wield little explanatory power. Granted, the September 11, 2001 terrorist attacks did trigger an abrupt change in the American public mood. But international terrorism has been around for centuries and has been shaping U.S. interests for many decades. America's recent military misadventures cannot be sufficiently explained by the rise of terrorism. The costly expedition into Iraq had nothing to do with terrorism, notwithstanding contorted efforts by the promoters of that war to capitalize on the martial post–9/11 public mood.

A traditional explanation for resorting to arms focuses on the vested interests of particular stakeholders. In the United States, this thesis has been most popular on the left, but has had a wider cachet ever since Dwight Eisenhower spoke about a military-industrial complex. Of course institutional blases exist, but the attitudes expressed by the U.S. institution most involved in the use of force—the military—do not support the thesis. The military tends to favor full application of resources to assigned missions, not the undertaking of new missions. It was a civilian policymaker, Madeleine Albright, who asked the nation's top military officer, Colin Powell, "What's the point of having this superb military that you're always talking about if we can't use it?" Today's senior military officers are exhibiting some of the same caution that Powell did. In a recent hearing of the Senate Armed Services Committee that addressed the possibility of establishing a no-fly zone in Syria, the vice chairman of the Joint Chiefs of Staff, Gen. Paul Selva, remarked that "we have the military capacity to impose a no-fly zone," but "the potential for miscalculation and loss of American life in the air" render the idea unwise. The hawkish and disappointed committee chairman, John McCain, referred to this testimony as "one of the more embarrassing statements I have ever heard from a uniformed military officer."

The infrequent use of military force in America's earlier history informs today's frequent use. Blessed with physical separation from foreign threats, Americans adopted the non-Clausewitzian habit of thinking about military means and political ends as two separate realms. They thought about war as the last resort, sallying forth abroad to eliminate whatever threat was sufficiently serious to justify such an expedition. Unlike the Europeans living with continuous threats at close quarters, Americans did not have to develop ways of thinking about security and military force that were more balanced and sustainable over the long term even with more permanent and intense engagement with the outside world.

But after World War II, the American superpower *did* become permanently and intensely engaged with the rest of the world. It was the sort of engagement that Americans were used to associating solely with wars, some "colder" than others. Thus an irony of American history is that the infrequency of wars in the nineteenth century helped to shape a national outlook that, combined with requirements of America's global involvement in the twenty-first century, has brought

Americans close to believing themselves to be in perpetual war. The belief has helped foster the reality.

The optimism that post–World War II Americans have exhibited as to what can be accomplished through force is rooted in the remarkable success that the United States enjoyed while rising to a position of unparalleled power. After all, military force produced an impressive winning streak through World War II. Even the one earlier war that should be scored as a draw—the War of 1812—was perceived by many Americans at the time as a win because combat ended with a smashing American victory at New Orleans. Even the Civil War that tore the nation apart later in the nineteenth century was ultimately a successful application of arms: a rebellion was quelled, the union was preserved and the country emerged freer than before.

America's military successes have been so obvious, so long-standing and so deeply embedded in American culture and lore that they still shape current discourse on the use of force. That history, ingrained in American habits of thought, impedes the learning of lessons from more recent and less successful uses of force. The history is part of what lies behind McCain's belief that it should not be too hard for "the most powerful nation on Earth" to set up a no-fly zone or to "take out" the so-called Islamic State.

Most of the wars the United States fought while still on a winning streak did not confront it directly with the nationalism-soaked problems that U.S. military interventions have encountered since the streak ended. The United States got its first real taste of such problems dealing with a stubborn insurgency in the Philippines after taking the islands from Spain following an easy win in the Spanish-American War. The lessons from that experience were not fully applied to a bigger insurgency elsewhere in Southeast Asia half a century later. Robert McNamara, the U.S. secretary of defense during the first half of the Vietnam War, wrote many years afterward with insight and anguish:

> We underestimated the power of nationalism to motivate a people (in this case, the North Vietnamese and Vietcong) to fight and die for their beliefs and values—and we continue to do so today in many parts of the world.

In many of America's more recent foreign expeditions, resistance to applications of U.S. military power stems not only from such strong nationalist sentiment but also from widespread perceptions of U.S. power as threatening rather than helpful. The difficulty most Americans have had in recognizing such perceptions and the problems they pose for U.S. military campaigns emanates from the benign American exceptionalist self-image. It also has historical roots in the geographic isolation that gave citizens of a younger and weaker United States the luxury of not having to think much about how someone else's projected power can feel threatening.

What should have been sobering lessons from the more recent and less successful military interventions have tended to be swept aside in favor of the historically based optimism about the utility of force. The "Vietnam War syndrome"—a public hesitance about such interventions after the nation got so badly burned in that war—was largely blown away by the inspiring success of Desert Storm. Although the Iraq War is deeply relevant to the ISIS situation, the lessons of that costly expedition have been compartmentalized and largely lost.

Some who supported that war explain it away as all about a mistake, not to be repeated, concerning nonexistent weapons of mass destruction. Donald Trump has tried to inoculate himself by claiming, with some exaggeration, always to have opposed the Iraq War, but such opposition has not deterred him from calling on Washington to "bomb the sh-t" out of ISIS. Ted Cruz's attempt to do something similar with his criticisms of neocons has not stopped him from calling for carpet bombing in Syria. Many Republican opponents of Barack Obama cling to the myth that the president snatched defeat from the jaws of victory by implementing the troop withdrawal agreement negotiated by the Bush administration—a myth that disregards both the substantial pace at which the Iraqi civil war was still being fought at the time and the failure of earlier military efforts to resolve the political conflicts that underlie instability in Iraq today.

Beyond all of this is a frequent admonition not to "overreact" to the bad experience of the Iraq War, an admonition voiced so frequently that it has become an overreaction about overreaction. Coupled with that theme are efforts to depict any proposals for more military intervention in the Middle East as much different in cost and duration from the quagmire that the Iraq War became. Typical is the urging by James Jeffrey, ambassador in Baghdad and a White House policy adviser in the George W. Bush administration, to initiate a U.S. ground war against ISIS, which he assures us would be a "short," "crisp," "rapid takedown" of the group. Similar spin comes from columnist Richard Cohen, who is more interested in using force against the Assad regime than against ISIS and says that a no-fly zone and "maybe taking a shot or two at a key government installation" would do the job. The relevance of lessons from the Iraq War simply gets defined away with unrealistically sanguine images of what the next war would look like.

Certain other rhetorical dynamics of current debates about the use of force in Syria and Iraq add to the historically based bias in favor of using it. One is the American habit of discussing almost any serious issue overseas as a problem that the United States can and should solve. A related rhetorical asymmetry is the greater appeal of positive, confident-sounding calls for the United States to do just that, compared with the lesser appeal of caution or skepticism about whether the United States really *can* solve other people's civil wars. Saying anything that sounds like, "that's a nasty problem, but given the downsides of our available options, we'll have to live with it" does not win American political leaders votes.

The public and political appetite for action usually means specifically visible, forceful action. That means that military responses have greater appeal than less visible policy tools, such as behind-closed-doors diplomacy. Amid today's Middle East security issues, the "war on terror" concept continues to weigh heavily on American debate and foreign-policy discourse. It is a metaphor that has shaped reality. It has led to the false syllogism that if a problem is serious then America is at war, and if America is at war, and if America is at war then it needs to use military force to solve the problem. The influence of this line of thinking is heard in the frequent declarations from Republican presidential candidates and others that "we are at war," notwithstanding the absence of a congressional declaration of war.

A related pseudologic equates leadership with toughness, and toughness with military force. Barack Obama has been especially vulnerable to criticism of his leadership along these lines, given his image as a pedantic law professor who came into office eager to withdraw from existing wars and whose administration has been said to "lead from behind." The lack of appeal, emotionally as well as politically, of this presidential style has led commentators not normally hostile to Democrats to complain about Obama's unwillingness to amp up his rhetoric. Dana Milbank of the *Washington Post* calls him "President Oh-bummer" and says although tough talk won't defeat terrorists "it will rally a nation." Milbank's *Post* colleague Richard Cohen says Obama's approach leaves him "empty and cold." Cohen observes that Obama "is a cautious man who fears his rhetoric running away from him"—an accurate statement about the president's concerns that also points to an actual process of rhetoric pushing policy, another reason that the use of military force has gone beyond what is in the nation's best interests.

Other dynamics compound this trend in Washington's approach to the Middle East. One is the luxury that political opponents have, and incumbent policymakers do not, of sounding appealing themes without having to voice less appealing cautions about long-term complications and consequences. Amid fears of terrorist groups and a presidential election, the rhetorical energy drives predominantly in the direction of more rather than less reliance on military force.

Another factor is the universal human tendency to treat sunk costs as investments. This tendency has especially affected American discourse about Iraq, and all the more so given propagation of the myth that the United States was on the verge of a victory there in 2009. Politicians and military veterans alike relate news about the latest fighting in Iraqi cities to sacrifices that U.S. troops made in the same locales during an earlier phase of the war. Such connections are drawn even though sunk costs really *are* sunk and past ill-advised expenditures have not bought any current opportunities.

At some level of consciousness the Pottery Barn rule—if you break it, you buy it—has affected American thinking about troublesome military expeditions, adding to the impetus to escalate and extend rather than to retrench and curtail. By itself the rule is laudable and teaches responsibility. The trouble is that the rule tends to get applied only after breakage has occurred. And with Americans thinking of themselves as builders rather than breakers, some commitments have been made with insufficient advance thought about what was likely to be broken.

All of the aforementioned factors have contributed to Washington's current state of unending warfare and of perpetuating the costly pattern of using military force beyond what careful consideration of U.S. interests would dictate. Among recent military expeditions, the invasion of Iraq remains a glaring example of how not to apply force—blind to the troubles that would spill out once Iraqi pottery got broken and with unrealistically rosy assumptions about how liberalism and democracy would fall into place after a dictator's ouster. But that war was an extreme case, given the extraordinary absence of any policy process to consider whether launching the war was a good idea and thus insufficient opportunity within the government to question the rosy assumptions and to consider all the possible costs and consequences.

Perhaps more illustrative of the general point about the American bias toward war have been the policies of, and pressures upon, Obama, who by contrast has deliberated meticulously ("dithering," to some) about applications of military force. He has tried to resist demands to expand the unproductive record of unending warfare. He has succeeded in resisting some, but has succumbed enough to disappoint followers who wanted a president who would be getting Americans out of wars rather than keeping the nation immersed in them. The political pressures from those followers have been much weaker than pressures coming from the opposite direction. Obama has had to deal with a Congress in which one chamber for most of his presidency, and both chambers for his final two years, have been controlled by an opposition party whose foreign policies have been dominated by neoconservatism. His first secretary of state and aspiring successor is more hawkish than he and is part of an element in his own party that favors armed intervention on humanitarian grounds, which was the rationale for the operation in Libya. The perceived trait that Obama, fairly or unfairly, continually has had to counteract is wimpiness, not recklessness.

The administration's first test was the war in Afghanistan. Long before President Obama entered office, the United States had failed to find an off-ramp. Once the Taliban had been ousted from Kabul and Al Qaeda rousted from its haven, the United States could have opted for an honorable conclusion to its justified military response to a major terrorist attack, before the operation morphed into a nation-building exercise in the graveyard of empires. The more time that passed after the successful ousting and rousting in the first few months of Operation Enduring Freedom, the less honorable any exit would have seemed. Moreover, for Obama in particular, Afghanistan was the "good" war in contrast to the "bad" war in Iraq, which to his credit he had opposed from the beginning. So a complete exit while Afghan factions continued to wage their civil war was not in the cards. The policy response included a surge that always made more domestic political sense than military sense, being too small and quick to accomplish much on the ground. The administration's response also has come to include a scotching of any idea of an exit in the foreseeable future, an apparent acceptance of indefinite extension of what already is America's longest war. All this in a country that, notwithstanding the association with 9/11, has taken its place in modern history because of an insurgency more than three decades ago against a client regime of the Soviets. Afghanistan is not inherently destined to be enmeshed in international terrorism, and whatever strategic significance it has is incommensurate with the longest ever U.S. war.

Some of the same psychological and political tendencies in the American approach to countering terrorism have been apparent in the use of unmanned aerial vehicles, or drones, to kill suspected terrorists. Lethal operations with drones began in 2002 under George W. Bush, and the Obama administration has increased their pace. The appeal of drones is partly as another splendid hammer that cries out for nails to be struck. More significantly and defensibly, drone strikes have been the only practical way to reach some suspected terrorists in remote places. Adding to their appeal is the same attraction that gives any other use of armed force an advantage over less kinetic tools of statecraft: it brings direct, immediate, tangible results, in this case in the form of dead terrorists. More indirect and intangible are the negative effects, including resentment and radicalization stimulated by collateral damage from the operations. The asymmetry that favors more attention to the first effect than the second—even though the longer-term radicalizing impact may ultimately shape terrorist threats against the United States more than any number of bad guys the drones kill—probably already has pushed the drone strikes past a point of diminishing returns. The results have not been encouraging in, for example, Yemen, where the number of violent radicals has increased during the same period that drone strikes have, even before the effects of the current civil war there began to be felt.

The most intense debates about the use of U.S. armed force are now centered on ISIS and its enclaves in Iraq and Syria, where the ISIS problem is superimposed on a complicated civil war in which a mélange of other opposition groups are also fighting against the Assad regime. Given that ISIS has supplanted Al Qaeda in American perceptions as the embodiment of international terrorism, discussion of what to do about ISIS is heavily weighed down by the baggage of 9/11 and the "war on terror." Among the consequences are the presumption that military force is the primary tool to wage this "war" and an assumption that if ISIS is not dispatched in the Middle East then it is very likely to harm Americans. A tone of urgency has infused calls to destroy ISIS before it conducts a major terrorist attack in the United States.

More sober consideration would begin by recalling what should be one of leading lessons from the Iraq War: that ISIS did not exist before that war, and that the group (originally Al Qaeda in Iraq) came into existence as a direct result of the civil war that the U.S. invasion and overthrow of Saddam Hussein ignited. Careful consideration of the problem would note that ISIS, unlike the main Al Qaeda organization from which it openly split, rejected the "far enemy" strategy of Osama bin Laden and Ayman al-Zawahiri. ISIS has focused instead on building and defending its so-called caliphate (from the "near enemy"), with any terrorism against the West fulfilling the secondary goals of revenge, recruitment, diversion, and deterrence.

Amid the sense of urgency about destroying ISIS's enclave, little is said publicly about exactly what difference a group's control of that kind of distant real estate makes for counterterrorism in the United States and the West. Even if some such real estate makes a difference, there is nothing sacred about the ground that ISIS has been occupying in Iraq and Syria. The broader history of Al Qaeda suggests that if there is going to be any base of operations for anti-Western terrorism, it is as likely to be somewhere on the periphery (such as Yemen), as in the group's original sanctuary. More fundamental is the question of how a terrorist group's control of *any* piece of territory affects the West. Experience indicates that such territorial control is neither necessary nor sufficient for significant international terrorist operations. Most of the preparation for 9/11 took place in apartments and flight schools in the West, and in cyberspace, rather than in the Afghan haven. Looking at counterterrorism through a war-tinted lens leads naturally to the equating of progress against ISIS with the movement of front lines on a map, as in conventional war.

What happens in ISIS's caliphate does affect the group's ability to inspire violent acts in the West. But these inspirational links may well be a matter of already radicalized individuals looking for a prominent brand in whose name they might commit violent acts they would have committed anyway. The mass shooting in San Bernardino, California in December 2015, which played a major role in stimulating the sense of urgency and alarm about possible ISIS-related attacks in the United States, is instructive. Although the shooters invoked the ISIS name, no evidence has emerged of any organizational connection with ISIS itself. Reportedly, the male half of the shooting pair had sought contact with different extremist groups, including Jabhat al-Nusra and al-Shabaab.

Of the two countries where ISIS has established its enclave, Iraq carries for Americans the baggage of the Iraq War and associated attitudes about sunk costs, but Syria is nonetheless the more complicated situation because of the uprising against the Assad regime. The revolt has regime-change juices flowing, stimulating an American itch to weigh in militarily, rather like what happened with Libya. This itch has spread to the Syrian regime itself, even though the Assads have ruled in Damascus for nearly half a century, so there would not seem to be a reason for urgency in toppling their regime. The impulse to use military force against the regime nonetheless has been strong, as suggested by how much American domestic opponents criticized the Obama administration for making use of a peaceful channel brokered by Russia to dispose of the Syrian regime's chemical weapons rather than going to war over the issue.

Much of the urging to do more militarily in Syria constitutes inchoate expressions of toughness by politicians or of displeasure with the Syrian mess by others who assume this is yet another problem the United States ought to be able to solve if it applies its power. The relative priorities of confronting the Syrian regime and of dealing with ISIS are often left unclear, as are details of exactly what sort of additional military action the United States might take. The closest things to specificity have been mentions of a no-fly zone and calls for initiation of a ground war against ISIS. For the latter purpose, for example, McCain and former Republican presidential candidate Lindsey Graham have talked about deploying ten thousand U.S. combat troops each to Syria and Iraq.

The idea of a no-fly zone—embraced by, among others, Hillary Clinton—has the attraction of being responsive to the urge to apply more U.S. military force in Syria while sounding less costly than another quagmire on the ground. But although such a zone can be useful where (as with Iraqi Kurdistan in the past) a friendly and well-established authority on the ground could use protection from a hostile force with air power, that is not the situation in Syria. Left unanswered in most calls for a no-fly zone are questions about who controls the ground underneath the prohibited airspace and who will do the fighting to ensure the control stays the way America wants it. Moreover, even just the air component entails a much bigger military commitment—i.e., initiating direct hostilities with the Syrian regime—than those suggesting the idea seem to realize. (Given that ISIS has no air force, a no-fly zone would be useless against that group.) Enforcement of the zone would probably include attacks against Syrian air-defense capabilities and would entail significant risk of direct combat with Russian aircraft flying missions in support of the Syrian regime.

Proposals for U.S. ground operations against ISIS are based on the false premise that "taking out" the group with a quick assault on its positions would be the end of the task. It would not. It would mark the beginning of a new phase of the war characterized by guerrilla attacks, terrorism, and other asymmetric operations. Chaos and instability left where the self-styled caliphate once stood would be a fertile garden for additional violent extremism, whether it bore the ISIS name or some other label. There would be no more justification for declaring "mission accomplished" after toppling the ISIS command structure than there was for declaring it in Iraq after toppling Saddam Hussein's regime. Political scientists Stephen Biddle and Jacob Shapiro assess that taking and holding ISIS's territory would require not ten or twenty thousand U.S. troops but instead one hundred thousand. In other words, it would be another large, costly, and, perhaps, interminable counterinsurgency and nation-building effort.

For the United States to plunge into the Syrian war would play into ISIS's hands. It would confirm the group's narratives about it leading Muslim defenses against a predatory West and about apocalypse between itself and the leader of the West. The inevitable collateral damage from increased lethal operations would foster the sort of resentment that aids terrorist recruitment.

Barack Obama, when pressed to do more militarily, has explained the situations in Syria and Iraq in terms that indicate he understands well the aforementioned costs and risks. In his last year in office, he has resisted the pressures to go beyond the approximately four thousand U.S. troops he has reinserted in Iraq, a very small ground presence in Syria and anti-ISIS air operations in both countries. His successor, however, is likely to be someone who will not only have more hawkish views but also, as a first-term president, be more easily moved by the urges and impulses that have pushed the United States into its state of perpetual warfare.

Those urges and impulses are deeply rooted in American history and, thus, in American habits of thinking. Occasionally, as after the Vietnam War, the sheer magnitude of the costs has led to a temporary departure from those habits.

Given the nature of the current debate, such a departure does not appear forthcoming. Quite the contrary. The United States appears destined, for reasons related to what makes it exceptional, to continue using military force beyond what serves its interests. It will take exceptional leadership to limit the resulting damage.

DISCUSSION QUESTIONS

1. Those who insist that the threat ISIS poses in the United States is overblown often compare the number of people killed in terror attacks inside the United States (an average of about 25 per year since 2010, although the number varies depending on what is defined as a terror attack) to the number killed by automobiles or guns (about 33,000 per year), drownings (about 3,500), or any number of other causes. Is this a meaningful argument? Is it right to argue that we should not worry about terrorism because—today—there are other things that pose a higher risk of harm?

2. Is there any common ground between Olson and Pillar? Is it possible to address the threat that ISIS poses without committing to major military action in Syria and Iraq?

Permissions Acknowledgments

Greg Abbott: "Restoring the Rule of Law with States Leading the Way," by Governor Greg Abbott. Office of the Governor Press Release, January 8, 2016. Reprinted by permission of the Office of the Governor, State of Texas.

Yoni Appelbaum: "America's Fragile Constitution," *The Atlantic*, October 2015. © 2015 The Atlantic Media Co., as first published in The Atlantic Magazine. All rights reserved. Distributed by Tribune Content Agency, LLC.

Peter Beinart: "Should the Poor be Allowed to Vote?" *The Atlantic*, October 22, 2014. © 2014 The Atlantic Media Co., as first published in The Atlantic Magazine. All rights reserved. Distributed by Tribune Content Agency, LLC.

Campaign Legal Center Staff: "Why Our Democracy Needs Disclosure," Campaign Legal Center Blog, August 18, 2011. Reprinted by permission of the Campaign Legal Center.

David Cole: "The Angry New Frontier: Gay Rights vs. Religious Liberty." From *The New York Review of Books*. Copyright © 2015 by David Cole. Reprinted by permission of The New York Review of Books.

Shikha Dalmia: "A State's Rights Approach to Immigration Reform," Reason Magazine and Reason.com, December 7, 2015. Reprinted by permission of the Reason Foundation.

Larry Diamond: "Ending the Presidential-Debate Duopoly," *The Atlantic*, May 8, 2015. © 2015 The Atlantic Media Co., as first published in The Atlantic Magazine. All rights reserved. Distributed by Tribune Content Agency, LLC.

The Economist: "Hamilton's heirs: Donald Trump's administration could deport millions of undocumented immigrants, using a system perfected under Barack Obama,"

The Economist, December 10, 2016. © The Economist Newspaper Limited, London 2016. Reprinted with permission; includes figure from "5 facts about illegal immigration in the U.S," Pew Research Center, (November, 2016) http://www.pewresearch .org/fact-tank/2016/11/03/5-facts-about-illegal-immigration-in-the-u-s/. Reprinted with permission.

Chris Edwards: "Options for Federal Privatization and Reform Lessons from Abroad," *Cato Institute Policy Analysis*, No. 794, June 28, 2016. Reprinted by permission of the Cato Institute.

John Fund: "Voter Fraud: We've Got Proof It's Easy," *National Review*, January 12, 2014. Copyright 2016 National Review. Used with permission.

Allen C. Guelzo and James H. Hulme: "In Defense of the Electoral College," from *The Washington Post*, November 15, 2016. Reprinted by permission of Allen C. Guelzo, Gettysburg College and James H. Hulme. James H. Hulme is an attorney in private practice in Washington, DC. He has been a partner with the law firm of Arent Fox LLP for thirty years.

Pratheepan Gulasekaram and Karthick Ramakrishnan: "Forget Border Walls and Mass Deportations: The Real Changes in Immigration Policy are Happening in the States," *The Washington Post, Monkey Cage*, September 24, 2015. Reprinted by permission of the authors.

Tara Helfman: "The Religious-Liberty War." Reprinted from COMMENTARY [May/2015], by permission; copyright © 2016 by Commentary, Inc.

A. Barton Hinkle: "How to Fix the Economy, and Income Inequality, The Libertarian Way," Reason.com, August 10, 2015. Reprinted by permission of Richmond Times-Dispatch.

Jihii Jolly: "How Algorithms Decide the News You See." This article by Jihii Jolly originally appeared online in the *Columbia Journalism Review*, May 20, 2014, as part of a series on News Literacy. Reprinted by permission of the author.

Robert P. Jones, Daniel Cox, E.J. Dionne Jr., and William A. Galston: "What it Means to Be an American: Attitudes in an Increasingly Diverse America Ten Years after 9/11," Governance Studies at Brookings Institution and Public Religion Research Institute, 2016. Reprinted by permission of Brookings Institution, Washington D.C. and Public Religion Research Institute.

About the Editors

David T. Canon is professor and department chair of political science at the University of Wisconsin, Madison. His teaching and research interests focus on American political institutions, especially Congress, and racial representation. He is the author of several books, including the introductory text *American Politics Today* (with William Bianco), now in its fifth edition; *Actors, Athletes, and Astronauts: Political Amateurs in the United States Congress*; *Race, Redistricting, and Representation: The Unintended Consequences of Black Majority Districts* (winner of the Richard F. Fenno Prize); *The Dysfunctional Congress?* (with Kenneth Mayer); and various articles and book chapters. He served a term as the Congress editor of *Legislative Studies Quarterly*. He is an AP consultant and has taught in the University of Wisconsin AP Summer Institute for U.S. Government and Politics since 1997. Professor Canon is the recipient of a University of Wisconsin Chancellor's Distinguished Teaching Award.

John J. Coleman is dean of the College of Liberal Arts and professor of political science at the University of Minnesota. His teaching and research interests focus on political party coalitions, factions, and organizations; elections and campaign finance; and the intersection of politics and economic policy. He is the author or editor of several books, including *Party Decline in America: Policy, Politics, and the Fiscal State*, and numerous articles on topics such as political parties, legislative-executive relations, campaign finance, and the politics of economic policy. Professor Coleman is a past president of the Political Organizations and Parties section of the American Political Science Association. At the University of Wisconsin, he received a Chancellor's Distinguished Teaching Award, held a Glenn B. and Cleone Orr Hawkins Professorship, and was a Jeffrey and Susanne Lyons Family Faculty Fellow.

Kenneth R. Mayer is professor of political science at the University of Wisconsin, Madison, with research interests in the presidency, campaign finance, and election administration. He is the author of *With the Stroke of a Pen: Executive Orders and Presidential Power* (winner of the Richard E. Neustadt Award), *The Political Economy of Defense Contracting*, and *The Dysfunctional Congress? The Individual Roots of an Institutional Dilemma* (with David Canon). In 2006, he was the inaugural Fulbright-ANU Distinguished Chair in Political Science at the Australian National University and the recipient of a University of Wisconsin System teaching award.